JB JOSSEY-BASS

Bill Joiner

Stephen Josephs

Leadership Agility

Five Levels of Mastery for Anticipating and Initiating Change

John Wiley & Sons, Inc.

Published by Jossey-Bass

A Wiley Imprint

989 Market Street, San Francisco, CA 94103-1741   www.josseybass.com

Jossey-Bass books and products are available through most bookstores. To contact Jossey-Bass directly call our Customer Care Department within the U.S. at 800-956-7739, outside the U.S. at 317-572-3986, or fax 317-572-4002.

Jossey-Bass also publishes its books in a variety of electronic formats. Some content that appears in print may not be available in electronic books.

Library of Congress Cataloging-in-Publication Data

Joiner, Bill, 1950-
  Leadership agility : five levels of mastery for anticipating and initiating change / Bill Joiner, Stephen Josephs.
      p. cm.
  Includes bibliographical references and index.
  ISBN-13: 978-0-7879-7913-3 (cloth)
  ISBN-10: 0-7879-7913-9 (cloth)
  1. Leadership—Psychological aspects. 2. Organizational change—Psychological aspects.
  3. Maturation (Psychology) 4. Leadership—Psychological aspects—Case studies.
  5. Organizational change—Psychological aspects—Case studies. 6. Maturation
  (Psychology)—Case studies. I. Josephs, Stephen, 1945- II. Title.
  HD57.7.J649 2007
  658.4'092—dc22
                                                                    2006020996

Printed in the United States of America
FIRST EDITION
PB Printing   10 9 8 7 6 5 4 3 2 1

—ᴧᴧ— Contents

We dedicate this book to
Debbie and Noah, Alice and Sean,
and to our parents:
Frances (Bunny) Joiner (1921–1999)
Billy Joiner (1920–)
Teddy Josephs (1914–2006)
Israel Josephs (1904–1981)

—∿— Introduction:
The Master Competency

Leadership agility isn't just another tool for your toolkit. It's the master competency needed for sustained success in today's turbulent economy. This book, richly illustrated with real-world examples, shows what leadership agility looks like in action. It will confirm your best instincts and introduce you to new forms of leadership currently practiced by only a small percentage of highly agile leaders.

Leadership Agility draws on a strong research base and three decades of experience consulting, coaching, and training leaders in companies based in the United States, Canada, and Europe. Although most of our stories and examples come from the business world, this guide is also designed for managers in the government and nonprofit sectors, in professional firms, in academic and religious institutions, in fact, for anyone interested in developing as a person and becoming a more effective leader.

If you're a leadership development professional, and you sense that our global economy demands new personal capacities as well as new leadership competencies, this book is also for you. It not only provides the first in-depth examination of leadership agility, it also describes five distinct levels that leaders move through as they master this much-needed competency.[1] Strikingly, the research reported in this book indicates that less than 10 percent of managers have mastered the level of agility needed for sustained success in today's turbulent business environment.[2]

AN INTEGRAL APPROACH

The prevailing approach to leadership development moves from the outside in: You identify a leader's external challenges and then determine the competencies required to meet these challenges effectively.

An inside-out approach has also emerged in recent years, focusing on the mental and emotional capacities needed for effective leadership.[3]

Leadership Agility is based on an integral perspective that approaches leadership development from the outside in *and* from the inside out.[4] From an outside-in perspective it highlights the skills needed for agile leadership in complex, rapidly changing environments. More specifically, it identifies agile leadership competencies in three distinct action arenas:

- *Pivotal conversations:* Direct person-to-person discussions where important outcomes are at stake.
- *Team initiatives:* Initiatives intended to improve a team and/or its relationship with its larger environment.
- *Organizational initiatives:* Initiatives designed to change an organization and/or its relationship with its larger environment.

This book also approaches leadership agility from the inside out: It identifies the mental and emotional capacities that work together to enable agile leadership in all three action arenas. These capacities, which we describe in Chapter Three, make you more agile in anticipating and initiating change, working with stakeholders, solving challenging problems, and learning from your experience.

STAGES OF PERSONAL DEVELOPMENT

From an inside-out perspective, this book reveals a significant set of findings about the relationship between personal development and leadership effectiveness: As adults grow toward realizing their potential, they develop a constellation of mental and emotional capacities that happen to be the very capacities needed for agile leadership. For example, as adults develop, they get better at understanding and appreciating viewpoints that conflict with their own. This capacity is an essential ingredient in what we call "stakeholder agility," the ability to lead successfully in situations where stakeholders have views and interests that conflict with your own.

Our understanding of the capacities that emerge as human beings develop is so central to leadership agility that we want to explain where it comes from. At the beginning of our careers, we studied and trained in a range of disciplines, both Eastern and Western, that enabled us to help managers develop both as human beings and as leaders. We also had the good fortune to discover a field called stage-development psychology, which shows that, as people develop, they evolve through a series of recognizable stages.

Take a moment to imagine the full spectrum of human growth, from humans at their most infantile to those who are the wisest, most mature, most fully developed on the planet. For more than eight decades, stage-development psychologists have researched and clarified this continuum. Studying this field and testing it against our real-world experience, we found that it provides an exceptionally useful map for understanding the journey of human development. The following sections present a brief overview of this map.[5]

The Pre-Conventional and Conventional Stages

By the end of the 1950s, psychologists including Jean Piaget and Erik Erikson had mapped the stages through which infants evolve into adults. These begin with the so-called pre-conventional stages, which mark the process of growth from infancy through the end of the grade school years.[6] Then come the three conventional stages, which we call Conformer, Expert, and Achiever, respectively.[7]

Most children enter the Conformer stage about the time they start middle school. At this stage, preadolescents develop the ability to engage in the most basic level of abstract thought and the ability to vividly imagine how they're seen by others. They have a keen desire to be accepted as members of groups to which they're attracted. Consequently, they are strongly motivated to conform to the social conventions that govern these groups.[8]

Some people remain in the Conformer stage for the rest of their lives. However, what we might consider true adult development—becoming an independent individual—begins with the Expert stage. At this stage people develop a strong problem-solving orientation. They want to differentiate themselves from others by developing their own opinions and areas of expertise. The great majority of those who finish high school and go on to college begin to grow into this stage during their late teens or early twenties.[9]

A smaller but still sizable percentage of people then grow into the Achiever stage. Adults at this stage develop a strong individual identity and work out a consciously examined system of values, beliefs, and goals to live by. By conventional standards, the Achiever stage represents full adult development. Most top executives and administrators, state and national politicians, influential scientists, and other highly successful professionals have stabilized their development at this stage. Even in the world's most economically advanced societies, few adults grow beyond it.

The Post-Conventional Stages

Over the past thirty years, researchers have identified further stages of adult development, sometimes called *post-conventional* stages, reached by only a small percentage of people.[10] Research has shown that people at these post-conventional stages are more deeply purposeful, more visionary in their thinking, and more resilient in responding to change and uncertainty. They're more welcoming of diverse perspectives and have a greater capacity for resolving differences with other people. They're also more self-aware, more attuned to their experience, more interested in feedback from others, and better at working through inner conflicts.

Some of the people who've identified and described these stages are beginning to become known in leadership circles: William R. Torbert, author of *Action Inquiry* and other books; Robert Kegan, author of *The Evolving Self* and *In Over Our Heads;* Don Beck and Chris Cowan, authors of *Spiral Dynamics;* and Ken Wilber, author of over a dozen books based on a stage-development framework.[11] Wilber's ideas, in particular, have become popular among a growing global network of leading-edge thinkers and change agents.[12]

Levels of Leadership Agility

During the early 1980s, a series of academic studies produced statistically significant correlations, showing that the capacities managers develop at the more advanced stages carry over into the way they exercise leadership. These studies also found that, in the great majority of cases, post-conventional managers are more effective than conventional managers. Why? Because they are more strategic in their thinking, more collaborative, more proactive in seeking feedback, more effective in resolving conflicts, more active in developing subordinates, and more likely to redefine problems to capitalize on the connections between them.[13]

As we incorporated these insights into our work, we found that developmental stage usually has a significant impact on a manager's ability to adopt new leadership practices. For example, managers at post-conventional stages usually find it relatively easy to encourage direct reports to participate in making key decisions. Taught the same practice, Achiever-stage managers are likely to solicit input, hoping to gain buy-in, but they may balk at allowing direct reports to significantly influence their thinking.

As time went on, we wanted to gain a more systematic understanding of the relationship between developmental stages and effective leadership. To clarify the current state of knowledge on this topic, we created the grid shown in Exhibit I-1, which mapped five stages of adult development against the three action arenas mentioned earlier: pivotal conversations, team initiatives, and organizational change initiatives. When we put existing knowledge into the grid, we found that a number of the boxes were essentially blank.

To complete this grid we initiated a multi-year research project that used questionnaires, in-depth interviews, client case studies, and student journals to examine the thought processes and behaviors of hundreds of managers as they carried out initiatives in each of the three action arenas.[14] An overview of the completed grid is presented in Chapter One. Additional detail is provided as the book unfolds.

Two core questions guided our research: What is it, exactly, that changes as a person grows from stage to stage? and How do leaders become more effective as they grow into more advanced stages? In a nutshell, here's what we learned: As you grow from one stage to another, you develop a distinct set of mental and emotional capacities

Developmental Stage	Pivotal Conversations	Team Leadership	Organizational Leadership
Expert			
Achiever			
Catalyst			
Co-Creator			
Synergist			

Exhibit I-1. Leadership Impact of Developmental Stages.

that enable you to respond more effectively to change and complexity. In other words, leaders become more effective as they grow into the more advanced stages, because, in doing so, they become increasingly adept at responding to the degree of change and complexity that pervades today's workplace. In sum, the research shows that, as leaders move from one stage to another, their level of *leadership agility* increases.

To these inside-out observations, we need to add some outside-in considerations: As you might expect, experience counts. Often because they lack experience, some managers haven't yet developed the leadership competencies that correspond to their stage of personal growth. For similar reasons, some managers don't function at the same level of leadership agility in all three action arenas. These findings underscore the importance of taking an integral approach to developing leadership agility: The most effective way to increase your agility is to use your everyday initiatives to develop stage-related capabilities and leadership competencies at the same time. We'll have much more to say about this in Part Three.

HOW TO USE THIS BOOK

Using the framework of five levels of leadership agility, this book is designed as a stage-by-stage guide to realizing your potential both as a person and as a leader.

Part One

In Chapter One we explain the "agility imperative"—the deep trends in today's global economy that demand greater agility of virtually all organizations and their leaders. This chapter presents a vivid example of agile leadership, outlines five levels in developing this master competency, and shows what these agility levels look like in three action arenas: pivotal conversations, leading teams, and leading organizational change. You can use this chapter to develop an initial understanding of the five agility levels and to think about which levels are used most frequently in your organization.

Chapter Two, "The Five Eds," uses a set of five scenarios to give you a more complete understanding of the five agility levels. It begins by describing a common leadership challenge: Ed, a bright, experienced manager is hired as the CEO of a faltering midsized company. Inspired by the classic movie *Groundhog Day,* the scenarios begin by showing how Ed would respond to this challenge if he functioned at the Expert level of agility. Ed then relives this experience four times, each time at a more advanced agility level. You can use this chapter to make an informal assessment of your own level of leadership agility, as well as that of the managers with whom you work.

The first two chapters approach leadership agility from the outside in. In doing so, they introduce you to two parts of the conceptual model underlying this book: the five levels of agility and the three action arenas. Chapter Three introduces you to the rest of the model: the four leadership agility competencies and the mental and emotional capacities that support them.

Part Two

The five chapters in Part Two use real-life stories to present the five levels of leadership agility in greater detail. Each chapter begins with a short story that shows what leadership means to a manager at a particular level of agility. Additional stories show what that chapter's agility level looks like in the three action arenas: pivotal conversations, leading teams, and leading organizational change. Each chapter ends with an overview of the mental and emotional capacities that support that level of agility. These chapters will help you fine-tune your self-assessment from Chapter Two, and they'll clarify what it takes to move to the next level.

Part Three

The final two chapters of this book will help you use what you've learned in Parts One and Two to increase your leadership agility. Chapter Nine walks you through a more individualized assessment, helping you identify areas where your agility is already strong and areas where it needs improvement. Chapter Ten begins with a story that shows how you can become more effective within your current level of agility. It presents a second story that shows what it takes to move from one level to another. Both stories are accompanied by guidelines based on our research and our years of experience working with leaders.

Additional Resources

At the back of the book, you'll find two appendices. Appendix A describes the multi-decade research effort that underlies this book, and it describes our research methods. Appendix B describes the stages of personal development as we define them, and it provides a chart that compares our model with those of other experts in the field.

The "Notes for Inquiring Readers" section provides more detail about many of the key points in the book. Unless you're a leadership development professional or are already familiar with the fields of leadership or stage-development psychology, you'll probably want to stay with the flow of each chapter and not try to read the notes, unless you come to a point you'd like to learn about in more detail. You can always come back and delve into the notes later.

At the end of the book, you'll find a Resources page that shows you where you can find a variety of aids for developing your leadership agility and that of the managers with whom you work.

A FEW WORDS ABOUT WORDING

It's worth taking a few moments at the outset to clarify some of the language we've used in the book.

Beyond the Leader/Manager Dichotomy

Throughout the book, we use the terms *leader* and *manager* interchangeably to refer to a person's *role* in an organization. We do, however, believe that the now-popular distinction between leading and managing, as two different kinds of *activities,* is a meaningful one. For the past thirty years, this paradigm has served a useful purpose. However, our framework of levels of leadership agility now provides a way to look at this distinction through a more refined lens.[15]

Generally speaking, the Expert level of leadership agility is closer to a supervisory mode of leadership than to full-fledged management. The capacities needed for managing in the classic sense of the word develop at the Achiever level. The more visionary approach to leadership (which some people simply call *leadership*) emerges at the Catalyst level. The Co-Creator and Synergist levels represent ways of exercising leadership that are relatively unknown in the current literature.

Throughout the book we use the term *leadership* to refer to a way of taking action, not to an organizational role or position. Because we distinguish between five different levels of leadership agility, our definition is a broad one, designed to apply to all five levels: Leadership is action taken with a proactive attitude and an intention to change something for the better.[16]

A *leadership initiative,* we say, is any action you carry out with this attitude and intent. This means that you don't need to be in a position of authority to exercise leadership. Leaders at all levels of agility have found that this way of thinking about leadership helps them to approach their work in a way that is more proactive and intentional.

Competencies and Capacities

"Competencies" is a term that's widely used to refer to the knowledge, skills, and abilities needed to perform effectively. In this book, when we look at leadership from the outside-in, we talk about the competencies associated with each level of agility. When we look at leadership from an inside-out perspective, we talk about the mental and emotional capacities that make these competencies possible. We find that using these terms in this way is helpful in maintaining an integral approach to leadership development.

Anonymous Real-Life Stories

This book contains twenty-two real-life stories, based on our experiences with clients and on in-depth interviews. By making the people in each story anonymous, we've been able to provide important details without violating confidentiality. To ensure anonymity we changed the names of people and organizations. We often changed demographic identifiers such as industry or company location, and we occasionally changed gender or ethnic identity. In a few cases, we fictionalized certain aspects of a leader's background to fit the "cover identity" we provided.[17]

Quotes

The great majority of the quotes in the book come from interviews with leaders. When people are interviewed, they do tend to ramble a bit. Consequently, we edited many of the interview quotes, not to change their meaning, but to make them clearer, crisper, and easier to read.[18]

PART ONE

What Is Leadership Agility?

CHAPTER ONE

Agility in a World of Change and Complexity

~~~

Robert faced the biggest leadership challenge of his career. An executive in a Canadian oil corporation, he'd just been named president of its refining and retailing company. Competitively, his company was positioned around the middle of the pack in a mature, margin-sensitive market where long-range demand was projected to be flat. With little to distinguish it from other regionals, it was watching its earnings go steadily downhill. In fact, its future looked dismal.

Within the company, morale was at an all-time low. People at all levels were frustrated and unhappy. The previous president had taken many steps to make the company more efficient, including a series of layoffs, but these steps had not produced the desired results. The whole organization was in a state of fear. Privately, the outgoing president had been considering which division would have to be sold or shut down. As Robert moved into his new position, everything was truly up for grabs.

Over the next three years, Robert led his company through an amazing turnaround. At the end of this period, it not only survived without selling any of its divisions, it entered a phase of aggressive growth, clearing $71 million a year more than when he took over. In the business press, the company went from being a "bad bet" to "one of the darlings of the stock market." Why did Robert succeed when his predecessor did not?

The company badly needed a short-term increase in its stock price. But Robert wanted to do much more than that. He wanted to transform an admittedly lackluster company into the best regional in North America. In fact, his vision was to develop an organization whose business performance and innovative ways of operating would be benchmarked by companies from a wide variety of industries. By putting the stock price goal in this larger context, Robert overturned his predecessor's assumption that the company's options were limited to difficult but familiar cost-cutting solutions. Instead, he decided to create a set of break-out strategies that would develop a more innovative organization.

Realizing that he and his top management group might not have all the answers, Robert hired a world-class strategy firm. He also set up ten "idea factories": creative strategic-thinking sessions, where employees and other stakeholders developed ideas for the top team to consider. People responded with enthusiasm, generating a huge number of ideas.

Robert then held a two-day retreat where he and his top management group synthesized the strategy firm's ideas with those generated by the idea factories. As he put it later, "We tried to involve as many people as possible in the strategic review process. We invested time and energy up front to listen to people, build trust, and get everyone aligned. It paid off, because we started to think with one brain. Instead of being at cross-purposes, we could understand and support each other's decisions."

The new strategies that emerged went well beyond those Robert, his team, and the strategy firm would have generated on their own. They resulted in a smaller, more focused organization with a much stronger "people strategy" designed to catapult the company into the ranks of high-performing organizations. When the new game plan was ready, Robert and his team presented it to the employees before they announced it to the market.

The presentation included some bad news, but the employees gave it a standing ovation. Over the months that followed, Robert and his team repeatedly communicated their new vision and its implications for employees in many different forums. As the new strategies were implemented, the top team kept everyone updated on the performance of the business. Every year, Robert met with each of the company's twenty management teams to discuss objectives and strategies and check for alignment.

Robert's participative approach to transforming his organization not only led to innovative strategies, it also developed the commitment, trust, and alignment necessary to implement them reliably and effectively. As a result, during his first three years as president, annual earnings went from $9 million to $40 million, and cash expenses were reduced by $40 million a year. A once-faltering company had become one of the most efficient and effective refiners in North America and one of the top retailers in its marketplace.[1]

THE AGILITY IMPERATIVE

Robert's story is part of a much larger drama: The struggle of organizations around the globe to adapt to a turbulent world economy. Underlying this turbulence are two deep global trends that have radically altered what it takes to achieve sustained success: accelerating change and growing complexity and interdependence.

Every year, new technologies, markets, and competitors emerge at an ever-increasing pace. As change accelerates, so does uncertainty and novelty: future threats and opportunities are harder to predict, and emerging challenges increasingly include novel elements. Further, with the globalization of the economy and the spread of connective technologies, it's increasingly clear that we live in a diverse planetary village where everything is connected with everything else.[2] In this interdependent world, the most successful companies will be those that create strong, timely alliances and partner effectively with customers, suppliers, and other stakeholders.

This means that, while specific future developments are increasingly difficult to predict, we can make two predictions with great certainty: The pace of change will continue to increase, and the level of complexity and interdependence will continue to grow. For more than a decade, organizational change experts, acutely aware of these powerful trends, have stressed the need to develop "agile" companies—organizations that anticipate and respond to rapidly changing conditions by leveraging highly effective internal and external relationships.[3]

Robert is one of those rare, agile leaders who succeeded in developing his management group into a cohesive leadership team that could transform their company into an agile organization. However, as many companies have discovered, developing truly agile teams and organizations is an unfamiliar and demanding task. Left to their own devices, the vast majority of today's managers would not approach Robert's challenge in the way that he did. Consequently, very few firms have developed the level of agility needed to keep pace with the ever-increasing degree of change and complexity in their business environment.[4]

A major reason for this continuing "agility gap" is the need for more agile leaders, not just in the executive suite but at all organizational levels. In a recent survey of CEOs in North America, Europe and Asia, 91 percent said that developing leaders is the most critical success factor for the growth of their business.[5] In another survey, senior executives in Fortune 500 companies identified "agility" as a leadership competency "most needed" for the future success of their business.[6] Yet although leadership development programs are a priority for most larger companies, very little attention has been given to understanding and developing the specific capacities and skills needed for agile leadership.

Leadership agility is directly analogous to organizational agility: It's the ability to take wise and effective action amid complex, rapidly changing conditions. In the last-mentioned survey, executives said they much preferred agility to similar-sounding competencies like flexibility and adaptability. Why? By themselves, flexibility and adaptability imply a passive, reactive stance, while agility implies an intentional, proactive stance.

FIVE LEVELS OF LEADERSHIP AGILITY

Based on data collected from more than six hundred managers, we've found that there are five distinct levels in the mastery of leadership agility: Expert, Achiever, Catalyst, Co-Creator, and Synergist.[7] In Table 1.1, you'll find profiles that show how managers at each agility level carry out initiatives in each of the three action arenas described in the Introduction: pivotal conversations, leading teams, and leading organizational change. Note that the competencies you need for agile leadership evolve further with each new level of mastery. Yet each time you move to a new level, you retain the ability to use those competencies you developed at previous levels.

The Expert Level

The name we've chosen for each agility level is intended to emphasize its strengths. Experts are so named because they're strongly motivated to develop subject-matter expertise, and because they assume that a leader's legitimate power comes from expertise and positional authority. Experts (roughly 45 percent of all managers) are the least agile of those profiled in the chart, but they're more agile than about 10 percent who remain at Pre-expert levels. With their tactical orientation and their capacity for analytic problem solving, the Experts' agility level is best suited for environments where success can be achieved by making incremental improvements to existing strategies.

The Achiever Level

About 35 percent of today's managers have developed to the Achiever level of agility. These managers are highly motivated to accomplish outcomes valued by the institutions with which they've identified themselves. They realize that a leader's power comes not only from authority and expertise but also from motivating others by making it challenging and satisfying to contribute to important outcomes. With their capacity for strategic thinking, Achievers can be highly effective in moderately complex environments where the pace of change requires episodic shifts in corporate strategy.

Heroic and Post-Heroic Leadership

In their book *Power Up: Transforming Organizations Through Shared Leadership,* David Bradford and Allan Cohen distinguish between "heroic" and "post-heroic" leadership. We found that managers at the Pre-expert, Expert, and Achiever levels (about 90 percent of all managers) operate from a heroic leadership mind-set.[8] That is, they assume *sole* responsibility for setting their organization's objectives, coordinating the activities of their subordinates, and managing their performance.

Level of Agility	View of Leadership	Agility in Pivotal Conversations	Agility in Leading Teams	Agility in Leading Organizational Change
Heroic levels				
Pre-expert (~10%)				
Expert (~45%)	Tactical, problem-solving orientation. Believes that leaders are respected and followed by others because of their authority and expertise.	Style is either to strongly assert opinions or hold back to accommodate others. May swing from one style to the other, particularly for different relationships. Tends to avoid giving or requesting feedback.	More of a supervisor than a manager. Creates a group of individuals rather than a team. Work with direct reports is primarily one-on-one. Too caught up in the details of own work to lead in a strategic manner.	Organizational initiatives focus primarily on incremental improvements inside unit boundaries with little attention to stakeholders.
Achiever (~35%)	Strategic outcome orientation. Believes that leaders motivate others by making it challenging and satisfying to contribute to larger objectives.	Primarily assertive or accommodative with some ability to compensate with the less preferred style. Will accept or even initiate feedback, if helpful in achieving desired outcomes.	Operates like a full-fledged manager. Meetings to discuss important strategic or organizational issues are often orchestrated to try to gain buy-in to own views.	Organizational initiatives include analysis of industry environment. Strategies to gain stakeholder buy-in range from one-way communication to soliciting input.
Post-heroic levels				
Catalyst (~5%)	Visionary, facilitative orientation. Believes that leaders articulate an innovative, inspiring vision and bring together the right people to transform the vision into reality. Leaders empower others and actively facilitate their development.	Adept at balancing assertive and accommodative styles as needed in particular situations. Likely to articulate and question underlying assumptions. Genuinely interested in learning from diverse viewpoints. Proactive in seeking and applying keep as is feedback.	Intent on creating a highly participative team. Acts as a team leader and facilitator. Provides and seeks open exchange of views on difficult issues. Empowers direct reports. Uses team development as a vehicle for leadership development.	Organizational initiatives often include development of a culture that promotes teamwork, participation, and empowerment. Proactive engagement with diverse stakeholders reflects a belief that their input increases the quality of decisions, not just buy-in.

Co-creator (~4%)	Oriented toward shared purpose and collaboration. Believes leadership is ultimately a service to others. Leaders collaborate with other leaders to develop a shared vision that each experiences as deeply purposeful.	Integrates assertive and accommodative sides in pivotal conversations and is agile in using both styles. Able to process and seriously consider negative feedback even when highly charged emotionally.	Develops a collaborative leadership team, where members feel full responsibility not only for their own areas but also for the unit or organization they collectively manage. Practical preference for consensus decision making but doesn't hesitate to use authority as needed.	Develops key stakeholder relationships characterized by deep levels of mutual influence and genuine dedication to the common good. May create companies or organizational units where corporate responsibility and deep collaboration are integral practices.
Synergist (~1%)	Holistic orientation. Experiences leadership as participation in a palpable life purpose that benefits others while serving as a vehicle for personal transformation.	Centered "within" not "with" assertive and accommodative energies, expressed as appropriate to the situation. Cultivates a present-centered awareness that augments external feedback and supports a strong, subtle connection with others, even during challenging conversations.	Capable of moving fluidly between various team leadership styles uniquely suited to the situation at hand. Can shape or amplify the energy dynamics at work in a particular situation to bring about mutually beneficial results.	Develops and maintains a deep, empathetic awareness of conflicting stakeholder interests, including the leader's own. Able to access synergistic intuitions that transform seemingly intractable conflicts into solutions beneficial for all parties involved.

Table 1.1. Quick Reference Guide to Five Levels of Leadership Agility.

Note: Each level of agility includes and goes beyond the competencies developed at previous levels. The percentage figures refer to research-based estimates of the managers currently capable of operating at each agility level.[9]

Heroic leadership can be highly effective in certain situations. The predominant combination of Expert and Achiever leadership worked relatively well for most companies until the waning decades of the twentieth century, when the globalization of the economy ushered in an era of constant change and growing interdependence. In this new environment, with its increased demand for collaborative problem solving, teamwork, and continuous organizational change, heroic leadership overcontrols and underutilizes subordinates. It discourages people from feeling responsible for anything beyond their assigned area, inhibits optimal teamwork, and implicitly encourages subordinates to use the heroic approach with their own units.

In this new century, sustained success will require post-heroic leadership. Leaders who develop beyond the Achiever level of agility retain the ultimate accountability and authority that comes with any formal leadership role. At the same time, they work to create highly participative teams and organizations characterized by shared commitment and responsibility.[10] Unfortunately, as noted in the Introduction, only about 10 percent of today's managers are functioning at post-heroic levels of agility: approximately 5 percent at the Catalyst level, 4 percent at the Co-Creator level, and 1 percent at the Synergist level.

The Catalyst Level

Robert's story provides a clear example of post-heroic leadership at the Catalyst level. When appropriate, he exercised Expert and Achiever power, but he led his company in a way that emphasized the power of vision and participation. While his Achiever-level predecessor took the company's existing culture as a given, Robert, like other Catalysts, was strongly motivated to create a participative culture capable of achieving valued outcomes over the longer term. Catalysts, with their openness to change, their willingness to rethink basic assumptions, and their visionary orientation, represent the first level of agility capable of sustained success in today's highly complex, constantly changing business environment.

The Co-Creator Level

Co-Creator leaders derive their name, in part, from their understanding that everything in business and in the rest of life is interdependent. Because of their principled commitment to the common good, many of the Co-Creators in our sample have pioneered new forms of organization where corporate responsibility is integral to their bottom line. Whether or not they establish new organizations, Co-Creator leaders are committed to developing genuinely collaborative team and organizational relationships rooted in a deep sense of shared purpose. With their emotional resilience, their capacity for dialogue, and their ability to generate creative, win-win solutions, Co-Creators are well-equipped for long-term success in the rapidly changing and often disruptive global economy of the early twenty-first century.

The Synergist Level

In conducting the research for this book, we found that the differences between the agility levels become more subtle as leaders move to each successive level. This is particularly true of the distinctions between Co-Creators and Synergists. More than any other, the Synergist level is best understood from the inside out. Part of what distinguishes the leaders who function at this level is their ability to enter fully into the moment-to-moment flow of their present experience. As this capacity for present-centered awareness develops, it gives leaders the ability, in contentious and chaotic situations, to stand in the eye of the storm. This ability to remain centered amid competing demands allows them to access "synergistic intuitions" that transform seemingly intractable conflicts into solutions that are beneficial for all parties involved. We believe that the capacities and competencies developed by these men and women represent the cutting edge of leadership development for the twenty-first century.

AGILITY LEVELS AND PERSONALITY TYPES

In the next chapter, we provide a more detailed walk-through of these five levels of leadership agility, designed to help you identify your own agility level and that of the people with whom you work. Part Two will allow you to fine-tune these initial assessments by reading real-life stories that illustrate each level of agility.

Before we turn to the next chapter, we'd like to address a misimpression people sometimes have when they first hear about the five levels of leadership agility: The assumption that we're talking about different personality types or management styles. Over the past few decades, a number of frameworks that distinguish between various personality types and management styles have found their way into the workplace. (Two prominent examples are the Myers-Briggs Type Inventory and the DISC Personal Profile System).[11] Influenced by this way of thinking, you might assume that some people grow up with an Expert personality, while others grow up with a Synergist personality, and so on.

We believe it's important to understand how personality types influence leadership styles. However, the levels we've just described are not personality types. As you may remember from the Introduction, each level of leadership agility correlates with a particular *stage* of personal development. Decades of research have confirmed that human beings move through these stages in a particular sequence. Similarly, the levels we've outlined represent sequential stages in the mastery of leadership agility. This means, for example, that leaders don't skip from the Expert level to the Co-Creator level. To operate reliably at the Co-Creator level of leadership agility, you first need to master the Achiever and Catalyst levels. So far, we've found no exceptions to this pattern.[12]

All our research indicates that level of agility and personality type are completely unrelated variables. Every personality type can be found at each level of leadership agility. This means that, no matter what your personality type happens to be, you have the potential to master advanced levels of agility—an important thought to keep in mind as you read the next chapter.[13]

CHAPTER TWO

The Five Eds

At this point, you may be asking yourself: What's my current level of leadership agility, and what would it be like to move to the next level? You may also want to assess your colleagues' agility levels. Chapter One provided a brief introduction to each level. This chapter offers the opportunity to assess yourself and others using a more complete, real-life picture of each agility level. It presents five scenarios designed to show you how a leader at each of the five agility levels would respond to the same leadership challenge. In Part Two, you'll read about each agility level in greater detail.

A LEADERSHIP CHALLENGE

Ed is the new CEO of Overmyer AMT. During the 1990s, the company was an industry leader in designing and installing advanced technology used in manufacturing plants. Cecelia Overmyer, who ran her own publishing company, became board chair of the family business when her father died in an automobile accident. She quickly realized that the company had lost its innovative edge and that the current CEO was a big part of the problem. The search for a new top executive led the company to Ed.

Ed is a bright manager in his mid-forties, well-qualified for the job. He has a bachelor's degree in engineering, an MBA, and many years' experience in the industry. He has a track record of successful assignments and is known for his initiative and his ready grasp of business and technological issues. In his last job, he led a small advanced manufacturing technology firm that made inroads into Overmyer AMT's customer base.

Cecilia Overmyer has given Ed a clear mandate: Restore profitability within two years and reclaim market leadership within three to five years. Overmyer AMT's larger size and its more complex array of products and customers will make this a bigger challenge than the one Ed faced in his previous job. Competition will be fierce, and customer requirements for new advanced manufacturing technologies will continue to change rapidly.

"What we need now," Cecilia tells him, "is real leadership. I'm confident that you're the man for the job." She only hopes that she's right.

A Little Imagination

As you read the five scenarios, we're going to ask you to use a little imagination. Taken as a whole, they're a bit like the 1993 movie *Groundhog Day*. In that film, Bill Murray plays Phil, a jaded weatherman who's covering the annual groundhog ceremony in Punxsutawney, Pennsylvania. After a very frustrating day in a town he hates on sight, he wakes up to find himself reliving the day's events all over again. This bizarre time loop recurs morning after morning, until it dawns on Phil that he can learn from his experience. Once he decides to use each day as an opportunity to change his life, he gradually transforms himself. In the end, with a few basic quirks still intact, he becomes a happier, wiser, and more compassionate person, open to the wonder and uncertainty of life.

Reading the five scenarios will be a little like watching Phil gradually transform as he repeats the "same" day. Each new scenario will show the same person (Ed) responding to the same leadership challenge. The only difference is that, for each successive scenario, we imagine that Ed has developed to the next level of leadership agility. Throughout all the scenarios, Ed will remain exactly the same age and have the same IQ and personality type.

Assessing Your Level of Leadership Agility

As you read about "the five Eds," ask yourself which scenario best describes the way you would respond to a similar kind of leadership challenge. This will allow you to make an initial assessment of your current level of leadership agility. Reading the scenario that follows the one with which you most identify will show you what it'd be like to move to the next level.

If you're like the vast majority of managers, you have one agility level that represents your home base—a way of operating you gravitate to again and again throughout your day. But your agility level can also vary somewhat over the day. For example, you might function mostly at the Achiever level, sometimes at the Expert level, and occasionally shift into the Catalyst level.

Each scenario shows how a leader at a particular agility level would typically lead an organization, build a team, and conduct pivotal conversations. In reading these scenarios, notice whether your own level of agility tends to change as you move in and out of these three action arenas. For example, you might identify with the Achiever level of team and organizational leadership, but when it comes to pivotal conversations, you might identify more with the Expert.[1]

Here are a few more details to set the stage: You and Ed are friends but you don't see each other that often. Seven months into his new role as CEO, he invites you to dinner to catch up on things. Each scenario will take the form of a brief, informal conversation. Each time, you'll ask Ed the same questions about how things are going at work.

The first evening, you'll talk with Ed1, who's spent the last seven months leading at the Expert level. When that conversation is over, you'll take a few moments to reflect on it. Then you and Ed will have a "groundhog day" experience: The next evening at the same table, you'll talk with Ed2, who's just spent seven months operating at the Achiever level. You'll continue this way until you've talked with all five Eds. One more thing: You can remember each conversation, but Ed has "groundhog day amnesia"—he can only recall his current agility level.

Here we go . . .

ED1: THE EXPERT

YOU: Well, Ed, you've been at it for seven months. How's it going?

ED1: You know that expression, when you're up to your butt in alligators, it's hard to remember you're there to drain the swamp? Well, this place is full of alligators. It's a tough job, but it's the kind of pressure I thrive on—having to use my industry know-how to fix a business. I'm a quick study, and I like solving problems. Wind me up and I drill down, figure out the problems, and come up with the right solutions. The fact is, I've got a damned good track record with this kind of thing.

YOU: How did you get started?

ED1: I went right away after the information I needed to wrap my head around the business. I met with each of my directs, but I concentrated on the main functions—R&D, Manufacturing, and Sales and Marketing. I studied reports—got up to speed on sales projections, financials, manufacturing efficiencies, and the product development pipeline. I kept in shape lugging two briefcases stuffed with reports back and forth between home and the office!

I have to admit, though, we have so many different products for so many different kinds of customers, this business is a little more complex than I'd expected. The learning curve's been a real bear and I haven't climbed it quite as fast as I thought I would.

But it didn't take me long to figure out some obvious things that needed to be done. I got R&D to accelerate development on a couple of products that could really be big for us, and I got Sales and Marketing to support faster launches. I told my Manufacturing VP he needed to cut costs for the year by 15 percent, and I showed him a few specific budget items to prune. Looking toward improving next year, I told my R&D VP and my Sales and Marketing VP to work with me on a profitability analysis of all our products. Also, I told my VP of Finance to start getting me the monthly numbers on time. I gave him a new way to format the data to make it easier for me to analyze our costs.

YOU: What's it been like working with your executive team?

ED1: I get more real work done with my directs when I meet with them one-on-one. Getting everybody together on a regular schedule, whether we need to or not, just isn't productive. Don't get me wrong. If we need a group meeting, I call one, but I use those meetings mainly to keep everybody informed about my latest thinking and review progress. I usually start with Sales and Marketing, then focus on Manufacturing, then R&D.

By and large, though, group meetings usually don't get you that much. People tend to hold back. When you do progress reviews, people focus more on making a good impression than on getting down to the real facts. Everybody else sits back and looks like they don't want to be there. I've tried all the usual techniques to get people engaged—

forceful arguments, provocative questions. I've even tried to get them to debate issues. But I usually leave thinking, "No wonder this place is in trouble. Everyone just sits back and plays it safe."

To be honest, I'm frustrated. My VPs don't seem to share my sense of urgency. I'm also not sure we have all the right people in the top few levels of management. But I don't think this is the time to shake things up with a lot of personnel changes. Right now what I need to focus on is getting this business back on track and under control.

YOU: Have you had any conversations so far that have been especially challenging?

ED1: What pops to mind— Last week, my HR VP asked if she could talk to me about company morale. I said OK, and she started talking about this meeting I'd just held with the group that runs R&D. Apparently, some people were offended by some of the comments I made about how to run a first-class new product development process. Something about my cutting people off when they reacted to what I was saying. Well, I had to stop her right there, because the real problem was that they were defending business-as-usual. I've gotta say, I was pretty disappointed to see how closed-minded they were to new ideas. I mean, why did Cecilia Overmyer hire me in the first place? Because in my old job I was taking market share away from this company! I just wish more people here shared my passion for making this a first-class operation. Sometimes I wish I could clone myself.

After you and Ed1 go your separate ways, you reflect on what he said. He expressed a lot of pride in his knowledge and expertise. But you get the distinct impression that he's focusing on issues in so much detail, he's getting overwhelmed by the complexity of the business. You wonder how much the executive team's passive stance is a business-as-usual mind-set and how much it has to do with Ed1's behavior. Finally, there was that conversation with his HR VP, where he cut her off just as he did with the R&D managers. You know he's always been successful in the past, but you can't help but wonder how things will work out this time.

ED2: THE ACHIEVER

YOU: Well, Ed, you've been at it for seven months. How's it going?

ED2: It's moving forward. The big challenge is shifting people's mind-sets. This place has an interesting history. In his own time, Cecilia

Overmyer's father was a pretty innovative guy. During the 1990s this company was a real industry leader. But they fell into the success syndrome mentality. You know, everything's working, you have a lot of pride in what you do, and you just keep doing it. Pretty soon, you lose your external focus, you miss changes in the marketplace, then competitors start to eat your lunch. That's the basic problem here. I'm working on getting everyone's head back into the marketplace, thinking further out and looking at things from the customer's point of view.

YOU: How did you get started?

ED2: For the first six weeks or so, I mainly just took a lot in. Got to know the executive team, did skip-level interviews, talked with current customers and ones we'd lost, walked around the factory, and generally made myself visible. Even did a town meeting. I think leadership has a lot to do with the personal qualities you bring to your mission, that ability to challenge and inspire others to go beyond what they think is possible.

I know the industry quite well. The company's biggest strategic problem is that it's lost its innovative edge. In this industry new technologies quickly become commodities, so we need to reignite Overmyer's tradition of innovative leadership. We need to revamp our new product development process and some of our other business processes so we can be more responsive to our customers. From a strategic point of view, we also need to deal with commodification by improving and expanding the services we offer.

The other thing I did at the outset was look at our people. Having the right strategy and infrastructure is essential, but to execute, you've gotta have the right people.

YOU: What's it been like working with your executive team?

ED2: We usually meet once a week, unless something major comes up. I start by doing updates and sharing important information, but I try to reserve most of the time for group discussion of important topics, either strategic or operational. I know I need to motivate them to focus more externally, so in every meeting I try to introduce at least one agenda item that stretches them in that direction. For example, I instituted a more meaningful customer survey process, and I make sure we talk at the executive level about results and implications.

Several months after I got here, I started a strategic planning exercise, and that's worked really well. Nothing too detailed or ponderous. I used it mainly to make sure my team and their directs are all working off the same data. Even more important, we're driving for the same outcomes. By having them work on *how* we're going to achieve Cecilia's mandate, I got them to buy into the mandate itself! Not only that, I got them to sign off on some new strategies that really worked for me in my last job.

I can't say that it's all been smooth sailing, though. I don't think everyone's going to be up to the challenge in front of us. One guy in particular I got very concerned about—Ray, my VP of Manufacturing. I could tell he hadn't really bought in to the need to change, that he was just going through the motions. A few others in the top ranks are question marks right now. But Ray's performance really stuck out like a sore thumb, so I knew I had to deal with it.

YOU: Have you had any conversations so far that have been especially challenging?

ED2: The meeting I had last week with Ray. These discussions are never easy, but I know from experience that if you avoid acting on major performance issues you can be sorry later. I had a number of conversations with Ray, starting early on. Before long, I was telling him what he needed to do if he was going to stay with us. I asked our HR VP to help me be sure I was handling this the right way. She was actually very helpful.

The previous VP of Manufacturing was a guy named Dan. When Cecilia's father went from being CEO and chairman to just being chairman, he promoted Dan to CEO, and Dan tapped Ray to take over Manufacturing. Unfortunately, Ray got promoted to a level over his head. He was hanging on, doing the old turtle routine, keeping his head in his shell and hoping no one would find out.

It finally came down to this: I realized I wasn't going to achieve Cecilia's mandate with Ray in that role. Last week, I finally told him he had to move on. We got him a good package, and I'm probably going to replace him from outside. We may need to let a few other people go as well.

Afterward, comparing this conversation to the one before it, it strikes you that Ed2's approach is quite different from Ed1's. While Ed1 focused mainly on discrete problems, Ed2 is more outcome-oriented. His top priority is achieving Cecilia's mandate. Whereas Ed1 seemed to lead primarily by giving orders, Ed2 wants to motivate people to adopt a strategic mind-set that's more focused on customers and marketplace dynamics. Ed2 also seems more prepared for the give-and-take of tough conversations: Unlike Ed1, he initiates discussion about major performance issues, and he accepts feedback and advice from his VP of Human Resources.

Then a few questions come to mind: Are his VPs really as supportive of his objectives and strategies as he thinks they are? Will the strategies that worked so well for his previous company be on target for the new one? What about the managers at the next level, which include people managing the company's overseas offices? Is Ed2 placing his VPs in a situation where they'll wind up getting things done by giving Ed1-style orders to their organizations?

ED3: THE CATALYST

YOU: Well, Ed, you've been at it for seven months. How's it going?

ED3: It's quite a challenge, but I'm excited about where we're going! Overmyer AMT definitely lost its edge after Cecilia's father stepped out of the CEO role, but I've always respected this company's tradition of excellence and innovation. In the martial arts, they say you need to aim right through and beyond your target. That's what I want to do with Cecilia's mandate. I envision a company that will not only regain its status as industry leader but also become a benchmark for other industries—a participative, high-performing organization that's a great place to work. To do that, people need to learn to lead and manage this place in new ways. It's going to be challenging for everyone, but I think the great majority will be able to rise to the occasion.

YOU: How did you get started?

ED3: I got to know people at the top levels, but I also walked around a lot and started following some of the social networks. I sought out the innovators, learned what they're doing, and gave them some encouragement. I also met with key customers, including some former customers, and I've asked my VPs and their people to do the same. Then we talked about what we learned.

A couple of months in, I had a two-day off-site with my directs and their directs, a good-sized group that included our top overseas managers. To help design and facilitate the meeting, I brought in a facilitator I worked with in my previous job. I started by saying a few things about myself and my respect for this company and its people. I said I'd been in their place a few times before when a new leader came in, and I could easily imagine the questions they might have about the company's plans and their own future. I reiterated our mandate to achieve profitability and industry leadership, and I said, "To achieve these objectives, we need everyone to contribute their best work and their best ideas. That's what's going to secure your job and mine, starting right here in this meeting."

Then I said that, these days, sustaining industry leadership takes more than innovative know-how and a can-do attitude. If you look out across different industries, I believe that the best companies are those that intentionally set out to establish an organizational culture based on participation, mutual respect, and straight talk—and that's what I intend for us to do, starting with this meeting. Of course, that kind of talk makes people nervous, because they're not used to managing or being managed that way. But I got right into it by asking for questions. A few brave souls spoke up, and we were off and running. It was a hugely productive two days. We only touched the tip of the iceberg, but our facilitator captured everything in writing, and it really opened things up.

YOU: What's it been like working with your executive team?

ED3: In many ways it's like a laboratory. I'm trying to develop an executive team that can serve as the prototype of a participative culture, which they can then disseminate to the rest of the organization. This is so important that I try to spend two hours a week with the team engaging in important strategic and operational issues. They know I make the final decisions, but they have a lot of influence. I may put my ideas on the table and ask for their critique, or I may just throw out a topic and let them go at it for a while. They may have fallen asleep at the wheel before I got here, but they know a hell of a lot about this company. Sometimes I wind up changing my mind, and sometimes I don't. But the main thing is that they see I can be influenced by their ideas, and they know it's not just a game to get their buy-in. I've already made some better decisions with their input than I would've made on my own. Not only that, it creates an environment where anyone can step in and exert constructive leadership. It also models what they can do with their teams.

Another vehicle I'm using is the strategic planning process. In addition to the usual process with the executive team, with their people playing supporting roles, I said I wanted to set up a way to get meaningful input from a cross-section of people at all levels. Not just as a feel-good thing, but because I think people at all levels can come up with interesting ideas—strategic as well as operational—that can be really useful.

The team batted the idea around a while, then dove in. A few weeks ago, we started a series of focus groups to capture ideas from a broad cross-section of employees. We also tasked a couple of groups to get ideas from outside stakeholders. This process is generating a lot of positive energy, which we really need right now, and I know from past experience that we'll get some ideas that will really make us think. When my VPs see what this generates, I think it's going to help change the way they lead their own organizations. That's the first step toward creating a new culture.

We also need to reexamine our core business processes, especially product development. We've also got some huge opportunities to make our manufacturing processes more efficient and more environmentally responsible at the same time. Lots of cost savings possible there.

YOU: Have you had any conversations so far that have been especially challenging?

ED3: I can think of several. I've been coaching some of my VPs. But about three months ago, I asked my executive team for feedback on my leadership approach. After some hemming and hawing, some people actually spoke up! Parts of that discussion were a little difficult, but it was very helpful overall.

The most challenging was a series of meetings with Ray, my VP of Manufacturing. After a couple of months, I saw that we weren't going to turn this place around if he stayed in that position. These conversations are always tough, but I finally just told him, very straight, what I'd observed about his attitude and his performance. I checked out a few assumptions I had, asked him how he saw the whole situation, and gave him a lot of room to respond. Pretty soon he opened up and acknowledged that he was over his head trying to manage an organization on an international scale.

After we reached that level of honesty, I said, "If you could invent any job you wanted, what would it be?" Turns out that Ray loves being a plant manager. After I talked it over with other key players, I concluded that he'd be a great asset back in a plant manager role. He said he'd love to do that, even with the pay cut. I won't go into detail about how it's all going to work, but it's opened the door to several other important personnel changes.

After you part company with Ed3, you reflect on the differences between this conversation and the previous one. Ed3 has a more ambitious vision that involves creating a company that not only is an industry leader but also has a model organizational culture. In fact, in just seven months, he's already doing things to shift the culture in that direction: that first three-level meeting, the way he's leading his management team, and the strategic thinking process he and his team have instituted. This participative approach might go a long way toward addressing the commitment and execution questions you had after your dinner with Ed2.

The other thing that strikes you is the difference between how Ed2 and Ed3 dealt with the VP of Manufacturing. Both confronted the issue, but when Ed3 got Ray to open up, it led to a more creative solution. Actually, Ed3's whole approach sounds pretty good. You just wonder how he'll handle the tension that might develop between the people who commit themselves to the transformation he's starting and those who'd rather continue with business as usual.

ED4: THE CO-CREATOR

YOU: Well, Ed, you've been at it for seven months. How's it going?

ED4: It's challenging and exciting at the same time. Something of a roller coaster. But I feel like we're already revitalizing this place. The company's tradition of excellence and innovation gives us a lot to build on. The other night, just as I was drifting off to sleep, I got this image that brought together everything I'm trying to do here. The image was three waves. The first, short-term wave returns us to profitability, and we become an industry leader. On the medium-term wave we develop the culture and the infrastructure of an agile, high-performing organization that's a magnet for the kind of people we need. The long-term wave establishes us as the leader in creating the AMT industry of the future, not just in technical innovation but also in social and environmental responsibility.

For example, if you look at the future of advanced manufacturing, you see highly skilled computer-control jobs driving out lower-skilled jobs. Yet here in the States, our students are way behind their worldwide counterparts in math and science. I put together a task force to see what we can do about this, and they tapped people from the education sector and some of our client companies. They've already identified a lot of good ideas, like IBM's practice of developing new career options for senior employees. Instead of retiring, they stay with the company and get certified to teach technical subjects to the next generation.

Each wave is longer than the one before it, all starting now and building over time. I think this could be the most meaningful assignment of my career. As far as I'm concerned, I'm in this for the long haul.

YOU: How did you get started?

ED4: During the first six weeks or so, I got out and felt the pulse of the place—learned a lot and had lots of "vision conversations," where I told people what I think this company can become and elicited their dreams for this place. My vision for the company is so far-reaching that I was surprised to find so many kindred spirits—including quite a few closet environmentalists—along with many who're stuck in the mind-set that being environmentally responsible automatically makes you less competitive.

I also met with key customers—and some former customers—face to face, I sought out a number of other stakeholders, and I encouraged my VPs and their people to do this, too. I also instituted a process where, every month or so, we pick a customer company in the area, and we invite a few people—like a plant manager and a manufacturing engineer—to spend an hour with us talking candidly about ways to strengthen our relationship.

A couple of months in, I had a two-day off-site with my executive team and their direct reports, including our top overseas managers. By then I'd connected with just about everybody in the room, so when I talked about where we can go as company, I knew I wasn't just speaking for myself. Then we moved into some facilitated discussions that helped us get the company's issues on the table. The two questions I kept asking were: Where are the internal and external obstacles to reaching our potential? and How can we overcome them?

YOU: What's it been like working with your executive team?

ED4: If the three waves of change are really going to happen, I can't lead them by myself. I need to build a collaborative leadership team, where every one of my VPs feels accountable not only for their own function but also for the company as a whole. I have no intention of giving up my final decision-making authority, but I want my executive team to function much like a collective CEO, where company-wide issues aren't just my purview—they're everyone's responsibility. A real team where each of us helps all of us succeed.

We're still in the early stages of development, but I already see signs we're moving in the right direction. A few months ago, we decided to create a scenario-based strategic thinking process that will incorporate input from a broad cross-section of employees, plus some outside stakeholders. We had a big meeting to launch the process, where people from all levels made presentations. During the week before the meeting, there was this incredible buzz as people prepared—lots of energy and excitement. I was really impressed—moved, actually—by the panel of manufacturing supervisors. They were so nervous and so real. They had lots of good ideas, and you could see what it did for them to be thrust into that role.

Ever since, we've been hearing how much our people liked the meeting. But it was also a great opportunity for the VPs. They got to experience themselves as a leadership team—empowering others but also empowering themselves. It also gave me a chance to see how they interact with people at different levels.

I also want the executive team to get to the point where we have enough trust in each other that anyone can step in and exercise leadership. I don't want to be the only person in the room who confronts Ray when he doesn't walk his talk. I can do the tough one-on-ones when they're necessary, but I'd want to see a more collective sense of responsibility, and I've told them that. I think we're getting there, but it's still early days.

YOU: Have you had any conversations so far that have been especially challenging?

ED4: The toughest I've had so far was a conversation with Cecilia about social and environmental responsibility. The first time the subject came up was during the interview process, when I mentioned that I'd cut costs in my old company by increasing energy efficiency and cutting environmental waste. I could tell that this whole way of thinking was unfamiliar to her, and we didn't pursue it further at that point.

Later, when I discovered some environmental co-conspirators in one of our local plants, I gave them some money from my own discretionary budget so they could do a pilot program, under the radar, and demonstrate how environmental efficiency cuts costs. But some good old boys from the plant got the word to Cecilia that I was "wasting money on nonessentials," and she called me on the carpet. She was very angry, insulting actually. Said she'd explicitly told me to hold off on doing anything like that. In fact, she hadn't told me that explicitly, but I knew well enough how she felt.

I just sat there at first, listening to her, aware of some very negative feelings her rant kicked off in me. I didn't agree with what she said, but I think I managed to respond without being too defensive. I reflected back what I heard her say, then I asked if she'd be willing to hear my rationale for doing the pilot. She said OK and seemed to calm down. I explained how I'd done this on a larger scale in my old job and gotten some fairly quick and impressive returns on the investment. Long story short, she agreed to withhold judgment until we could review the results of the pilot together.

I guess that's a pretty good overview of how things are going. Have any advice for an old friend? I can use all the help I can get.

You think for a moment and then say, "You seem to be spending a lot of time on what many managers might consider peripheral issues. You're trying to create a collaborative culture, and you've got teams focusing on social and environmental issues, when the company is struggling with profitability. Are you really sure about starting all three waves at the same time?"

"That's a very good question," he replies. "In fact, it's come up in our executive team meetings. In terms of environmental efficiencies, there's enough low-hanging fruit in this area that it will help us, not hurt us, in becoming more profitable. Things like the IBM idea that have short-term costs and longer-term paybacks—we'll have to play those by ear. I'm trying to develop an executive team that can raise and manage exactly these kinds of dilemmas. For me to be truly strategic as a CEO, I think participation and collaboration are essential. The faster we develop a cohesive, straight-talking executive team, the faster we'll return to profitability and industry leadership."

ED5: THE SYNERGIST

YOU: Well, Ed, you've been at it for seven months. How's it going?

ED5: It's been exhilarating and almost all-consuming. Right now, I'm in search of a little more balance between work and the rest of my life.

At this moment, I'm just enjoying this opportunity to clear my head, reconnect with you, and savor some good food!

When I was first offered this job, I wasn't at all sure about it. I actually had a lot of questions about staying in the industry. In my last job I had a lot of success demonstrating how much money an AMT company can save by being environmentally efficient. But when I looked at what's happening globally, changing one company seemed like just a drop in the bucket.

I thought about becoming a corporate responsibility consultant, but I'm really more of a leader than a consultant, and manufacturing is in my blood. Then one morning, just as I ended my morning meditation, this question hit me from out of the blue: What would a manufacturing industry look like that's *really good for people and the planet*—both in the products it produces and in how they get produced? Could I develop a new kind of AMT company with an overarching mission to help create a truly sustainable manufacturing industry on a worldwide scale? What if we started by becoming a model company and then added consulting services to help our customers follow our example?

The more I thought about it, the more exciting and scary the whole idea became. It seemed like way more than I could possibly accomplish. But I also had this persistent feeling that, somehow, this was what I needed to do.

YOU: How did you get started?

ED5: I did all the usual things—the stuff that, by now, feels very natural: Got to know my direct reports, started to build relationships, and tried to understand the social networks. Had conversations throughout the company, many about vision and innovation. Found quite a number of highly competent self-starters and a number of co-conspirators and gave them all a lot of encouragement.

I talked with customers and other stakeholders and got my VPs and their people to do the same. I also held "opportunity conversations," where I've pulled our executive team and other groups of managers together. We pooled our knowledge about emerging customer needs, new technologies, what competitors are doing, and environmental issues—even had a few speakers in. Then we brainstormed where our best opportunities might lie.

A couple of months in, I had a two-day off-site with my executive team and their direct reports, which included people from overseas. I gave a short talk to help them get to know me and let them know I'd been in their shoes. I focused on profitability and industry leadership, and then I planted a little seed that I've been watering ever since: Being an industry leader isn't just about market share. This industry is constantly changing, sometimes in very new and disruptive ways. Being a true industry leader means influencing how the AMT industry evolves, which could mean influencing the future of manufacturing itself. I was brief—just planted the idea.

After some Q&A, we spent the rest of the time in roundtable discussions on two sets of topics: First, what are our strengths? What initiatives are already moving us toward industry leadership, and how can we build on those? Second, what are the obstacles to regaining industry leadership, and how can we remove them? It felt like a great start. I could feel the energy shift as we began to talk about our strengths and how we can build on them.

YOU: What's it been like working with your executive team?

ED5: My aim is to transform the executive group into a truly collaborative leadership team that can essentially function as a collective CEO, which will free me to focus more on long-term vision and external relationships. They're already showing a lot of promise. They designed a very successful meeting to kick off the scenario-based strategic thinking process we initiated. That meeting generated a great deal of buzz and lots of good ideas. Great developmental opportunity for the VPs.

Within the first month, I knew we had the wrong guy as VP of Manufacturing. We had some heart-to-heart discussions, and he actually acknowledged that he was in over his head. By mutual consent we moved him back into a plant manager role and this allowed us to make some other needed personnel changes. We're about to replace him with an extremely competent and innovative guy, someone who shares my audacious vision for the company. He has extensive experience creating high-performance, team-based manufacturing plants—exactly what we need going forward. Very exciting!

YOU: Have you had any conversations so far that have been especially challenging?

ED5: The most challenging and interesting conversations have been with Cecelia. In the early months it was extremely important to her to see that we were taking tangible steps to return the company to profitability. However, as she's gotten more comfortable with me and more confident about what I'm doing, she's been able to relax enough to have some heart-to-heart conversations about what she wants as her family's legacy. I've encouraged her to talk about her values, and we've also started to talk about ways we might begin to integrate those values more fully into how the company operates.

For example, she was willing to support the pilot we've started, where we've added environmental efficiency criteria into some process redesign work we're doing in one of the manufacturing plants. Down the road, she'd like to be doing something to support better education in math and science. But what really sparked her interest is this wild idea a few of us came up with: Just before I was hired, my predecessor was thinking about selling off the company's old tool and die unit, the last vestige of the Overmyer Tool & Die Company founded by Cecelia's great-grandfather. Our idea is to take the unit into the third world where it can be used to support the development of micro-enterprises among the poorest of the poor. It's kind of a crazy idea, but once we're profitable again, we might just find a way to make it work.

Overall, I'd say I have a tiger by the tail! You've been a very patient listener. I'm interested in your perspective on all this.

You tell him you think he's pretty gutsy, and you ask him if he ever worries that he's being too idealistic—that he'll overreach and wind up crashing if others don't ultimately share his vision.

"Yeah, sometimes I worry about that," he replies. "Sometimes I feel very confident. At other times, I feel I'm being stretched beyond my capacity. Who knows how this will turn out? The thing is: The underlying vision is so compelling, I feel like I just have to go for it. It sure keeps me on my toes!"

You respond and continue the conversation and before long you realize that you're talking about important things in your own life. Ed5 has become the listener.

INITIAL SELF-ASSESSMENT

Some people who read these scenarios wonder if the post-heroic levels we've portrayed aren't a bit idealistic. A few even want assurances that these levels are based on sound research.[2] In fact, although the preceding scenarios are fictional, each one is research-based, crafted to be consistent with what clients and interviewees operating at that agility level have said and done in similar situations. When you get to

Part Two, you'll see many connections between the scenarios presented here and the real-life leadership stories presented in those chapters.

This would be a good time to flip back through the five scenarios and consider which one best represents the way you exercise leadership.[3] (You could also use Table 1.1). As we noted earlier, you may find that you function at somewhat different levels of agility in different kinds of situations. If so, it's helpful to note where these variances tend to occur. Does your level of agility change mainly when you move from one action arena to another, or are there other situational factors that cause you to act from different levels of agility?[4]

You can also begin to ask yourself: Having seen the full spectrum of leadership agility levels, am I satisfied with where I am now? Suppose you usually operate at the Achiever level, and you'd like to move to the Catalyst level, but you're not sure you'd ever want to be a Co-Creator or Synergist. That's fine. To shift fully from one level of leadership agility to another requires time and intentionality. So take it one step at a time. Once you're firmly established in the next level, subsequent levels may or may not attract your interest. You won't know for sure until you get there.

CHAPTER THREE

Four Competencies for Agile Leadership

H ow can you become a more agile leader? We address this question more completely in Chapter Ten, but here's the short answer: The fastest and most reliable way is to use an integral approach, one that combines the usual outside-in approach to leadership development with an inside-out approach. Fine, you may say. But what, exactly, does that mean?

You can increase your agility from the outside-in by developing agile leadership competencies and putting them repeatedly into action. The scenarios in Chapter Two identify behaviors associated with each of the five agility levels. However, they only hint at the mental and emotional capacities that make these competencies possible. Why, for example, does Ed3, the Catalyst, lead his organization in a more participative manner than Ed2, the Achiever? To answer this kind of question, we need to understand leadership agility from the inside-out.

As we noted in the Introduction, leaders develop the capacities needed for a particular level of agility when they grow into the corresponding stage of personal development. Through extensive research and analysis, we have discovered that each developmental stage is essentially a constellation of eight mental and emotional capacities. Each time you grow into a new developmental stage, this constellation of capacities matures to a new level. Further, all eight capacities contribute directly to your effectiveness as a leader.

An example of a developmental capacity is stakeholder complexity, the ability to understand and empathize with perspectives that differ from your own, whether or not you agree with them. One reason that Ed3's leadership is more participative than Ed2's is that Ed3 has a greater capacity for understanding the perspectives held by his stakeholders. Achiever-level leaders are frequently advised by coaches and consultants to act more like Ed3. Yet these behaviors often don't stick. Why? It's usually because achievers haven't developed the mental and emotional capacities needed to support participative leadership.[1]

As you'll see in Chapter Ten, an integral approach to leadership development makes it possible to develop new capacities and learn new leadership behaviors at the same time. When you use this approach, new leadership behaviors come more easily, and they feel more natural.[2]

THE LEADERSHIP AGILITY COMPASS

To help take full advantage of this integral approach, this chapter introduces you to a graphic tool called the Leadership Agility Compass. Through our research, we have discovered that those leaders who are most successful in turbulent organizational environments exhibit four mutually reinforcing competencies:

- *Context-setting agility* improves your ability to scan your environment, frame the initiatives you need to take, and clarify the outcomes you need to achieve.

- *Stakeholder agility* increases your ability to engage with key stakeholders in ways that build support for your initiative.

- *Creative agility* enables you to transform the problems you encounter into the results you need.

- *Self-leadership agility* is the ability to use your initiatives as opportunities to develop into the kind of leader you want to be.[3]

The Leadership Agility Compass shown in Figure 3.1 provides a way to visualize these four competencies. Each quadrant symbolizes one of the four competencies. The outer circle represents the leadership tasks associated with each competency. The middle circle represents the capacities that make each competency possible. In this chapter, we walk you around the four quadrants of the Compass, describing each competency with brief examples from the "five Eds." As we do so, we also describe the pair of inner capacities that underlie each competency. Toward the end of the chapter, we present another version of the Compass that displays all eight capacities.

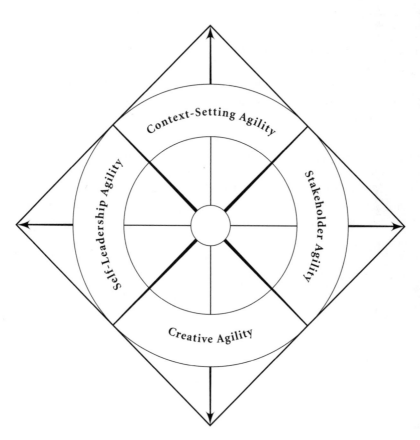

Figure 3.1. The Leadership Agility Compass.

Context-Setting Agility

Viewed as a set of leadership tasks, the competency we call context-setting agility includes scanning your environment, anticipating important changes, deciding what initiatives to take, scoping each initiative, and determining your desired outcomes.[4] As with all four competencies, context-setting agility evolves through five levels. Your level of agility in carrying out these tasks depends on how fully you've developed two capacities: *situational awareness* and *sense of purpose.*

When you're taking a leadership initiative, your situational awareness refers to the quality of your attention to the larger context that surrounds it. This capacity gives you the mental equivalent of a zoom lens: You can step back from an issue, view it in a larger context, and then zoom in on the issue, keeping this broader perspective in mind. As you develop your situational awareness further, you gain an increased appreciation of the impact of your initiatives on their larger social context and on the natural environment.

As your sense of purpose develops, it becomes increasingly important to you that your leadership initiatives serve others' needs in truly meaningful ways.[5] You find these initiatives highly motivating, even if their ultimate outcomes lie in the long-term future. As your sense of purpose develops, you also find that you can move back and forth between different time frames with greater ease.[6]

For example, each of the post-heroic Eds has a level of context-setting agility that allows him to launch visionary initiatives that take into account factors beyond his particular industry. As a Catalyst, Ed3 has aspirations for Overmyer AMT that include but go beyond achieving specific strategic outcomes like profitability and industry leadership.[7] He wants to create a culture that will be benchmarked by companies in a variety of industries. Ed4 and Ed5 envision a business where corporate responsibility is a central strategic and operating principle.[8]

Stakeholder Agility

As a set of leadership tasks, stakeholder agility involves identifying your initiative's key stakeholders, understanding what they have at stake, assessing the alignment between your objectives and theirs, and finding ways to increase alignment. Your level of agility in carrying out these tasks depends on the development of two capacities: your *stakeholder understanding* and your *power style.*

Your level of stakeholder understanding determines how deeply you can understand the viewpoints and objectives of those who have a stake in your initiatives, especially when they differ from your own. Your power style is determined partly by your assumptions about power and authority. It's also expressed in the way you typically respond when your views and interests conflict with those of key stakeholders. Most leaders have a power style that emphasizes one of two basic forms of power: *Assertive power* takes the form of advocating your own views and interests. *Receptive power* may initially seem like a contradiction in terms. But it's a more subtle form of power, based on a willingness to understand and seriously consider others' views and objectives. Most managers at heroic levels of agility have a power style that's considerably more assertive than receptive, although a surprising minority rely primarily on receptive power.[9]

As we've seen, the Eds with post-heroic levels of stakeholder agility have a capacity to enter deeply into frames of reference that differ from their own while still honoring their own perspective. This capacity is related to their enhanced ability to integrate assertive power and receptive power. The post-heroic Eds are intent on developing participative teams and organizations not simply to gain buy-in but because they feel that genuine dialogue improves the quality of their decisions.[10]

Creative Agility

Successful leadership initiatives transform actual or potential problems into desired results.[11] The problems you encounter in complex, rapidly changing environments are what cognitive scientists call "ill-structured," meaning that they're complex and have novel features. An ill-structured problem isn't predefined. You have to define it yourself. Rather than having one right answer, it has a number of plausible solutions. You rarely have access to all the information you need to solve the problem just when you need it. Problems become even more ill-structured when they cross disciplinary, organizational, or cultural boundaries and when they need to be solved in conjunction with other problems.[12]

Ill-structured problems are best solved using a competency we call creative agility: problem solving that uses both critical and breakthrough thinking to generate uniquely appropriate responses.[13] Viewed as a set of leadership tasks, creative agility involves applying this kind of thinking as you identify and diagnose key issues, generate and develop possible options, and decide on the best solutions.[14] Your level of creative agility depends on two personal capacities: *connective awareness* and *reflective judgment*.[15]

As you diagnose and solve problems, connective awareness is what allows you to hold different ideas and experiences in mind, compare and contrast them, and make meaningful connections between them. It's what allows you to step back from the problems you face, so you can understand how they're related, prioritize them, or see how they're similar to and different from those you've faced in the past. Connective awareness also allows you to discover what apparent opposites have in common—a noted hallmark of creative thinking.[16]

When you take leadership initiatives, reflective judgment is the thought process you use to determine what's true and decide the best course of action to take. It also includes the rationales you use to justify these conclusions to yourself and to others.[17] As your level of reflective judgment develops, you become increasingly aware of the subjectivity inherent in all human perception and decision making. You also begin to see ways in which your own judgment, and that of others, is shaped by nonrational factors such as temperament, family upbringing, and cultural background. As these realizations sink in more deeply, you develop the ability to question underlying assumptions and seriously consider a range of diverse viewpoints.[18]

The post-heroic Eds see the same strategic problems and solutions that Ed2 sees. However, their level of reflective judgment makes them less attached to any single frame of reference as they think about these issues. This orientation makes it easier for them to step outside conventional wisdom and think more creatively. In addition, their level of connective awareness enables them to hold the mental and emotional tension between differing frames of reference. This capacity gives them the ability to transform conflict into true win-win solutions by making useful connections between ideas and objectives that appear to oppose one another.

For example, consider Ed3's approach to his VP's performance problem. Rather than limit his options to those considered by the heroic Eds (keep him in his current role or fire him), Ed3 surfaces the VP's frame of reference (his operational rather than strategic orientation) and uncovers a win-win option: move the VP back to his plant management role. This solution is actually win-win-win, because it allows Ed3 to make other personnel changes, simultaneously solving a wider range of problems.

Self-Leadership Agility

In *Mastering Self-Leadership* Charles Manz and Christopher Neck say, "If we ever hope to be effective leaders of others, we need first to be able to lead ourselves effectively."[19] As a set of tasks, self-leadership is a cyclical process: You determine the kind of leader you want to be, use your everyday initiatives to experiment toward these aspirations, reflect on your experience, and fine-tune the changes you'd like to make.[20] Your level of agility in engaging in this process depends on two personal capacities, your *self-awareness* and your *developmental motivation.*

Your level of self-awareness refers to the quality of attention and reflection you bring to your own thoughts, feelings, and behaviors. In a more general sense, it also refers to the accuracy and completeness of your self-knowledge, including how well you understand your current strengths and limitations as a leader. Each time you move to a new stage, the quality of your self-awareness evolves, and what motivates you to develop as a person and as a leader also changes.[21]

Particularly at the heroic levels, your developmental motivation is shaped by three key factors: your primary source of professional self-esteem, your leadership ideals (images of the leader you want to be), and the emotional tone you use to assess your progress. When you feel you're living up to your leadership ideals, or making progress toward them, your self-esteem typically goes up. When you feel you're not living up to them, or not making adequate progress, your self-esteem typically goes down. In moderation, either reaction can provide motivation to move toward your leadership ideals.

At the Expert level, your underlying developmental motivation is to improve yourself as a leader so you'll be admired for your astuteness and expertise. At the Achiever level, you want to gain the competencies needed to achieve outcomes that will advance your career and bring success to your organization. At the post-heroic levels, you develop an intrinsic motivation to grow as a person. You want to find greater personal meaning in your work and in all aspects of your life. Particularly at the Co-Creator and Synergist levels, you want to lead in a way that serves others while bringing a deeper sense of purpose to your own life. For example, Ed4 and Ed5 envision a company that can achieve a greater good and provide everyone involved with ways to make meaningful contributions.

At post-heroic levels of self-leadership, you reach new levels of self-awareness. You become conscious of habitual behaviors, feelings, and assumptions that escaped your attention at heroic levels. You discover that harsh self-judgment makes you feel defensive and discourages true self-knowledge. Paradoxically, the more self-knowledge is accompanied by an acceptant attitude, the easier it is to find the inner strength to make the changes you need to make.[22] With this outlook, it's more natural to be proactive in seeking feedback. For example, we see Ed3 soliciting feedback on his leadership style from his executive team.

PUTTING IT ALL TOGETHER

Highly agile leaders orchestrate the four competencies we've just described so they work in concert. It's best to begin an initiative by explicitly setting the context, but it's often wise to communicate with key stakeholders before you complete this step. This is also a good time to think about the opportunities your initiative may provide to experiment with new and more effective leadership behavior.

Creative agility is particularly useful when you're working on the specific issues you encounter in planning and implementing your initiative. To maximize your effectiveness, you need to engage key stakeholders in creative problem solving, and you need to be proactive in learning from your experience throughout the initiative. Also, keep in mind that new developments in the larger context may require you to use your context-setting agility to reconsider your initiative's scope and objectives.

The relationships between the four leadership agility competencies and the eight capacities that support them are depicted in Figure 3.2.

The outer circle on this graphic represents the tasks carried out using the four leadership agility competencies. The middle circle represents the four pairs of capacities that support these competencies.[23]

LEVELS OF AWARENESS AND INTENT

Distilled to its essence, each leadership agility competency involves stepping back from your current focus in a way that gives you greater perspective, followed by full engagement in what needs to be done next:

• *Context-setting agility* entails stepping back and determining the best initiatives to take, given the changes taking place in your larger environment.

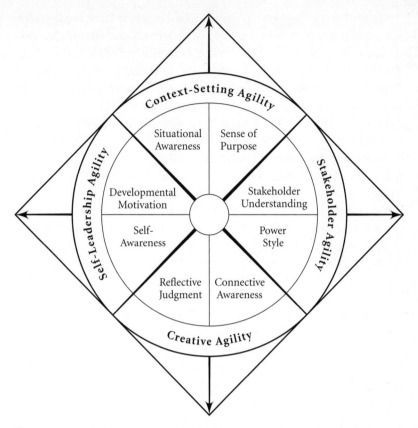

The innermost circle represents the level of awareness and intent that underlies each level of leadership agility.

Figure 3.2. The Leadership Agility Compass: Supporting Capacities.

- *Stakeholder agility* requires you to step back from your own views and objectives to consider the needs and perspectives of those who have a stake in your initiatives.

- *Creative agility* involves stepping back from your habitual assumptions and developing optimal solutions to the often novel and complex issues you face.

- *Self-leadership agility* entails stepping back; becoming more aware of your thoughts, feelings, and behaviors; and experimenting with new and more effective approaches.

At any level of leadership agility, when you step back from taking action, you step back into the "level of awareness and intent" that corresponds to that level.[24] For example, when you step back at the Achiever level, you activate a robust reflective capacity and an intention to achieve desired outcomes. Repeatedly using this level of awareness and intent in your leadership initiatives helps you develop Achiever-level capacities, such as the ability to think strategically.[25]

As you move to the Catalyst level, you activate an additional level of awareness and intent: You learn to step back and reflect "on the spot." This new capability increases your awareness of assumptions, feelings, and behaviors you'd otherwise overlook. You also develop an intention to create contexts that enable the sustained achievement of desired outcomes. Applied to your leadership initiatives, this new level of awareness and intent helps you develop a new level of agility: As we saw in Robert's story in Chapter One, you gain an increased capacity for visionary thinking, and you create opportunities for key stakeholders to participate in shaping your strategies.

To return to the Leadership Agility Compass: The innermost circle represents the level of awareness and intent that underlies your level of leadership agility. Applied repeatedly in action, this level of awareness and intent develops the eight mental and emotional capacities identified in the middle circle. These capacities, in turn, bring the four leadership agility competencies to a new level.

The five chapters in Part Two use real-life stories to give you a more complete understanding of the five levels of leadership agility. Each chapter ends with a section that shows how the eight capacities just mentioned evolve at a particular level of agility. That section also includes a description of the level of awareness and intent that underlies these capacities, a topic we return to in Chapter Ten, when we show how you can become a more agile leader.

Five Levels of Leadership Agility

CHAPTER FOUR

Expert Level

Solve Key Problems

T ony was a sales manager in his early thirties who worked for a company that made personal care products. After gaining experience in various sales management positions, he was promoted to trade marketing manager for Warehouse Clubs.[1] Like about 45 percent of today's managers, Tony operated at the Expert level of leadership agility.

WHAT LEADERSHIP MEANS TO AN EXPERT

How does an Expert-level manager understand leadership? Tony wanted to distinguish himself as a leader in the minds of his boss, his customers, and his team. When asked what it meant to be a leader, he said:

> The kind of leader I most respect is someone who is sought out to solve problems and does so with self-assuredness and style. These leaders consistently make the right choices. They aren't afraid to stand alone and defend their positions when they know they're in the right.

They defend, support, and instruct weaker teammates and maintain a positive team spirit. If they do make mistakes, they immediately take responsibility and make things right again. When things get hard, they redouble their efforts. When things are good, they continue to press for growth and further success rather than resting on their laurels.

That's the kind of leader I want people to see me as being. I want to be respected as a real expert in my position, someone with a lot of business acumen, who really understands our business, our customers, and our category. I want to be the first person sought by Marketing and by the field on any issues pertaining to our business. If I can do that, I think I'll be considered, maybe even recruited, for a position within our brand marketing department or a high-level field sales position for a top ten customer.

Asked what he thought he needed to do to become a better leader, Tony responded:

I've already demonstrated that I can learn the salient nuances of new products and classes of trade. What I need to do now is get fully up to speed on brand directions and divisional initiatives. I think I can speak in public with a good deal of poise, but I need to have a better command of the facts when I'm dealing with peers and colleagues.

When asked if he'd like to improve in any other areas, Tony acknowledged that he was sometimes stubborn and opinionated, and that he needed to work at keeping an open mind. Then he added, "But a healthy skepticism toward others' opinions generally serves me well, because it forces me to think critically."

In a moment, we'll complete the picture of the Expert-level leader with stories about three other managers: Beth, a team supervisor in a bank's Corporate Actions department, who learns how to have more effective pivotal conversations at the Expert level. Carlos, an accounting manager in a young architectural firm, who confronts his limitations as an Expert team leader. Kevin, the CEO of a regional hospital council, who struggles to improve his organization. Taken together, these stories illustrate both the strengths and the limitations of Expert-level competencies. We'll briefly summarize these competencies now, so you can keep them in mind as you read.

If you're an Expert-level manager, you have a strong problem-solving orientation, and your thinking is more independent and analytical than it was at pre-Expert levels. In taking leadership initiatives, your orientation is likely to be more tactical than strategic. You tend to focus on the organizational unit under your formal authority, and you rarely take the initiative to improve relationships with other units.

At the Expert level, you don't yet have a full appreciation of the extent to which the motivations and expectations of key stakeholders can influence the effectiveness of your initiatives. If the goals and assumptions that drive your initiative conflict with those of your stakeholders, you tend to assume that your perspective is the correct one. As we'll discuss in a moment, the way you handle this conflict depends upon whether your power style in a given relationship is predominantly assertive or accommodative.

When carrying out an initiative, your strong problem-solving capacities kick into gear. However, rather than stepping back to see how various problems might be related, you tend to tackle one problem at a time, each as an isolated task. As you move from problem to problem, innovative thinking takes a backseat. Although you don't realize it, limiting personal biases are likely to influence your approach. Because you tend to assume that your judgments are correct, you're not likely to test your views against objective data or differing viewpoints.

As you grow into the Expert level, you develop an introspective awareness that allows you to recognize recurring inner moods and fashion a more independent image of yourself. Just being part of a group, a central motivation at the previous level, is no longer enough. You now derive your self-esteem from developing your own beliefs, advancing your knowledge and skills, and being respected as someone who can improve and accomplish things. When you feel you're not making adequate strides to improve yourself, you can be quite self-critical. Together, your tendency to judge yourself harshly and your need to be right make you hesitant to seek feedback from others.

PIVOTAL CONVERSATIONS
AT THE EXPERT LEVEL

Pivotal conversations are discussions whose outcomes either contribute to or detract from achieving important organizational objectives. Almost inevitably, people come to these conversations with differing views and priorities. The best outcomes occur when there's a good give-and-take, with each participant articulating their own perspective but also taking the others' views into account. However,

Expert-level managers often find this kind of conversation difficult to initiate and sustain.

As an Expert, when you find yourself disagreeing with others, you have a strong tendency to believe that your view must be correct. How you handle this assumption depends on your power style. If you have an assertive power style, you try to influence others without being influenced by them. If you have an accommodative power style, you may politely express your views, or you may withhold them and outwardly defer to others. With either style, you find it difficult to step back and see the strengths and limitations of others' perspectives as well as your own. Consequently, you often adopt an either/or mind-set, assuming that every argument must have its winner and its loser.

Research shows that most managers use the assertive style much more frequently than the accommodative style.[2] For example, consider Tony's description of the way he typically conducts himself in his manager's staff meetings:

> I formulate opinions on issues and topics very quickly. I usually wait for a few people to speak and then assert my opinion fairly aggressively. I try not to be offensive, but I try to be pointed enough to trigger a response from the group—either for or against. Unless I feel really strongly about a particular issue, I try to be tactful enough that I have an "out" or a face-saving means of retraction or repositioning. That enables me to quickly move back into the group dynamic without alienating people. But it needs to be strong enough to get a reaction. This is something I do frequently. It can be a liability on occasion. But at least it gets things moving!

Tony's approach, typical of many Expert-level managers, was predominantly assertive. He recognized the need for some kind of give-and-take in discussing important issues, but he didn't entertain the possibility that he might change his mind. Like most Expert managers with an assertive style, he frequently overlooked, minimized, or rationalized anything that implied he might be wrong, make mistakes, or have a weakness.[3]

Almost everyone uses some version of their less favored style at least some of the time, and Tony was no exception. While he was assertive with subordinates, he was much more accommodative with his boss. As the preceding quote indicates, when he worked with peers, he tried to temper his assertions with just enough accommodation that he didn't alienate anyone.

However, because Tony didn't ask for or receive feedback from his coworkers, he didn't know how his style affected them. To grow as a leader, he needed to develop a more balanced power style that combined assertiveness with an ability to seek out others' views and take them more fully into consideration.

Beth had the opposite challenge. A supervisor in one of the oldest private banks in the country, she enrolled in a semester-long leadership course taught as part of an evening MBA program. The course used an action learning format, which included readings, class exercises and discussion, weekly application of class learnings, journaling, coaching, learning teams, and an organizational improvement project. Throughout the course, students were encouraged to use what they learned to improve their effectiveness as leaders in their everyday work environment.[4]

Beth supervised the notification team in the bank's Corporate Actions department. Her manager, Kathleen, had recently given her a mixed performance review. Beth had the analytical skills needed to monitor the specialists on her team, and she was good at keeping people informed about volume spikes and corporate actions like stock splits and tender offers. But she was so absorbed in her monitoring work that she was rarely available to answer specialists' questions, provide coaching, or think about ways to improve the notification process.

From an assessment she did early in the course, Beth knew that she functioned at the Expert level with an overly accommodative power style. For example, she avoided telling specialists about their mistakes and often corrected their work herself without telling them. Reflecting in her journal, she realized that she did this not only because she knew they were short-staffed and overworked, but also because she was afraid that pointing out their errors would strain her relationships with the specialists.

When she and her learning team discussed her highly accommodative supervisory style, she saw that it increased her own workload, stress level, and error rate. This style also gave her no time to think about ways to improve the notification process. In addition, it was self-reinforcing, because the specialists continued to repeat mistakes that she then had to fix.

With further introspection, Beth realized that she avoided asserting herself because she was afraid others wouldn't listen. Despite her fears, she decided that she had to become more assertive. With the support of her learning team, she stopped correcting the specialists' mistakes and started to give them feedback and coaching. Whenever these interactions didn't go well, she used her journal and her learning team to rehearse ways to improve them. Within a month or two, she completely shifted her role to that of a coach. As a result, the specialists became more productive.

Beth now had the time to approach Kathleen about solving an important problem in the notification process. At that time, the unit had no reliable way to prevent the most costly errors the team could make, many of which cost the bank more than a million dollars with each occurrence. Beth proposed that she develop the new tracking and "tie out" methods needed to solve this problem. Once these were approved, she would create and execute an implementation plan.

Kathleen, who'd been too busy fighting her own fires to address this issue herself, was more than pleased to approve the project. Beth then used a class assignment to do a simple analysis of her project's two key stakeholders: Kathleen and the relatively large group of specialists on the notification team. When she asked herself what kind of support she needed for the project to succeed, Beth realized that she needed to get input both from her manager and from the team.[5]

After she got these inputs and designed the new methods, Beth developed an action plan that highlighted the costs and benefits of implementation. Although her learning team felt Kathleen was very likely to approve her proposal, Beth prepared for the meeting as if it were a high-stakes conversation. Over the preceding month, she had practiced a pair of pivotal conversation skills taught in the leadership course: advocacy and inquiry.[6] Because she'd found these skills useful, she decided to organize her presentation around them.

Advocacy and Inquiry

Advocacy is expressing what you think is true or what you think should be done. You advocate when you describe how you see a situation, what you think the causes of a problem are, what the goals should be, what the options are, what the solution should be, or what would happen if a particular course of action is followed. Advocacy can also include giving feedback or advice to others. Advocacy statements can be about external situations, other people, or even yourself.

Inquiry, as we use the term, has a somewhat more specialized meaning than its usual one. Here, to inquire means explicitly to invite others to express their views on a particular issue. To be genuine, inquiry is more than a request for another person's views. It also involves really listening to what others say and trying to take what they say into account. Inquiry usually takes the form of a question, but inquiries don't always take the form of a question: "Kathleen, I'd like to know what you think about my proposal" would be an inquiry. Similarly, not every question is a true inquiry. Leading questions and comments disguised as questions are not inquiries. For example, "You'd agree with what I'm proposing, wouldn't you, Kathleen?" is a poorly disguised advocacy statement, not a true inquiry.

In the meeting with Kathleen, Beth used these skills to advocate the cost-benefit for the improvements she proposed and to inquire about Kathleen's approval. She used them again to advocate the implementation plan she'd developed and to inquire about her manager's reaction. While this is a fairly standard protocol for getting approvals, it was good practice for Beth, who later found this approach useful in a wide variety of conversations. Kathleen was impressed with Beth's work and approved her entire proposal, clearing her to present it to the notification team.

When the day came for Beth to present to the team, she felt quite anxious, but she took a deep breath and plunged ahead. She presented her proposed implementation plan, answered questions, and incorporated some minor suggestions for improvement. She then asked for the team's support and received their unanimous approval. She ended the meeting by offering to speak with anyone who had further questions or suggestions.

About a month later, Beth received her annual performance review. Kathleen was extremely pleased with Beth's progress, saying that she'd "greatly matured" in her new role. She noted that Beth had overcome her pattern of avoiding confrontation and was now giving specialists direct feedback. She also observed that Beth had developed new competencies through the "admirable job" she'd done to improve the notification process. Beth was now viewed as a leader, not only by the notification team but also by management. Kathleen told her she was well on her way to receiving a promotion.

Beth emerged from this experience with a new sense of self-confidence. She still needed to learn to use advocacy and inquiry in more challenging, unstructured conversations. But she was well on her way to developing a style of interaction that was more balanced between assertion and accommodation. In our experience, this is one of the most important steps you can take to increase your effectiveness in pivotal conversations at the Expert level. In the next chapter, we show how developing to the Achiever level further enhances your agility, especially in more challenging conversations.

TEAM LEADERSHIP AT THE EXPERT LEVEL

Carlos had lived and worked in the Southwest most of his life. Now in his mid-thirties, he managed the Accounting Department of a small, five-year-old architectural firm in Santa Fe, founded by renegades from a large firm headquartered in San Francisco. Carlos had joined the firm at its founding and now managed a department of sixteen people.

Carlos was a participant in a customized leadership development program conducted for the firm's managers.[7] Early in the program, Carlos entered into a coaching relationship that began with a 360-degree feedback process. The feedback showed that he was seen as a bright, sincere, committed employee with high ethical standards and mastery of accounting procedures. He was already considered a valuable asset, and his superiors viewed him as someone with great potential to grow with the firm.

The feedback also indicated that Carlos had room for improvement. Top managers said he had trouble "seeing the big picture," because he was too much into the details of his own job. They wanted him to "be more of a manager" and take greater initiative to make departmental improvements.[8] People within his department said he seemed too busy with his own job to provide the leadership they needed. Several wanted him to hold regular department meetings "where everyone can discuss problems that need to be addressed."

Carlos told his coach he agreed with all the feedback, both the positive and the negative. He and his coach then identified his current level of leadership agility.[9] Together, they determined that Carlos had developed into the Expert stage during his freshman year of college and fully established himself as an Expert-level manager during his twenties. Now in his mid-thirties, he'd developed a few Achiever-level capacities. However, in his professional life, he operated almost exclusively at the Expert level.

Carlos's department included the three managers who reported to him directly and twelve additional employees at the next level. At the Expert level, when you head a department, you're aware of its larger organizational environment. However, like Beth, you tend to limit your focus to your department's internal operations. In addition, your tendency is to focus much more on the work of each individual than on the working relationships among group members.

Carlos's approach to managing his department fit the typical Expert team leader profile with remarkable precision: He had fallen into a hub-and-spokes approach to working with his managers. He was the hub, meaning that most of their work was not coordinated among themselves but in his head and at his direction. The spokes represented his habit of interacting with his direct reports one-on-one. This configuration is sometimes called a "staff group," because subordinates are treated largely as extensions of their manager, and they function more as a group than as a team.[10] As is typical of this approach, the few sporadic meetings Carlos held with his managers focused almost exclusively on sharing company-level information and getting individual updates.[11]

The HR Department had instituted a process where the firm's managers set goals with their direct reports and formally reviewed performance once a year. Carlos was up-to-date in clarifying his managers' individual performance goals. However, he had set no goals for the department as a whole. He felt that the individual goals he and the CFO had set for himself were sufficient for that purpose. Even so, he hadn't communicated these goals in any of the one-hour information-sharing meetings he held for the department as a whole.

Carlos found it hard to shift into a more strategic orientation because he was caught up in the details of his work. Two Expert-level characteristics made him particularly vulnerable to this malady. First, he focused much more on accounting tasks than on managing his organizational unit. Second, it was difficult for him to step back from his tasks and prioritize them. Consequently, whole workdays were frequently consumed fighting fires. As Carlos observed, "Working nose-to-the-grindstone can feel really productive while I'm doing it, but sometimes when I'm driving home, I get this sinking feeling: Did I really accomplish anything important?"

The supervisory styles of Expert team leaders range from hands-on to hands-off. Those who are assertive are often so hands-on that they micromanage their subordinates. Experts who are accommodative tend to use a more hands-off style, unless a crisis arises. At that point, they usually flip and become very hands-on, sometimes stepping in and taking over tasks originally assigned to subordinates.

According to his assessment, Carlos's power style was predominantly accommodative. On the positive side, he was calm and composed, a great listener who took others' feelings into account. However, people at all levels said he had an overly laid-back management style and needed to become a more direct, proactive, decisive leader. His subordinates didn't want him to micromanage them, but they did want him to provide clearer direction and to confront a few long-standing performance issues.

When Carlos combined his 360-degree feedback with what he'd learned about his leadership agility, his development path became clear: He needed to learn how to lead as an Achiever. In the next chapter, we show how Carlos's approach to leadership changed when he developed to that level.

ORGANIZATIONAL LEADERSHIP AT THE EXPERT LEVEL

Kevin, a bright and highly opinionated manager in his mid-fifties, had been president and CEO of a Midwestern state's regional hospital council for more than three years. He'd previously served as a hospital administrator and then as a VP for the hospital council. In his present position, he was quite disappointed with the performance of his seven-member management team. They, in turn, did not like his management style.

Bart, Kevin's most senior direct report, was a genial silver-haired man who headed the council's lobbying efforts at the state and local levels. Because of his experience, knowledge, and connections, he was the one VP whom Kevin considered indispensable. Although Bart loved his work in government relations, he was deeply concerned about how well the council was serving the hospitals and medical practices it represented. The council's members had differing views and priorities, and those at the extreme ends of the spectrum always seemed to speak the loudest. To cope with these conflicting stakeholder pressures, Kevin had retained the council's rather innocuous mission statement, and the objectives he set were not sharply defined. To further protect himself, during his three years at the helm he had packed the council's Board of Trustees with people unlikely to challenge him.

Kevin did not involve his management group in setting direction or in making key decisions. Consequently, they weren't aligned with his priorities, and they didn't always do things as he would. Partly for this reason, Kevin was critical of the performance of most of his direct reports. In fact, with the exception of Bart, he often felt he couldn't trust his VPs to do the right thing. It didn't occur to Kevin that their behavior might stem, at least in part, from unclear objectives or his failure to engage with them as key internal stakeholders. As far as he was concerned, the organization's problems lay entirely with them. This perception reinforced his habit of micromanaging their work.

Kevin mainly worked with his subordinates one-on-one or in small task groups, but he also held a weekly staff meeting. About six months into his tenure, the group complained that he set all the agendas unilaterally, so he instituted a procedure that allowed group members to add agenda items prior to each meeting. Nevertheless, people rarely contributed anything.

Kevin used his staff meetings almost exclusively for information sharing. In addition, these meetings included a go-round where each person shared important information and reported progress. During this part of the meeting, Kevin often grilled people, expressed his displeasure, or engaged a direct report in intense debate. Group problem-solving discussions were rare, and people sometimes left meetings wondering whether or not decisions had been made.

At one point, one of his VPs said she felt too much meeting time was spent on matters that weren't very relevant to the group as a whole. A few others agreed. What she really meant was that Kevin talked much more than anyone else, sometimes going off on irrelevant tangents. Not understanding her real meaning, Kevin cut the length of his staff meetings from an hour and a half to an hour, which made meaningful group discussion even less likely.

Because the VPs' roles were highly interdependent, their tasks required extensive coordination among themselves. Yet Kevin created very few forums where VPs could work together to solve problems and coordinate their work. For example, the council had to make a number of written public statements that required input from multiple VPs. They all worked in the same office, but when they had different opinions about these statements, they rarely got together face-to-face to resolve their differences. Instead, they e-mailed their edits and re-edits back and forth to one another. On top of this, Kevin insisted that he review all public statements before they went out. In fact, he spent a good deal of his time on this task alone.

Consequently, even as change accelerated in the council's organizational environment, the organization was slow to respond to current events. Because Kevin overlooked his contribution to this problem, he felt this lack of organizational agility was entirely the fault of his management group. For their part, management group members often complained to Bart about what they saw as Kevin's dysfunctional management style.

The VPs came to Bart because they were afraid to raise these issues with Kevin directly. Kevin usually had a reserved, low-key demeanor, but under stress he could yell at VPs and other employees, insult them, and make them feel like idiots. Not everyone was directly affected, but it happened often enough that it significantly dampened office morale. Kevin had already fired several VPs who clashed with him. Some of the remaining VPs feared for their jobs. Others were considering leaving. At the VP level, only Bart was entirely spared from Kevin's abusive behavior.[12]

While Kevin's micromanagement and his emotional outbursts created a good deal of conflict in the office, he often went out of his way to avoid conflict. For instance, whenever possible he tried to get Bart to address the performance issues of other VPs. Bart saw how everyone contributed to the organization's dysfunctions in their own way, but he was caught in the middle. One option was to leave, but he loved his government relations work. He could think of no job better suited to his experience and abilities.

So Bart sat down with Kevin and had some long heart-to-heart conversations. To depersonalize the issues, Bart emphasized that the organization needed to evolve so it could respond more effectively to its changing environment. At various points in these conversations, Kevin agreed that he needed to become more strategic, shift to a predominantly outside focus, set clearer objectives, become less risk-averse, and give his VPs more room to manage their own areas. But three months went by and Bart saw virtually no change in Kevin's behavior. The council continued to lurch from crisis to crisis.

Bart initiated another round of conversations. He asked Kevin to retain a leadership coach who could help him grow as a leader and build an executive team that could manage needed organizational changes. Kevin finally agreed to interview three candidates that Bart had screened. Their proposals had one key feature in common: After interviewing Kevin and his management group, each proposed to produce a report that would diagnose the present situation and make tailored recommendations. Then they'd lead a facilitated discussion of the report with him and the rest of the group.

Each consultant offered to meet with Kevin privately to help him process the feedback and prepare for the group meeting. However, when he learned that none of the consultants thought it appropriate for him to edit the report so that it didn't paint an "overly negative picture," he decided that he didn't need outside help after all.

EXPERT-LEVEL LEADERSHIP AGILITY COMPETENCIES

As we've seen with Carlos and Kevin, a great many managers who function at the Expert level need to develop into the Achiever level. Even supervisors, like Beth, are more effective when they operate as Achievers.[13] To help managers develop from the Expert to the Achiever level (or to do so yourself), it's essential to have a clear picture of the competencies and capacities associated with both levels of leadership agility. As an introduction, we begin by describing the core capacity of this and every level of agility: your level of awareness and intent.

Expert Awareness and Intent

As you grow into the Expert level, you develop a level of awareness characterized by a modest reflective capacity, a strong problem-solving orientation, and an ability to think more independently and analytically. Using this ability to make analytical distinctions, you modify the simple right-and-wrong imperatives you unconsciously incorporated from your environment earlier in life.[14] As a result, you develop a level of intent that's governed by high standards but also allows you to apply these standards in ways that take situational differences into account. At the same time, you find it difficult to step back from your standards and beliefs enough to compare, contrast, and integrate them with one another. For this reason, you haven't yet developed the coherent system of values and beliefs that emerges at the Achiever level.

Expert Context-Setting Agility

Your agility in setting the context for your leadership initiatives is supported by two capacities: *situational awareness* and *sense of purpose.*

SITUATIONAL AWARENESS. When you take a leadership initiative, your situational awareness refers to the quality of attention you give to the organizational context that surrounds the issue you're addressing. At the Expert level, your situational awareness isn't very well-developed. It's something like a still camera lens that gives you a clear picture of your subject with just enough background to give you some sense of the surrounding situation. That is, whenever you focus on an issue, you know that it exists in a larger context, but you tend to tackle it as an isolated issue.

For example, Carlos was aware that his department operated within a larger organization that had important relationships with customers and suppliers. However, because he didn't yet have an Achiever's situational awareness, his initiatives focused entirely within the boundaries of his own department.[15]

SENSE OF PURPOSE. When Experts take leadership initiatives, their sense of purpose is typically more tactical than strategic. In this sense, Beth, Carlos, and Kevin are not true managers: They focus much more on ensuring the accomplishment of functional or technical tasks than on managing their team or organization.

In addition, in the midst of daily work pressures Experts find it difficult to hold multiple tasks in mind and prioritize them based on a comparison of the various reasons for doing each task. As with Carlos and Kevin, the Expert finds it difficult to step back from immediate, urgent tasks and prioritize work so that important but less urgent tasks also get the attention they need.

For similar reasons, at this level you rarely step back and set explicit success criteria. If, like Beth and Carlos, you work in an organization where managers at higher levels set company objectives and strategies, you usually take this larger strategic framework for granted. If you're a CEO, like Kevin, you operate without true strategic vision, focusing instead on short-term goals. Although it's no problem to think more than one or two years into the future, you rarely find goals beyond this time frame very compelling.

Regardless of your position, your tactical orientation places you in a reactive relationship to the deeper trends and more complex changes taking place in the larger environment. Even when you think about your future as a professional, you lack the career orientation that comes at the Achiever level, so you tend to focus instead on your current position and what might come next.

Expert Stakeholder Agility

The level of agility with which you engage with stakeholders is made possible by two capacities: your *stakeholder understanding* and your *power style.*

STAKEHOLDER UNDERSTANDING. At the Expert level, as you observe people over time, you can infer personality traits, abilities, and recurring emotional states that account for the regularities in their behavior. You also develop an initial level of tolerance for people whose backgrounds and viewpoints differ from your own.

Still, your capacity for understanding other perspectives is limited by some very real biases. As noted previously, you usually assume that your judgments are correct and not just a matter of opinion. Further, when you feel that others aren't living up to your standards, you have a strong tendency to criticize and blame. Kevin provides a particularly vivid example of this tendency.

POWER STYLE. Your power style is shaped partly by your assumptions about power and authority. At the Expert level, you focus on power based on expertise or organizational authority.[16] Because you tend to equate leadership and authority, you're likely to assume that you can lead only when you have formal authority over others. You also believe in the kind of authority that comes from expertise. As in Tony's case, your ideal leadership scenario may be one where people follow your lead—not just because of your position but also because your expert opinion is considered authoritative.[17]

When Expert managers describe what it means to be a good leader, they routinely articulate one of two sets of standards and beliefs. Some Experts focus on the successful completion of important tasks. They say a good leader "runs an efficient organization," "is a great asset to the business," "gets the most from the staff," and so on. Other Experts focus on the quality of working relationships. They say that a good leader "treats people fairly," "takes an interest in individual staff members," "can make people's jobs more interesting," and so on.[18]

This focus on *either* task completion *or* working relationships is directly related to the two power styles described earlier in this chapter. When you're focused on task completion, you act from the assertive side, trying to get others to follow your agenda. A focus on working relationships, wanting others to feel that their needs are taken into account, is consistent with an accommodative style.

Consistent with their tendency to focus on only one set of criteria at a time, Expert managers usually act as if they only must choose between being assertive or accommodative.[19] Given this choice, most, like Tony and Kevin, are distinctly assertive, while a significant minority, like Beth and Carlos, use an accommodative style. However, many Experts change their power style for different relationships. For example, given their assumptions about power and authority, it's very common for Experts to be accommodative toward their manager and assertive toward their direct reports.

As an Expert, how do you typically respond when the stakeholders in your initiative have views and interests that differ from your own? First, because your stakeholder understanding hasn't yet reached the Achiever level, you rarely see the importance of motivating others and managing their expectations. Instead, you rely on your assumptions about power, which tell you that others "should" follow you, because you have expertise or an authoritative position.[20] Second, at this level being right is so important that, when you say you respect others' right to disagree, what you usually mean (implicitly) is that you respect their right to be wrong.

Therefore, as an Expert, you're likely to treat your stakeholders in one of several ways. If your power style is assertive, you may opt for some form of unilateral communication: announce and explain your initiative, but don't ask for input or buy-in. If you get serious objections, and you can't resolve conflicting agendas by asserting your authority or expertise, you persuade and argue. This stance is vividly conveyed in Tony's description of the leaders he most admires: People who are "not afraid to stand alone on issues and to defend their positions when they know they're in the right."[21] Kevin's approach to organizational leadership represents a more extreme version of this stance.

If your predominant power style is accommodative, you're still likely to assume that you're right, but rather than openly disagree, you use a more indirect approach. This was the style that Beth and Carlos both adopted. While this style allowed them to earn points as good listeners, those who worked for them complained that they didn't meet performance issues head-on.[22]

Expert Creative Agility

Your level of creative agility is a reflection of two personal capacities: *connective awareness* and *reflective judgment.*

CONNECTIVE AWARENESS. Experts have a relatively low level of connective awareness, the ability to hold various ideas and experiences in mind, compare and contrast them, and make meaningful connections between them. For example, Expert managers are less likely than those at the Achiever level to make meaningful connections between ideas and experiences that have occurred at different times. When trying to solve ill-structured problems, they're also less likely to see cause-effect relationships that recur across different time periods.

Experts find it difficult to hold dissimilar ideas in mind and discern relationships between them. This is particularly true with ideas considered to be incompatible opposites. At the Conformer (pre-Expert) level, you see opposites as stark *black-and-white* absolutes: always true versus never true, always good versus always bad, and so on. At the Expert level, you continue to see polarities as mutually exclusive opposites, but you see that each polarity has its own gradations. For example, you recognize that there are *degrees* of goodness and *degrees* of badness. However, while this perspective represents an advance over the Conformer level, it still limits you to an either/or mind-set.

REFLECTIVE JUDGMENT. Reflective judgment refers to the thought process you use to determine what is true and what is the best action to take to solve the ill-structured problems you encounter in all leadership initiatives. It also includes how you justify these conclusions to yourself and to others.

Some of the best information about Expert-level reflective judgment comes from research on university students. A classic study at Harvard University found that when students began their freshman year, most had at least begun to develop Expert-level reflective judgment. The small percentage who entered as Conformers reacted to the problems they encountered as if they were, or should be, well-structured. In courses ranging from literature to economics, they saw their professors as truth-giving authorities.[23]

However, as their college careers progressed, they were repeatedly exposed, both academically and socially, to a range of different ideas and perspectives. As they grew into the Expert level, they developed a capacity for analysis that allowed them to think more independently and examine issues in greater detail. Because most of the problems they faced didn't have one right, preestablished answer, they gradually began to rely on their own judgment. However, once they developed their own opinion about something, they had trouble genuinely believing that other opinions might be equally valid.[24]

Expert managers, faced with an ongoing stream of ill-structured problems, treat some as if the right solution has already been determined, either by upper management, by their technical or functional training, or by "how we've always done things around here." However, they respond to most problems they face with a problem-solving approach: They analyze the specific situation in which they find themselves and use their own judgment to make a decision.[25]

For example, a study of factory supervisors at the Conformer and Expert levels showed that, faced with a personnel problem, Conformer supervisors talked only about what should and shouldn't be allowed, according to the work rules. The Expert supervisors felt that work rules were essential, but they didn't treat them as absolutes. Instead, they examined situational factors and considered multiple options before deciding how to proceed.[26]

That said, the Expert manager's capacity for reflective judgment is still rather limited. At the Achiever level, managers make a clear distinction between evidence (facts that can be objectively verified) and beliefs (which are inferred from the available evidence). Achievers recognize that, because inferences can be biased or mistaken, a belief needs to be substantiated by providing an evidence-based rationale. However, when Experts form opinions, they're often unaware of having made an inference. While they may say that their beliefs are "just my opinion," they tend to experience their opinions as if they were objective perceptions of reality.

As a result, if someone disagrees with the Expert's opinion and provides a coherent reason for a differing position, the Expert usually shows little interest in considering the alternative rationale. Instead, Experts are likely either to assume that the other person is wrong or to alter their own position without realizing what they're doing. This is the agility level where you're most likely to have biased opinions, to be unaware of your biases, and to see those who disagree with you as suffering from your own malady.[27]

Experts tend to overlook their own biases partly because they're often unaware of the tacit mental frameworks they use to diagnose problems and develop solutions. For example, most Expert managers have been trained in a particular professional function or technical discipline. When you're functioning at this level, the mental framework provided by past training becomes a taken-for-granted lens that strongly influences how you view organizational and business issues. This bias becomes most evident when you're placed in a situation where you need to work across functional boundaries to make organizational improvements. For example, if you're in sales, you see organizational issues exclusively from a sales mind-set; if you're in human resources, you see issues through an HR lens; and so on.

Expert Self-Leadership Agility

Your self-leadership agility is supported by two personal capacities: your *self-awareness* and your *developmental motivation.*

SELF-AWARENESS. At the Conformer level, self-awareness is quite limited. You have little capacity for introspection, and your image of yourself is still simple and stereotypical. However, as you grow into the Expert level, the analytical awareness you develop gives you a capacity for introspection that previously wasn't possible. The feelings you articulate, though still expressed in rather simple terms, have more shades of gray.

With this new introspective awareness, you recognize recurring inner moods and develop a more independent image of yourself, a budding sense of identity that includes what you stand for and believe. Your self-image as a leader encompasses your perception of your current role, your professional skills, and your personality traits. For example, Tony believed that he had some but not all of the knowledge and skills needed to be the leader he wanted to become. He thought he embodied many of the personality traits he admired in others, particularly a willingness to take a stand on issues and defend his position. At the same time, he acknowledged that he could sometimes be stubborn and opinionated.

DEVELOPMENTAL MOTIVATION. Your developmental motivation is shaped by the interaction of three key factors: your leadership ideal (the image you hold of the kind of leader you want to be), your primary source of professional self-esteem and satisfaction, and the emotional tone you use when you evaluate yourself. At the Expert level, your leadership ideal includes the knowledge, skills, and personality traits to which you aspire as a leader. For example, Tony wanted to be "an expert with a lot of business acumen, who really understands our business, our customers, and our category." He also wanted to be a leader who maintains a positive team spirit, who's unafraid to stand alone on issues, who takes responsibility for mistakes, and so on.

Your developmental motivation is also shaped by your primary source of professional satisfaction and self-esteem. This motivation is partly intrinsic: At the Expert level, you feel satisfied when you can solve short-term problems that require independent critical thinking and advice. But your self-esteem also comes from feeling that you stand out from others, that others admire you for your expertise and the astuteness of your point of view. In this sense, you're still strongly motivated by what others think of you.[28]

The third factor that shapes your developmental motivation is the emotional tone you use when you assess your progress toward your leadership ideal. At the Expert level, you take your goals and standards very seriously. When you feel you're not living up to them, you have a strong tendency to blame yourself, often rather harshly, a tendency that can undermine your self-esteem. It can also lead you to amplify any negative feedback you receive from others.

To convey how Expert level self-leadership works in a real situation, we'll introduce you to Guy, a manager in his mid-thirties. In the late 1990s Guy was a director of customer service for a company in the semiconductor industry. Based in Austin, Texas, he reported to the VP of Quality and Customer Service for one of the firm's business units and managed an on-site call center with about eighty employees.

Guy was an Expert manager par excellence. A seasoned professional, he knew his part of the organization backwards and forwards. In many ways he'd fulfilled the dream we heard Tony articulate earlier. He was a go-to person who'd gained great respect for efficient, high-quality work. His boss would tell him she needed a new type of analysis done on his center's performance, by the next day. He'd stay up late at night to complete it. The next evening, she'd call him at home and say she needed the data sliced another way, by tomorrow. Guy always delivered.

Like Tony, Guy's self-ideal was to be seen as competent, knowledgeable, and efficient, capable of handling any demand. What he didn't see was that this constant striving was largely motivated by fear—fear of how he'd feel about himself if others thought he wasn't capable or efficient. Because he constantly guarded against this danger, when his boss made unreasonable demands, he always complied. In situations where he felt he wasn't living up to his self-ideal, he judged himself harshly. Whenever he felt let down, he noticed a relentless stream of mental chatter going through his head, much of it self-critical.

There's nothing inherently wrong with wanting to be capable and efficient. What caused problems for Guy was the motivation behind this aspiration—the fear and self-judgment that are often such a big part of the Expert's striving for self-improvement. Guy's nose-to-the-grindstone work style prevented him from being strategic in his management of the call center, his work became progressively more stressful and less satisfying, and he wasn't sleeping well. Worst of all, he convinced himself that he was stuck where he was, incapable of doing anything new. In the next chapter, we show how Guy changed by growing into the Achiever level of leadership agility.

CHAPTER FIVE

Achiever Level

Accomplish Desired Outcomes

A fter Rachel completed her MBA, she worked at a consulting firm for several years, then held a series of marketing positions in financial services firms. During that time, she developed a talent for identifying high-value customer segments and finding ways to use company capabilities to attract and retain them. In the late 1990s a brokerage firm's senior VP of strategy and marketing realized they needed a better understanding of their customers. He hired Rachel to head a team to analyze the company's customer base and recommend ways to improve its business model.

Rachel began by focusing on the Fixed Income group. Considered the firm's weakest contributor, it had low profit margins, and it constituted only a small percentage of the company's business. The group initially resisted the project because people feared that Rachel would highlight their perceived inadequacies. But she explained that she'd already done an initial analysis that suggested Fixed Income's potential value was currently underrated. She stressed that her aim was to gain a better understanding of their customers' full potential value to the company.

In fact, when Fixed Income's customers were compared with those of the firm's other investment groups, Rachel's hypothesis was confirmed. Almost everyone who invested with the Fixed Income group did all their stock and mutual fund investing with the firm, whereas those who invested only with the company's stock and mutual fund groups also invested large percentages of their portfolios outside the firm. Further, when customers withdrew their fixed income investments, they pulled all their other investments with the firm. Yet the current business model subjected this customer segment to long wait times, and the employees to whom they spoke lacked the level of expertise found in other investment areas. When fixed income customers left the firm, poor service was the primary reason, and they rarely came back.

Rachel involved Fixed Income employees in developing a strategy for growing and retaining this important customer segment. Fixed Income customers would now enjoy a new level of service that included ready access to people with high levels of expertise. Rachel also guided the team in leveraging existing company capabilities to create more innovative services. For example, the team discovered that the firm already had a good deal of information, which, properly packaged, could help retain this vitally important customer segment.

WHAT LEADERSHIP
MEANS TO AN ACHIEVER

Reflecting on this and other projects she spearheaded at the brokerage firm, Rachel described what leadership means to her:

> For me, leadership doesn't necessarily mean being in a formal leadership role. It can be leading the thought effort for something that truly makes a difference for an organization or for a company as a whole. I think leadership has a lot to do with personal qualities that allow me to inspire, excite, and challenge myself and others to improve results in interesting and challenging ways.
>
> What gets me going is the newness, the interesting, the pushing. That's what's fun for me. And when others see I'm having fun, it can inspire them to take on things that interest them and that challenge them to do things they didn't think they could do. With the Fixed Income project I was very gratified to see people get excited about a new,

more powerful vision for their business—going from just selling a product to growing a market for the firm as a whole.

This statement is quite different from what we heard Tony, the Expert manager, say. Leadership is no longer equated with a position. We hear no references to defending your viewpoint, instructing weaker teammates, or being admired for your expertise. Instead, we hear an emphasis on creating an environment that draws others into an interesting and challenging enterprise, where they can reconceptualize their business and contribute in ways that make a difference.

If you've grown into the Achiever level, you've developed a robust reflective capacity that's enabled you to create an explicit, consciously examined system of values and beliefs to live by. You see the organization you work in as a system that operates in a large, complex institutional and societal context. You've learned to think strategically, and you're highly motivated by objectives that may take as long as two to five years to achieve.

You realize that the success of your leadership initiatives requires an adequate level of support from key stakeholders, and you're aware that their motivations and expectations are central to their willingness to provide this support. Your power style may be *assertive* (focused on persuading others to follow your agenda) or, less likely, *accommodative* (focused on getting stakeholder input and buy-in). Either way, it's likely that you often try to balance your predominant style with elements of its opposite.

Like Rachel, when you carry out a leadership initiative, you want problems to be diagnosed and solved using verifiable data. You see how individual problems are connected. You can rethink issues and arrive at innovative solutions by taking what was successful in one context and applying it to another.

Finally, you develop a level of self-awareness that allows you to reflect on recent events and understand why you acted as you did. Through these reflections and a newfound ability to recall what you were like in different periods of your life, you construct a solid sense of your own identity. Because you can also vividly imagine the future effects of your actions, you have a strong sense that you control your own destiny. Your professional self-esteem comes primarily from believing you've contributed to the achievement of significant outcomes.

In a moment, you'll read the stories of three Achiever-level managers who share Rachel's understanding of leadership. You'll find out how Guy and Carlos, two managers you met in the Expert chapter, each developed into the Achiever level. You'll also read about Mark, an Achiever-level CEO who led his HMO through a fundamental strategic change that required him to overcome initial resistance from key stakeholders. As in Chapter Four, these stories represent the three action arenas we introduced earlier: pivotal conversations, team leadership, and leading organizational change.[1]

PIVOTAL CONVERSATIONS AT THE ACHIEVER LEVEL

To show what Achiever-level competencies look like in pivotal conversations, we pick up our story about Guy, the Expert-level call center manager you met in Chapter Four. Just when everything seemed to be going downhill, Guy was promoted to a new position implementing a "knowledge capture" strategy developed by his business unit's top executives. The intent of the strategy was to collect the know-how generated by product development efforts so that future products and customized work could be produced more efficiently, making the unit more competitive.

Guy and his new team of direct reports were responsible not only for organizing product development knowledge and making it readily accessible but also for obtaining this knowledge from product managers. Once they'd thought through their basic approach, Guy invited the senior product managers to a meeting to launch the initiative. To his great disappointment, they responded to his presentation with skeptical questions and critical comments. Taken aback by the strength of their reactions, he felt he was facing an impenetrable wall of resistance. He finally invoked top management's mandate and essentially ordered them to comply. The pronouncement was met with stony silence. No one even looked at him as they filed out of the room.

When Guy tried to follow up, many of his calls and e-mails simply weren't returned. Those who did respond treated him like a presumptuous nuisance. He was extremely discouraged. He'd turned his prospective partners into enemies virtually overnight. It looked like the whole initiative might collapse before it even started.

Guy had initially hesitated to take the new job, afraid he didn't have the leadership skills needed to influence people over whom he had no direct authority. But the hiring VP had encouraged him, saying that if Guy ran into difficulty, he could use a leadership coach the VP had used himself to good effect. Now that all his worst fears seemed to be materializing, Guy decided he'd better meet this coach.

Guy and his new coach quickly decided to have an accelerated series of coaching sessions. During these meetings, they clarified his current leadership challenges, identified his present level of agility, and set leadership development goals.[2] Guy discovered that he'd been operating at the Expert level for many years, and he became convinced that to succeed in his new role he needed to grow into the Achiever level. He also saw that his power style with peers and subordinates was highly assertive, with little accommodation to others' priorities.

To get started, they focused on the pressing matter of his relationship with the product managers. With Guy's overall objective in mind, his coach asked a question to help him plan his next steps from an Achiever perspective: "What *outcomes* do you want from what you do next with the product managers?" "I want them to commit to implementing the knowledge capture procedures," he said. "I just don't know how to get there from here."

To help him bring more balance to his power style, his coach said: "It sounds like you're being held accountable for this initiative but the product managers are being held accountable for another set of objectives. Right now, you each have different things at stake. Given that this is the set-up, what would you like the outcome to be in terms of the kind of *relationship* you want to develop with the product managers?"

After reflecting a moment, Guy said he wanted to replace the feeling of mutual attack with a commitment to work together toward a common goal. Putting himself briefly in their place, he understood that, unless the product managers felt some sense of mutuality in the relationship, they weren't going to cooperate. He saw that he needed to listen, understand, and negotiate a more positive relationship. With this insight, he was positioned to bring more balance to his power style.

Guy's coach then introduced the pivotal conversation skills of advocacy and inquiry, described in Chapter Four. In the first meeting Guy had used advocacy to the exclusion of inquiry. Now, he could provide some balance by starting with inquiry: asking questions to better understand what was behind the product managers' concerns. Then he could respond to their concerns with curiosity and clarifying questions rather than defensive explanations. This would help rebuild the relationship, which was a precondition for securing their commitment to new procedures. However, at some point, he'd also need to advocate his own priorities. By using both advocacy and inquiry, he could stay balanced and work out a mutually agreeable way to proceed.

Guy decided that his next step would be to set up a meeting with the product managers who reported to Dennis, the senior manager who seemed least hostile to the new procedures. In preparation, his coach introduced him to the skill of framing, that is, describing the purpose and assumptions behind a meeting. Given how the first meeting had gone, what was the best way to propose this idea to Dennis? Then, how did Guy want to start the meeting?

The next day, he dropped by Dennis's office. Guy said he realized the first meeting had been strained, and he wanted to have a different kind of meeting, this time with Dennis and his direct reports, so he could understand their pressures and concerns. Dennis agreed to the meeting, but when Guy walked into the conference room several days later, the air was thick with tension. To frame the meeting, he spoke first directly to Dennis, then broadened his attention to the rest of the group:

> I've been thinking a lot about the meeting I had with you and the other senior product managers, and I feel I really started off on the wrong foot. I still believe knowledge capture can be of great benefit to your group and to all our product managers. But I think I was overly defensive in responding to your concerns. I should have stopped to understand the pressures and priorities you're facing, and how you think these new procedures will impact your projects. So that's what I'd like to do now.

Dennis said, "That's fine. I think that's what we're here for." Guy quickly got the group up to speed on the basics of the initiative. Then he said, "So, I'd like to know: What are the main pressures and priorities you're already dealing with?" After a few moments of awkward silence, Dennis led off with a little background on his group's work. Guy listened. When he asked for clarification on a particular point, another manager jumped in. Before long a number of people had spoken and the picture was clear: The product managers were held accountable for three objectives: cost, quality, and schedule. Speed to market was a huge priority, and they felt the knowledge capture procedures would slow them down.

Guy caught himself several times starting to correct what he felt were myopic views and erroneous assumptions. But he let the comments keep coming until the energy behind them begin to wane. He'd now spent more than thirty minutes asking questions and taking notes, probably more sustained listening than he'd ever done in his life. He thanked the product managers for their forthrightness and said he now had a much better understanding of their goals and concerns. He summarized what he'd heard and asked if he'd understood correctly. After correcting a few minor points, the group said he had it right.

Guy noticed that the group's body language had shifted dramatically. He had a receptive audience and a clear picture of the mind-set he needed to address. He then asked one more question: Could they make a ballpark estimate of how much time the new procedures would take, on a monthly basis? They said that, to determine the actual time impact, they needed to understand the procedures in more detail. Inwardly, Guy was greatly relieved. They'd implicitly acknowledged that their concerns were based on assumptions about the time the procedures would require—assumptions that he privately suspected were overblown.

To wrap up, Guy said he wanted to hold a brief series of working group meetings to assess how long the procedures would take and, if necessary, adjust them to reduce the time requirements while still meeting the objectives for knowledge capture. These meetings would be attended by a representative from each of the product management groups and some members of his own team. Dennis agreed to send one of his people to the meetings.

Positive reports about the meeting spread to the other product management groups and made them more receptive. His confidence buoyed, Guy used the same approach with them and got similar responses. Within a few weeks the working group was having productive weekly meetings. His initial mistake cost him some time, but now everyone concerned was committed to making knowledge capture work.

After just two meetings, the working group felt it had good estimates of the impact the proposed procedures would have on product development cycle time. They decided that only three procedures would cause real time problems, so they zeroed in on the best ways to change those procedures. Here, the group got stuck. Every time someone proposed an idea, someone else shot it down. Ideas weren't flowing, and people were getting frustrated.

When he described this last meeting to his coach, Guy said he wanted to find a better way to orchestrate the group discussion. His coach said:

> It sounds like the product managers are focusing on ideas consistent
> with the cycle time outcome, and your people are focused on the

knowledge capture objective. I think you need to frame the group discussion by referencing what's going on and establishing a norm that people need to provide rationales for their views—rationales that tie into the four shared outcomes you've already established.

The coach suggested that Guy come to the next meeting with an agenda that would take the group through three steps: brainstorm solution ideas, group and prioritize the ideas, then improve and evaluate them. Guy could remind everyone that "good ideas" would be those that helped capture the necessary knowledge with minimal impact on cost, quality, and—especially—time to market. He could review and enforce the basic ground rules for brainstorming and record the group's ideas on flip chart paper while adding his own ideas to the mix. For the last step, the group could identify the most promising ideas, and subgroups could do their best to improve those ideas before they were reviewed by the whole group.[3] His coach continued:

> The other thing that makes for a good rationale is when the person advocating an idea can show how it's consistent with facts that everyone can agree on. Let's say you're at the end of the meeting and you need to work through some disagreements. You can use the four objectives as one set of criteria, but you may also want to ask them to provide some relevant "data." If there aren't any objective data available, you can ask them to provide some other kind of concrete reference point, like describing an experience they've had where their idea worked. Of course, it would also help if you modeled this type of rationale by using it to illustrate some of your own points.

Guy thought this approach would go a long way toward getting people thinking along the same lines. But he was worried about how to respond if the group zeroed in on ideas he felt were unworkable. Keeping the Achiever level of leadership agility in mind, his coach said:

> You can tell them up front that you'll be making the final decision about what changes to make in your proposed procedures—that you're looking to the group for their recommendations. But I think the chances are good that you won't need to make more than small modifications in the group's recommendations.

Guy structured the next meeting the way his coach suggested, and he used some of the new skills they'd worked on. At the end of the meeting, everyone agreed about how two of the three procedures should be changed, and they agreed to pilot the proposed changes to a third procedure. Although the working group's task was now completed, they decided to meet again periodically to make sure the new procedures were capturing the knowledge needed without causing cycle-time problems. Guy felt very good. The product managers had now taken their share of the responsibility for making the initiative work.

TEAM LEADERSHIP AT THE ACHIEVER LEVEL

In Chapter Four, we introduced you to Carlos, the accounting manager at a small architectural firm in Santa Fe. For many years, he had functioned at the Expert level of team leadership. He preferred to work with his three direct reports one-on-one, and the infrequent meetings he held with his sixteen-person department were used for information sharing only. His 360-degree feedback said that, although he was bright and knowledgeable, he was so immersed in the details that he wasn't truly managing the department. The feedback also indicated that he needed to be more direct and decisive, set clear direction for the department, and confront some long-standing performance issues.

Agreeing that the feedback was valid, Carlos set three leadership development goals: become a full-fledged department manager; rise above the details and improve on prioritizing tasks; and develop a more proactive, direct, and decisive leadership style. In working with his coach, he discovered that he could accelerate his progress toward these goals by developing to the Achiever level of leadership agility.

As one step toward becoming a full-fledged department manager, Carlos changed the way he led meetings. He decided to hold meetings with his managers every other week and to focus discussion on department-wide issues. He also planned regular monthly meetings for the whole department. Each department meeting would function as a problem-solving forum, where people would identify, initiate, and monitor projects to improve the department and its relationships with other functions.

This was exactly what the firm needed from Carlos, and it was consistent with Achiever-level team leadership. However, it would be hard to do if he remained immersed in the details of accounting tasks, so his coach gave him something to read on this issue.[4] When they discussed it again, Carlos said he'd come to a realization: He'd been so driven to complete urgent tasks that important but not urgent work rarely got his attention.

Carlos decided he'd start getting to work fifteen minutes earlier. On Monday mornings, he'd spend thirty minutes planning his week. On the other mornings, he'd take fifteen minutes to set priorities and make an initial plan for his day. Throughout the week, he'd try to find a better balance between urgent and important tasks.

Two weeks later, Carlos had made progress in prioritizing his work, but he hadn't scheduled a meeting with his managers. His coach asked if he was concerned about what might happen if he made a decisive move toward managing his department. Carlos reflected for a moment:

> I've never liked managers who separate themselves and act like they're better than everyone else. There are a few people here at the firm who do that, and I have no desire to emulate them. One of the things I've always liked about my department is that it feels like a family. We sometimes have our squabbles, but no one acts like they're better than anyone else. I don't want to lose that feeling. It makes for a good work environment. I know I need to be more of a manager, but I do worry that it could be the beginning of the end for some of the positive relationships I've built with the people in my department.

Like most Expert-level managers, Carlos held the assumption that assertive and accommodative leadership styles are either/or alternatives. When he committed to becoming more assertive, he assumed he'd have to abandon his existing style and adopt its opposite. In fact, he was wrestling with some basic questions: Can you be an assertive leader and still empathize with the people who work for you? Do you have to act like you're above them, or can you still stay connected and continue to have fun?

As he discussed these concerns with his coach, Carlos saw that he wasn't being asked to drop his ability to listen and empathize. His challenge was to *balance* these strengths with more assertive leadership. A more balanced leadership style was actually likely to improve his working relationships, and he could still do the ski trips that had become a department tradition.

Within a month, Carlos had held two meetings with his management group and one with the whole department. People responded positively to his new leadership. Several months later, he used a department meeting to facilitate a visioning session as part of a company-wide effort to align departments with the firm's vision. This session got him to think two to three years out and see Accounting from the perspective of the outcomes needed by customers and subcontractors, an experience that took him beyond his usual tactical orientation and helped him to formulate clear departmental goals in a more strategic context.

Carlos's group meetings helped him shift from the Expert's focus on managing tasks to the Achiever's focus on managing people. To complete this shift, he needed to change the way he worked with individual direct reports. Instead of troubleshooting specific tasks, he needed to identify and address individual performance issues that persisted over time. To do this, he needed to be more direct in discussing performance problems with his subordinates, something his accommodative style had led him to avoid.

In the months prior to the visioning session, Carlos used the pivotal conversation skills he'd learned in the company's leadership development program to address some minor performance issues. But he still avoided the most glaring problem, a persistent set of issues with Lorie, his direct report in charge of employee payroll and benefits.[5]

Carlos told his coach he hadn't confronted the issue because he had conflicting feelings about what to do. On one hand, he thought Lorie simply couldn't deal with the more complex employee compensation issues brought on by the firm's steady growth. On the other hand, he wanted to be fair, and he realized that his assessment might be wrong. After he touched base with the firm's HR manager, his coach helped him develop an approach that took both feelings into account.

When Carlos met with Lorie, he set the frame for the meeting, illustrated the performance problems he saw, and asked her where she agreed and disagreed with his assessment. Although she took issue with some minor points, Lorie readily agreed that she was in over her head. They worked out a three-month action plan, beginning with training to get her up to speed, followed by weekly review meetings. However, after two months, Lorie realized that she was no longer a fit for the job, and she told him she needed to move on. A month later, Carlos was so pleased with the person who'd taken her place, he couldn't believe he'd waited so long to confront the issue.

Meanwhile, Carlos's coach built on the visioning session by asking him a series of questions to help him think further about his vision. In this conversation, Carlos reflected on a period in his life when several people challenged him to develop his academic and athletic abilities. Remembering how stimulating this was for him, he said:

Part of my vision for my department is that I want people to feel *motivated*, to go home and say they feel great about where they work. For that to happen, I need to be sure I'm creating a fun, challenging environment where people feel their opinion matters. I want to provide creative opportunities that challenge people to be their best. That's what I really want to get to. We're on the way, but sometimes I feel guilty because I feel like I'm not really there yet.

What stands out in Carlos's statement is a desire, similar to Rachel's, to create an environment that's both challenging and engaging. At this point, six months after Carlos decided to become an Achiever-level team leader, his coach interviewed everyone who'd provided his 360-degree feedback. The interviews made it clear that he'd come a long way toward realizing his aspiration. In describing the department meetings, an employee who reported to one of Carlos's direct reports said:

The meetings seem to get better each time. The one we had yesterday was about the atmosphere within Accounting. Carlos led us in an exercise where he had us write down all the things that were bothering us. These were grouped on a board and discussed by the group. He did a great job in dealing with a sensitive subject. We developed solutions, and one day later I can already see changes in people's behavior.

He's not dictating or monopolizing the time in these meetings. He's setting the stage and managing the discussion. It's a far cry from meetings in other companies where I've been, where you're afraid to say anything. He's built up a team concept—Carlos and the managers working as a team—and they all do a great job.

Now an Achiever-level leader, Carlos had transformed his management group and his department into what we call "orchestrated teams." At this level, managers still assume that they have *sole* responsibility for defining roles, motivating team members, ensuring individual performance, and orchestrating team efforts. They frequently enter decision-making meetings with a best solution in mind, but they often prefer to get everyone's views on the table, while orchestrating the discussion toward their desired outcome. They feel that group discussion can increase team member buy-in and provide a way to test their own ideas.

LEADING ORGANIZATIONAL CHANGE AT THE ACHIEVER LEVEL

In the mid-1990s Mark was CEO of a successful HMO based in Ohio. The health plan had grown into a highly respected midsized organization, now a major player in the region. A mature Achiever in his mid-forties, Mark had a strong management team, and board members were satisfied with the health plan's steady growth. Due in no small part to his leadership, the organization had a strong, cohesive culture shaped by a clear set of values. Employees considered it a great place to work.

In spite of his company's success Mark was quite concerned about its future. Knowing the industry as he did, he found it easy to look two to four years down the road and see what was at stake if emerging trends continued. New forces were at work: The managed care marketplace was about to be transformed by fierce competition and radical restructuring.

Strategies initiated by providers (hospitals and physician groups) and by corporate purchasers would put HMOs in a squeeze. To cope with declining revenues and high cost structures, hospitals and other providers were consolidating into integrated health systems that offered a whole continuum of care. Consolidation not only provided greater efficiencies, it also gave providers more bargaining leverage with HMOs. Meanwhile, purchasers were applying pressure from the other side. Many large corporations had decided to limit their health plan purchases to a small group of preferred suppliers, a move that stimulated increased competition among HMOs. In addition, new legislation in Ohio allowed small and medium-sized companies to increase their bargaining power by participating in large purchasing pools.[6]

As Mark looked around the country, he saw that some health plans were already responding to these pressures by increasing operating efficiencies, tailoring traditional products for individual corporate purchasers, and diversifying their product lines for one-stop shopping. But these HMOs believed that what would most differentiate them in the eyes of corporate purchasers was the cost and quality of their provider network. In pursuit of this objective, they were creating preferential relationships and exclusive alliances with physician groups and hospitals. Some were also enhancing their provider networks through mergers with other health plans.

Given this strategic assessment Mark believed that, if his HMO could form its own preferential and exclusive relationships with the right providers, it could differentiate itself from its competitors as never before. There was just one catch: Mark's health plan was originally founded by a group of physicians seeking an alternative to the traditional health insurance organizations that had dominated the region. His HMO had always welcomed virtually any qualified doctor who was part of a participating hospital staff, and it was committed to treating its physicians fairly and equally. The company was governed by a board of physicians as well as by a business board. Each of the doctors in its network had a vote, and many felt they should have a voice in its business plans and medical management policies.

Historically, this stance had served the company well, engendering strong physician loyalty and distinguishing it from large insurance companies and other HMOs. On one hand, Mark wanted to retain these attributes. On the other hand, some HMOs in the region had already begun to form exclusive alliances with large medical practices. If his company stood by as its competitors cherry-picked high-quality medical groups, it could find itself in serious trouble.

Mark was what leadership guru Jim Collins calls a "Level 5 leader," a person with unwavering resolve and understated presence, who channeled his ego needs away from himself and into the larger goal of building and sustaining a great company. As Collins points out, "It's not that Level 5 leaders have no ego or self-interest. Indeed, they are incredibly ambitious—*but their ambition is first and foremost for the institution, not themselves.*"[7]

Mark was like that. In many ways, he'd grown up with the company. He and a whole community of colleagues had worked long and hard to develop a company that reflected their values. Unless they made some major strategic changes, he feared they'd be acquired by a large corporation that didn't share their values.

In his own mind, Mark had concluded that the only way to maintain the company's identity and independence was to initiate a true "merger of equals" with a larger Ohio-based HMO that had a completely different provider network strategy. While many independent physicians had joined that HMO's network, it had its own clinics, and it had already formed preferential and exclusive relationships with some of the largest medical practices in the state. Together, they would have a diverse, high-quality provider network that could make them the premier health plan in the region. If they chose this path, he promised himself he'd do everything possible to maintain the strong employee-centered values that had been so much a part of his company's tradition.[8]

Mark was a bright, confident leader who also had strong "people values" and a realistic sensitivity to the need for stakeholder buy-in. His power style leaned to the assertive side but was highly balanced. He knew that championing this change would be a new and challenging experience. He also knew that, to be successful, he'd need the sanction of his boards and the unflinching commitment of his management team. Only then could he hope to generate the support he needed from his physician network and from the employees who'd made the company what it was today.

Mark's management team had the same concerns any top group would have about merging with a larger company. But they understood the issues and were generally supportive. The primary resistance would come from the two boards, who were locked into a traditional strategic mind-set and uninformed about new competitive realities.

Mark decided that a day-long retreat would be the best way to educate, motivate, and align the two boards and his top management team. Yet, he knew that simply standing up and trying to persuade the boards that he was right would only generate endless debate and continued resistance. So he chose a consultant to help design and facilitate the event.

Mark didn't want to make specific strategic decisions at the retreat. The outcome he wanted was for the boards to ask him and his team to seriously explore several new strategic options. He and his consultant designed the weekend so that the combined groups could do their own strategic analysis, and they prepared a packet of background information for participants to read before the event.

At the retreat Mark's consultant facilitated a series of activities that allowed the participants to identify the most important trends, threats, and opportunities the HMO faced over the next two to four years. The group then visualized what would happen two to four years out, if the company maintained its current strategy. Next, they assessed the pros and cons of incremental improvement versus major strategic change. They concluded that the organization needed to do both, but that fundamental change was essential. With this understanding, they brainstormed new strategy ideas and then distilled these into the five that looked most promising.

The highlight of the retreat was a series of fifteen-minute debates that took place in the afternoon. Five groups of eight were formed, each group focusing on one of the top strategy ideas. In each group the four who most strongly favored their group's assigned strategy became one subgroup. The four who had the greatest reservations became the other.

They were told to prepare for a debate, but with a twist: The subgroups in favor of the strategy idea were to debate against it, and the subgroups with reservations were to debate for it. Once the shock and laughter abated, the subgroups went to work, and a rousing series of debates ensued. The whole idea, of course, was to ensure full exploration of each idea, giving everyone an opportunity to examine issues from a new perspective.

When the retreat was over, the participants rated it a huge success. Mark was extremely pleased with the outcome: In a combined board meeting the following morning, he and his team were asked to explore two new strategic possibilities: merging with another health plan, and pursuing preferential relationships with physician groups. Within several months, Mark and his team were engaged in serious merger talks with the larger health plan. The talks had their tense moments, of course, but overall they went remarkably well.

Six months later, a true merger of equals was under way. For several months, each part of the new company was managed by two co-leaders, one from each company. This arrangement worked very well and was phased out as decisions were made about which of the two would head each function. Two years later, Mark became the CEO of the new company. At the top level, the merger was a great success. Mark and his newly configured management group initiated a new strategy that called for aggressive growth into neighboring states.

Unfortunately, Mark and his top group became so focused on their growth strategy that they overlooked the company's operational vulnerabilities. Incompatible computer systems had yet to be integrated, and many areas of the company still had separate business processes.

A year after Mark became CEO, the growth strategy began to strain the HMO's operational capacity, and real problems began to emerge. The new health plan's board, increasingly concerned, finally decided that new leadership was needed. Mark was asked to leave. His Achiever-level successor ultimately got the HMO through its post-merger phase successfully, and it became one of the leading health plans in the region.

Mark took an executive position in another health care organization where he performed admirably.

The merged HMO's early stumble was caused by a complex set of factors. But two factors concerning Mark's leadership are worth noting here: First, when he became CEO of the new health plan, he continued to exhibit the strong resolve and understated presence characteristic of the "Level 5 Leader," but he moved away from his balanced power style and adopted the more exclusively assertive style exhibited by executives from the larger HMO. His inclination to seek out and take in differing perspectives diminished accordingly. Second, once you read about leading organizational change at the Catalyst level, we think you'll agree that Mark's chances of succeeding during the post-merger phase would have been greater if he'd learned to operate at that level.[9]

ACHIEVER-LEVEL LEADERSHIP AGILITY COMPETENCIES

How do the four leadership agility competencies change when you develop to the Achiever level?

Achiever Awareness and Intent

Growth into the Achiever level of leadership agility begins when your reflective capacity deepens, allowing you to discern more abstract themes and relationships that persist over longer periods of time. You find yourself thinking about earlier periods of your life, noting how you've changed and how you've stayed the same. Your capacity for thinking about the people, organizations, and industries you encounter as a leader expands accordingly. This new level of awareness even affects the way you learn from your experience. For example, consider the following Achiever-level vignette:

> One evening, you go to an obligatory event where you're pleasantly surprised to find that the after-dinner talk is actually stimulating. The speaker is a retired CEO, and the talk is about leadership.
>
> Various things he says trigger vivid memories from different periods in your career. One of his points is a different spin on something you learned from an early mentor. A story he tells brings to mind an

uncomfortable episode you lived through in your previous position. A question from the audience makes you think of a leadership challenge you're about to take on. At one point he asks, "Have you ever thought about what you want your legacy to be?" For a few minutes, you project yourself into the future and imagine that *you're* now a retired CEO, giving your own talk. What *do* you want your legacy to be? Hmm.

Your attention wanders from time to time, but as the talk goes on, your reflections weave a web of connections between different ideas and experiences, jelling into a few basic themes that remain with you as you drive home from the event. The next day, you find yourself thinking about one of these themes—something about the importance of stakeholder buy-in—and you put it into action.

This is what it's like to reflect as an Achiever.[10] As an Expert, you're more likely to quickly evaluate the speaker's credentials, react to comments on a point-by-point basis, and pit the speaker's opinions against your own. As an Achiever, you take more in. You gain a more nuanced understanding based on connections made over longer time frames, and you take what you learn more to heart. Over time, this level of reflection allows you to step back from the standards and beliefs you developed at the Expert level, compare and contrast them, and integrate them into a coherent *system* of values and beliefs.[11]

Ellen, a businesswoman in her late forties, provides an example of what we mean. Recently promoted to president of one of America's best-known Fortune 100 companies, she entered the Achiever level of agility early in her career. She attributes much of her success to a leadership philosophy she developed over the years. A sought-after speaker and role model for others, she has distilled her values and beliefs about leadership into an explicit set of principles.

For Ellen, a leader has an obligation to "sound the trumpet"—to provide vision and direction—and to communicate with others in ways that are clear, concise, and candid. She believes that leaders also need to exemplify the values they expect others to follow, acting with integrity (being an honest and faithful steward of the money invested by the company's owners) and setting a tone of caring and respect, not only toward stockholders, but also toward customers and employees.

Ellen believes that, both publicly and privately, leaders should be bold, dynamic, and courageous but also courteous and appreciative.

She's happiest when her organization is solving problems and making money, and she says the best leaders are those who motivate others by expecting and celebrating high performance.

Even this highly condensed version of Ellen's principles shows how they differ from an Expert's laundry list of standards and beliefs. She has a conceptually coherent system of ideas and ideals that spans multiple action arenas, ranging from face-to-face relationships to the company's relationship with its larger environment.[12]

Although many Achiever-level leaders have a leadership philosophy similar to Ellen's, the specific values and beliefs embedded in their leadership philosophies can vary widely. What these philosophies have in common is the fact that they are *systems* of values and beliefs, developed as the result of robust personal reflection.

At the Achiever level, regardless of how much you respect external authorities, you understand that developing your own system of values and beliefs is ultimately a matter of personal choice and responsibility. Psychologists refer to this development as the full "relocation of authority within the self."[13]

Achiever Context-Setting Agility

We now turn to the two developmental capacities that shape the way you set the context for your leadership initiatives: *situational awareness* and *sense of purpose*.

SITUATIONAL AWARENESS. As noted in Chapter Four, at the Expert level your situational awareness is something like the fixed lens of a still camera.[14] It gives you a clear picture of your subject (the central issue of your initiative), but only a general sense of its immediate context. At the Achiever level, your situational awareness is more like an adjustable lens. You can focus on the issue at hand, but you can also zoom out and view it from a wider angle.

This level of situational awareness allows you to understand any issue or organizational unit in the context of its relationships with its larger environment. For example, this awareness guided Rachel's strategic analysis of the Fixed Income group, which identified business needs and opportunities at the interface between the company and its customers.

SENSE OF PURPOSE. As your situational awareness develops, your *sense of purpose* expands from tactical to strategic. Your Achiever-level reflective capacity not only allows you to look back and see things in greater historical context, it also allows you to vividly imagine possibilities that lie further down the road. As we saw in Carlos's story, at the Expert level you're rarely motivated by goals lying more than a year or so in the future, but at the Achiever level medium-term objectives (two to five years out) become quite compelling.

With this new level of context-setting agility, you understand that no team or organization can succeed over the longer term unless it anticipates and responds to the changes taking place in its environment. This understanding, along with your capacity for envisioning future possibilities, provides the foundation for strategic foresight, the ability to anticipate important environmental trends and scenarios. As we saw in Mark's story, organizational leaders at the Achiever level have the interest and ability needed to analyze the dynamics of their industry. They're particularly interested in discerning midterm trends, problems, and opportunities concerning customer needs, competitor behavior, and emerging products and services.

Achiever-level context-setting agility also entails a significant shift in the way you think about a team or organization's performance. At the Expert level, your primary focus is on "doing things right"—making improvements within a system's boundaries so that tactical goals can be achieved. At the Achiever level, you realize that a system's success over the longer term requires it to produce the outputs needed by its central stakeholders (owners, stockholders, customers). As a result, your primary focus as a leader becomes "doing the right thing," ensuring that the objectives set for the system are optimal *outcomes*.[15]

This outcome orientation allows you to think and plan strategically. Once your outcomes are clear, you identify the strategic initiatives needed to achieve them. You retain the ability to think tactically, but your tactics are now linked to strategic outcomes. Like a good chess player, you can think several steps ahead, see multiple pathways to your end game, anticipate potential obstacles, and plan ways to overcome them.

While the Expert focuses mainly on functional or disciplinary tasks, the capacities you develop at the Achiever level give you the mental agility needed to master the tasks classically associated with effective management: strategic planning, resource allocation, and staffing;

designing organizational structures and processes; and using information systems to monitor and improve organizational performance. You have a much greater appreciation of the way in which multiple functions, properly orchestrated, can contribute to the achievement of a common set of organizational outcomes.

Achiever Stakeholder Agility

Your level of stakeholder agility is directly supported by two personal capacities: your *stakeholder understanding* and your *power style.*

STAKEHOLDER UNDERSTANDING. At the Expert level, you can observe people over time and come to conclusions about their personality traits, abilities, and characteristic emotional states. Although you've developed an initial level of tolerance for people whose backgrounds and viewpoints differ from your own, you ultimately assess others according to your own set of high standards. You're often inclined to be very critical (inwardly or outwardly) when they don't live up to these standards.

At the Achiever level, as you become more self-reflective you gain a more specific awareness of your own feelings and motivations. Because your stakeholder understanding always deepens to the level at which you understand yourself, you now see that others' behavior is caused by specific motivations. This enhanced awareness of others' feelings and motivations allows you to be more empathetic than you were at the Expert level. You also develop a new interest in talking about your personal experiences and finding out how they compare with those of others.

As illustrated in each of the stories earlier in this chapter, Achiever-level stakeholder understanding makes you more attuned to the role that stakeholders' motivations and expectations play in determining their support for your initiatives. As a result, you realize that it's important to at least know who your key stakeholders are, anticipate their likely reactions to your initiatives, and consider the best way to influence their expectations and gain their support.

POWER STYLE. How you engage with stakeholders depends a great deal on your power style, which includes your assumptions about power and influence. At the Achiever level, you view formal authority structures as an important part of any organization's design, but you don't automatically equate leadership with a position of authority. While you view your own authority as a powerful tool, you realize that authority alone is rarely sufficient to accomplish anything of great consequence. As Rachel expressed it, your power is partly a function of certain personal qualities you bring to your role.

As an Achiever, you also realize that the real sources of power extend far beyond formal structures. You see that an organization is in many respects a political organism: an arena where multiple stakeholders—both internal and external—exercise power and influence, each trying to maximize its self-interest within a context of larger shared interests. It's clear to you that any time you initiate change, multiple interest groups will have a stake in what happens and, invariably, some will hold views and priorities that differ from your own and from one another.[16]

As you'll remember, Expert managers usually adopt either an assertive or an accommodative power style. In contrast, the reflective capacity that emerges at the Achiever level allows you to hold aspects of both styles in mind, compare their relative value, and work out ways to take both into account.

In spite of this capability, a small minority of Achievers adopt a power style of extreme assertion or extreme accommodation.[17] Those with extreme assertive styles pursue their own agendas without consideration for other views. The only legitimate stakeholders, in their mind, are those who are willing to support their agenda. They essentially treat those with opposing or competing agendas as enemies. The smaller minority who adopt an extreme accommodative style try to ensure that all stakeholders are happy, even if this means minimizing their own responsibility for setting clear direction and asserting appropriate authority.

Rather than viewing assertion and accommodation as complete opposites, the great majority of Achievers see a continuum that runs from one extreme to the other. Most adopt a style that's on the assertive side but that also incorporates certain elements of accommodation. The rest do the reverse. For example, earlier in this chapter we saw how two Expert managers, Guy and Carlos, developed a more balanced power style as they developed into the Achiever level, although Guy still leaned toward the assertive side and Carlos toward the accommodative side of the spectrum.

Whatever their primary stance, Achievers are more likely than Experts to develop a style that's relatively balanced between assertion and accommodation, as Mark did early in his career. Compared with Experts, Achievers also are more agile in moving back and forth along this continuum, depending on the specific situation they're facing.

How do Achievers with assertive power styles respond to stakeholders who have views and interests that differ from their own? Because they understand that the expectations and motivations of key stakeholders can have a big impact on an initiative's success, they usually find some way to engage with them. Some try to sell their change initiatives by relying primarily on various forms of one-way communication. Others, like Guy and Mark, also find ways to solicit stakeholder input, although this input isn't likely to alter their overall agenda in a significant way.

Less frequently, we find Achiever-level leaders whose strengths lie on the accommodative side of the spectrum. Compared with other Achievers, they're good listeners, coaches, and team-builders, and they often seek and seriously consider stakeholder input. They're often respected by others for not putting their own interests above those of the organization. At the same time, when these leaders aren't willing to take strong stands with their stakeholders, they limit their effectiveness in important ways.[18]

As an Achiever dealing with key stakeholders whose views and interests differ from your own, you're likely to visualize a continuum of options for resolving this conflict. At one end of the spectrum, you win. At the other end, you lose. In between are a number of possible compromise positions. Given this mind-set, the classic forms of negotiation become your primary means for resolving differences. Your style of negotiation may be assertive, accommodative, or relatively balanced, but until you grow beyond the Achiever level, you're unlikely to discover ways to resolve conflict that lie beyond the options of win, lose, or compromise.

Achiever Creative Agility

Invariably, the kinds of problems leaders face in carrying out their initiatives are ill-structured. The more complex your business environment and the more rapidly it's changing, the more ill-structured these issues will be. Creative agility is the ability to transform these ill-structured problems into desired results. Your level of creative agility is supported by two developmental capacities: *connective awareness* and *reflective judgment.*

CONNECTIVE AWARENESS. Connective awareness is the ability to hold various ideas and experiences in mind, compare and contrast them, and make meaningful connections between them. Just as scientists use experimental data to construct explanatory and predictive theories, Achiever leaders reflect on what they've learned in specific situations, see connections, and arrive at more general truths. Like their scientific counterparts, they realize that these insights are probabilistic (generally true, very likely to be true), not absolute.

While Experts are more attracted to procedural frameworks (lists, steps, and how-tos), Achievers appreciate the leverage that new ideas and conceptual frameworks give them in the world of action.[19] They aren't interested in systems of thought as ends in themselves. But they often have a strong interest in practical conceptual models that can help them interpret events and predict the future consequences of their actions.

At the Achiever level you also develop the ability to hold opposing ideas and experiences in mind, compare them, and, when needed, work out ways to take both into account. As we saw with assertive and accommodative leadership styles, at this level, you see that opposites are related to one another along a continuum. While circumstances sometimes call for either/or choices between opposing alternatives, Achievers can also envision solutions that represent a compromise between extremes. However, at this level it's unusual for a leader to develop true win-win solutions, where each party comes away with what they most need.

REFLECTIVE JUDGMENT. This capacity refers to the way you determine what's true and what's the best course of action for solving ill-structured problems—and to the way you justify these views to yourself and to others. At the Expert level, you often perceive ill-structured problems as if they must have well-established answers just waiting to be remembered or rediscovered. You also have a limited understanding of the extent to which biases of all kinds enter into the way you diagnose and solve problems. As a result, you can easily confuse your opinion with an objective perception of reality, and you don't fully appreciate the need to use factual information and other viewpoints to test the validity of your views.

At the Achiever level, your reflective judgment deepens. You have a greater appreciation of the ill-structured nature of business and organizational problems, and you're more aware of how easily bias and error can enter into attempts to solve these problems. Consequently, with important problems, you want to make sure your diagnoses are consistent with the available evidence. Similarly, when you solve problems, you want to consider any data that will help you predict which solutions best meet your success criteria.

At the same time, Achievers are typically unaware of the extent to which their own value and belief system influences their selection and interpretation of factual information. Once Achievers have arrived at a position that seems consistent with the available evidence, they often find it very difficult to seriously consider alternative interpretations of the same evidence. It's not until the Catalyst level that leaders begin to develop a genuine interest in value and belief systems that differ from their own.

Achiever Self-Leadership Agility

Your self-leadership agility is made possible by the depth of your *self-awareness* and your *developmental motivation.*

SELF-AWARENESS. Achiever-level reflective awareness not only generates a more complex understanding of the external world, it also activates a new level of self-awareness. As your reflective capacity deepens to include longer time frames, you're more likely to think about earlier periods of your life. Looking forward, you can vividly imagine what your life might be like in future decades.

The self-awareness you develop at the Achiever level also allows you to reflect on recent events and answer questions such as these: How did I contribute to that particular outcome? What were my motivations? What was I thinking and feeling at the time? When you remember past behaviors, emotional states, and motivations, you're able to call on richer and more specific detail than you would have at the Expert level.

Because you can now reflect on your life in greater depth and over longer time frames, you gain new insights about your most enduring traits. As a result, the self-image you developed at the Expert level evolves into an interrelated system of ideas about your personal strengths and limitations. Psychologists refer to this as the development of a "strong sense of identity."[20]

To illustrate this development, we turn briefly to the story of Karen, an Atlanta housewife who grew into the Expert stage in her mid-thirties, while she worked as an administrative assistant, got involved in political campaigns, and joined a women's support group. She then began to follow the promptings that would take her into the Achiever stage:

> I started getting really strong urges to have a career. I wanted to move toward being a self-reliant, independent person. I didn't want to isolate myself from other people—I just wanted to do something not out of need or dependence but because it was what I really wanted to be. Admittedly, I went through an overly selfish and rebellious period at that time. My husband and many of my friends found the "new me" pretty threatening. That was when I decided to dissolve my marriage. It was a really drastic step, and I sometimes had grave doubts about it, but to grow sometimes you have to risk letting go of what's familiar and realize that you'll have some doubts along the way.

During a period of concentrated journaling, Karen developed a more reflective self-awareness and a stronger sense of identity:

> After the divorce, I isolated myself for about two months and had these intensive sessions with myself. For the first time in my life, I was *really* honest with myself—what had motivated me and why certain things had happened. That's when I realized that many of the things I'd blamed on my marriage really had nothing to do with my husband. I'd used my marriage as an excuse not to risk going after what I wanted to do professionally.
>
> Part of what came out of this was a very sincere commitment to continue to get clear about who I really am, what I'm really like. I decided I'd actually write down all of my attributes. I came up with a very long list! Then I went through it and tried to be totally honest with myself, and I reduced the list considerably. What I learned is that the real me doesn't have nearly as much as I'd thought of either the positive or the negative. That's when I realized I could do anything I wanted to, as long as I was willing to acknowledge and deal with my limitations.

Karen went on to earn a master's degree in public administration and become an executive in a community development corporation.

DEVELOPMENTAL MOTIVATION. Your developmental motivation is shaped by your leadership ideal, by your primary source of professional self-esteem and satisfaction, and by the tone of your self-evaluation. At the Expert level, your leadership ideal includes your short-term professional goals and the knowledge, skills, and personality traits you want to have as a leader. At the Achiever level, it expands to include long-term career objectives and an explicit or implicit leadership philosophy.

At the Expert level your professional self-esteem and satisfaction come primarily from feeling that you're admired for your astuteness and expertise. At the Achiever level, your ability to visualize the future results of your actions gives you a strong (and sometimes exaggerated) feeling of responsibility for the impact you have on the world around you. For this reason and because of your newly developed outcome orientation, your professional self-esteem and satisfaction come primarily from your own belief that you've contributed to the achievement of significant outcomes.

At the Expert level, you take your self-ideal very seriously. As Guy's story illustrates, when you feel you're not accomplishing your goals or living up to your standards, you can easily become quite self-critical. Although this reaction can motivate you to change, it can also eat away at your self-esteem, often making it harder to change.

At the Achiever level, you still criticize yourself, but the tone of your self-criticism is not as harsh, so you're left feeling more guilty than ashamed. For this reason, developmental psychologist Jane Loevinger uses the term "conscientious" to describe the Achiever stage.[21] This less punitive form of self-criticism gives you a bit more mental space to reflect on your experience and decide how to respond to what's happened.

If you're coaching an Achiever, it's useful to know that they have a capacity for taking in feedback that's less developed at the Expert level. Achievers may even solicit feedback, something that Experts rarely do. Achievers are often most receptive to feedback when it takes their desired outcomes as givens and provides more effective ways to achieve them. Achievers may also be open to feedback that shows them how they can act more consistently with their leadership ideals. They are most receptive to specific examples where their behavior worked against their ideals or their self-interest, combined with concrete alternatives that will lead to their desired results.[22]

CHAPTER SIX

Catalyst Level
Mobilize Breakout Endeavors

A s the senior environmental health and safety officer for a global chemical corporation, Brenda was charged with implementing the company's worldwide commitment to sustainable
development.[1] A bright and spirited Catalyst-level leader, she felt
strongly that a genuine commitment to environmental responsibility
would not only benefit the planet, it would also make the company
more profitable. She described the chemical industry's historical stance
toward environmental issues in this way:

> Before the mid-1980s, the industry assumed that anyone concerned
> about chemical risks was either wrong or irrelevant. The only real
> stakeholders in their minds were shareholders and government regu-
> lators. The primary strategy for dealing with the public's concerns was
> to stonewall.
>
> Then in 1984 came the Bhopal disaster. Even without that, the in-
> dustry was finding that, when people were ignored or misled, they got
> distrustful and angry, and the pressure to change increased. They re-
> alized they had to deal with the public, so they adopted a PR strategy

to try to convince the people that chemicals are safe and chemical plants can make good neighbors.

The first real shift took place in the very late 1980s when there was a new wave of environmental consciousness, and the industry acknowledged that it needed to change. By 1990, a worldwide industry movement called Responsible Care was under way, and our company was part of that. A commitment to environmental responsibility and public accountability, two pillars of the Responsible Care movement, became conditions for continuing membership in the Chemical Manufacturers Association.

By the early 1990s, some people in the company understood that, in a whole host of ways, environmental responsibility is good for the bottom line, and these ideas were starting to get traction at the top level. They came up with a new set of global business principles, and they made a commitment to reducing the environmental impact of their products from cradle to grave: health and safety, greenhouse emissions, energy efficiency, the whole nine yards. Then, after several years of PR about how they were into sustainable development, they realized they had to actually deliver!

It was at this point that Brenda joined the company. A manager named Dan had volunteered to take over the company's lowest-performing facility in the United States, an operation that was also in deep trouble with the EPA. As a pilot project, he set out to transform it into a high-performing, environmentally responsible organization. He hired Brenda as his EH&S manager. They had anything but a smooth start:

> About a month after I took the job, a SWAT team of Feds with helicopters and guns burst into our offices waving their badges and saying, "Don't touch anything! You're under arrest!" I kid you not.

Yet within several years Dan, Brenda, and their respective teams turned their operation into a model facility:

> Everyone was very excited. We created this empowered organization that was just screaming off the charts on all the traditional performance measures—operating efficiency, quality, safety—*and* on all the new environmental measures. Plus, we put a whole lot of money in the bank. The EPA now loved us, and at the state level we were nomi-

nated for the Governor's Award for Environmental Health and Safety Excellence.

The corporation's officers were extremely impressed. Before she knew it, Brenda was living in Europe where she had a job at corporate headquarters, reporting to a top executive in her new role as Global Project Manager of the company's sustainable development initiative. She taught people throughout the company how to replicate what she and Dan had accomplished, and they had many similar successes.

> Then we were told to go to the company's *highest*-performing facility and work our magic there. This would be a test case to see if we should roll out this approach all across the corporation. I was wary at first. With such a high-performing operation, I was concerned that the improvements would be fairly minor. We had to generate a 1.8-year simple payback. That's big. It's hard to find a capital investment that'll do that for any facility. But I really believe in this stuff, so I decided to go for it.
>
> Sure enough, we helped them find a host of capital improvements for a clear 1.8 payback. They reduced their emissions by 55 percent and improved their operating efficiency, liability, and energy consumption by 45 percent. When we back-tested out across all the other facilities, it was a $60 billion opportunity for the corporation worldwide over seven to ten years. Not to mention a reduction in worldwide emissions that would take us below the levels to which the company had publicly committed.[2]

WHAT LEADERSHIP MEANS AT THE CATALYST LEVEL

Brenda's understanding of leadership is reflected in the way she approached her change initiatives. As one example:

> In the U.S. facility, my team identified our emission levels and where they came from. Traditionally, the next step is to give this analysis to the manufacturing engineers and have them fix the problems. But in my experience this doesn't create the best solutions, nor does it help employees adopt an environmental mind-set. Instead, we pulled together a set of cross-functional teams that included everyone from frontline people to the facility's most innovative thinkers—maintenance operators, operations people, process engineers, manufacturing

engineers, you name it. We told them what the problem was, the outcomes we needed, and we turned them loose to do their best and most creative thinking.

What this did inside the organization was remarkable. People felt empowered, people felt excited, people felt honored. Somebody was looking at them and saying, "You're not just a cog in the wheel. You're a smart, creative human being." People came alive in that environment. And guess what? They came up with a really inexpensive way to capture one of the largest emission sources and reintroduce it into the process in a way that significantly increased our daily output. That's like gold. We got rid of fifteen tons of toxic emissions. That's just one of over thirty major improvements they came up with. The whole approach we took, not just in that first facility but in many different facilities, is based on seeing the facility as a community, a place that can come alive when everyone is treated like a real human being.

This, in a nutshell, is the Catalyst's understanding of leadership. Catalyst-level leadership means creating new contexts where people can tap into their creative potential by participating in the development of solutions that benefit multiple stakeholders. It's the first level of "post-heroic" leadership.

The Catalyst leadership orientation is supported by the mental and emotional capacities that emerge at this level. When you grow into this level, you begin to feel more at ease with change and uncertainty, and you develop a broader, longer-term view of your organizational environment. Because you realize that what's made you successful in the past may not be what's needed now, you tend to be more visionary in your response to new leadership challenges. While you retain the Achiever's strong outcome orientation, you recognize that the sustained achievement of desired outcomes takes place within a larger context of human relationships (teams, organizational culture, alliances), and you make it a priority to enhance the quality of these contexts.

Your interest in engaging with stakeholders comes from the conviction that strategies and solutions are usually better when they're influenced by a diversity of relevant viewpoints. Your increased capacity for tolerating conflict, both within yourself and with other people, allows you to respond to stakeholder complexity with greater mental and emotional agility. Because you understand that you do not and cannot have all the answers, you're more likely than you were at the Achiever level to use participative decision making to empower and develop your people.

At the Catalyst level you develop a capacity for trying on differing frames of reference, and you see that diametrically opposed viewpoints can each be valid in their own way. This new perspective sparks your creative thinking and makes you more aware of the powerful role that frames of reference play in joint problem solving. As a result, you're more likely to question the assumptions you and others make when framing problems and developing solutions. You're also more likely to see a problem as part of a larger pattern caused by deeper organizational issues.

At this level, you develop a new capacity for self-observation. You can now step back from your image of yourself and recognize feelings, assumptions, and priorities that would otherwise escape your conscious awareness. You begin to see that your need to achieve comes, much more than you'd realized, from a desire for approval and recognition. At the same time, you discover that your self-esteem is determined primarily by your own reactions to your successes and failures. You also become more proactive in seeking feedback and in looking for ways to bring greater meaning into all aspects of your life.

You're now about to read the stories of three Catalyst-level leaders, each of whom was centrally involved in turning around a faltering company: David, an embattled software executive who became a leader in creating a highly collaborative organizational culture; Joan, who led the way in creating a new future for a small consulting firm; and Robert, the oil company president you met briefly in the first chapter.[3]

PIVOTAL CONVERSATIONS
AT THE CATALYST LEVEL

David put down the phone and looked up. John's tall figure loomed in his office doorway, frowning in frustration. "We've gotta talk about EDR," John said, referring to one of their most important new product development projects. David grimaced. *Oh no,* he thought, *not another problem with EDR!*

David was executive VP for systems development at Financial Software Systems (FSS), a young 250-person firm that developed sophisticated software for financial institutions. The company had been quite successful as a start-up, and revenue from initial products continued to be good, but its new products were chronically late. Customers were constantly complaining, and programmers were leaving the company at an alarming rate.

The corporation that owned FSS used two measures to assess the firm's performance: 75 percent was based on its annual revenues. The other 25 percent hinged on new product innovation. Because the parent company was rapidly losing confidence in FSS's ability to innovate, its product development budget was about to be cut, and the firm was in real danger of losing what autonomy it still had.

The company was organized into two major divisions. David, the company's technical guru, was in charge of the systems organization, which was responsible for the design of new software applications. David's organization interfaced with four sales and marketing units. Each unit, headed by a VP, was responsible for sales, installation, and customer service for a particular customer segment. Each part of the company had its own budget, performance measures, and standards of compensation.

EDR was the most complex new product development project the company had launched to date, and a great deal rode on its success. John had come to David's office because he'd just received a call from Elliot, a tech who worked with the equipment supplier for EDR. "The project plan says that what we charge for the equipment is supposed to include the first step of installation, provided by the equipment supplier," Elliot had said. "But I just found out they don't do that kind of work. They recommended a contractor, but, as I'm sure you know, contractors for this kind of work are really expensive."

John was stunned. David, who'd written the project plan before John was hired, had made a costly mistake, but because it concerned the installation budget, it was John's performance that would suffer. The meeting that ensued was subsequently written up by David as a "learning case" for a Pivotal Conversations program provided for FSS's top management group.[4]

In the introductory part of his learning case, David said his objective for the meeting was to solve the EDR installation problem as quickly as possible, in a way that would require as little as possible from his own people. Knowing that his people were already overcommitted and afraid that John would try to get him to accept full responsibility for solving the problem, he wanted to get John to agree that they shared responsibility for resolving the issue.

In the left-hand column of his learning case, David documented his conversation with John. In the right-hand column, he wrote what he was thinking and feeling at each point in the conversation. At the end of the case, he described where he felt he had and hadn't been effective:

CONVERSATION	DAVID'S UNSPOKEN THOUGHTS AND FEELINGS
JOHN: I just got a call from Elliot. There's a problem with the first step of the installation process. Elliot just found out the supplier doesn't do that kind of installation work. They recommended a contractor, but, as I'm sure you know, contractors for this kind of work are extremely expensive.	I immediately feel irritated and defensive. Having the equipment supplier take care of the first step of installation was just a working assumption. But I feel guilty about just dumping EDR in John's lap when he joined the company and not discussing it with him. Now he's going to try to pin this problem on me and my people. That's what he usually does. He never comes in here without telling me that Jessica is screwing up and he wants me to get her to change something she's doing.
DAVID: Come on in and sit down. Let's go over the facts and see what the options are.	My whole organization is operating beyond capacity. If my people took the time to help John on this issue, it would hurt their performance in other areas. They're already behind on enough projects. But I don't want to get into an emotional confrontation with John.
[We go over the project plan and budget. We figure out what things will and won't cause expense overruns.]	
JOHN: So here's where we're coming out: To know exactly what	

CONVERSATION	DAVID'S UNSPOKEN THOUGHTS AND FEELINGS

the costs will be, we need your people to coordinate getting the estimates. But, ballpark, it looks like this. If we could use our own contractor to do all the installations, we'd be over budget, but it wouldn't be that bad. The real kicker is we know some of our key customers are going to insist on having us pay for their own installation contractors to do the work, and that's going to involve expensive union labor. How do we handle that?

He's saying, "Whose problem is this?" I wish I'd anticipated that this was going to be so expensive. But what I really can't afford are solutions that take too much of my people's time. I'll try to put it back on him.

I don't think John will be able to get the customer to agree to my proposal. We're in a bad position.

DAVID: In those cases, let's see if we can get the customers to pay for this themselves. If that won't fly, we could offer to reimburse them an amount equal to having our contractor do it.

Well, that didn't work. He threw it back at me. I can't duck my responsibility to generate the estimates. John's people can't do that.

JOHN: I'll talk to the customers, but I seriously doubt they'll go for it. I want your people to coordinate getting all the estimates.

This is not good. I don't think John will be able to get the customer to agree to pay for anything.

DAVID: OK. My people will coordinate estimates, but I think you should push hard on the customer.

JOHN: All right. I'll need those estimates by Thursday.

Reflections: I wasn't effective in minimizing unplanned expenses or the impact of the installation problem on my people. The outcome, because

I didn't really believe we were going to get any money from the customer, really ended up with me carrying the ball on the whole problem. I didn't end up feeling that it was a shared problem and that we were going to work together on it. I believe that having it be a shared problem might have resulted in a more effective solution.

In the workshop, David readily acknowledged that he hadn't achieved his desired outcomes, and he asked how he could handle meetings like this more effectively. The initial feedback he received from his colleagues focused on the fact that both he and John kept trying to put the ball in the other's court. Because they didn't openly discuss their differing perspectives and priorities, neither felt satisfied with or committed to the steps they agreed on.

David's colleagues helped him see that he contributed to this outcome by repeatedly advocating his own ideas without ever inquiring about what would work from John's perspective. One of the sales and marketing VPs put it this way:

> David says, "Why don't we see if we can get the customers to pay for this themselves?" But in the back of his mind, he knows damn well they aren't going to do that. But he doesn't say that to John.
>
> [To David] Why are you proposing that John do that, when *you* know the customers aren't going to do that? It seems to me, not that it's a bad suggestion, but you ought to finish it by saying, "I know that it's going to be a bitch, and here are the reasons why. Do you think it's worth a shot, John? Is there anything I can do to help you get that done?" But it's more like, "Let me give him a half-assed solution, and let him go run off with it." I mean, that's how I interpret it.

Because a real solution to this project required a joint effort, getting the problem defined as a shared one was an important objective. However, as his colleagues pointed out, David didn't take the opportunity to frame the discussion this way. In fact, in the workshop David acknowledged that his attempt to establish joint responsibility had really been a defensive maneuver, a tactic to prevent him from taking full responsibility. His actual objective, in the moment, was to take as little responsibility for the problem as possible.

Like everyone else in their management group, David and John functioned at the Achiever level. For this reason, it's not surprising that each manager focused only on maximizing those outcomes used to measure his own performance. However, in pivotal conversations like this one, where the issue at hand crosses organizational boundaries, focusing solely on your own objectives often leads to results that satisfy no one.

To be effective in these types of conversations, David learned that he needed to shift from a unilateral intention (focusing on only what was good for him) to a collaborative intention (a willingness to develop a solution that took into account the priorities of all the key stakeholders—including himself). Put differently, he needed to shift from a predominantly assertive power style to one that balanced assertion and accommodation.

To make good on this collaborative intention, David needed to know how to initiate and sustain a problem-solving dialogue. He learned he could do this by advocating his position and then immediately inviting the other person to express his own views.

David also received feedback about his "unspoken thoughts and feelings." For example, David knew that the assumptions he'd made about installation costs were now going to hurt John's performance, but he didn't acknowledge this. Brian, the president of FSS and the person to whom both David and John reported, put it this way:

> The conversation is like a surface dialogue. The real conversation is in the unspoken thoughts and feelings. In other words, John is probably saying to himself, "David didn't set this up right, and now I'm bagged with the thing. That annoys the hell out of me. What can he do to help me?" And I'm just talking about the business aspects of it. And, David, you're probably saying in your own mind, "I'll bet that's where John's coming from." It seems to me it would have helped to get this out in the open. Then John could say to you, "I don't understand why you did this in the first place. Why was the deal structured this way? How did we get to this point?"

The fact that John was sitting across from David in the workshop gave them an opportunity to discuss this for the first time. John said that David's response in the meeting had angered him and reinforced his distrust of the systems organization. In his relatively short tenure at FSS, John felt that David's people constantly pushed him away and kept him in the dark. He didn't always trust their reasons for project delays, and when John asked David to intervene, it rarely made any difference. David sensed this distrust, but he never brought it up to see what they could do about it.

Had David and John been able to discuss these issues using the skills they were now learning, they would have discovered that they held different views about what David's role should be in solving the problems that arose on new product development projects. In fact, there was no commonly understood process for resolving these kinds of issues.

In the workshop, David and his colleagues were introduced to the Catalyst-level definition of *framing*, which went beyond the Achiever-level definition Guy's coach gave him in Chapter Five: At the Catalyst level, framing isn't just making your objectives and assumptions explicit at the beginning of a conversation. It's also the skill of explicitly describing the key priorities, feelings, or assumptions influencing your perceptions and actions at *any* key point in a conversation. David and his colleagues discovered that getting many of these internal thoughts and feelings on the table can be extremely useful, not only for solving the problem at hand but also for identifying and resolving underlying issues.

Pivotal conversations often provide unrecognized opportunities to surface important underlying issues regarding organizational structures and working relationships. Quite often these issues are problem generators. For example, the lack of clarity about how to resolve differences at the interface between the systems organization and the sales and marketing organization was a big cause of new product delays. Yet, partly because of the "Ping-Pong" discussions that were the norm at FSS, these issues remained undiscussed and unresolved.

Like his colleagues, David was initially much better at reflecting on conversations after the fact than he was at changing his behavior while it was happening. However, through practice, he gradually developed a Catalyst's level of awareness and intent: the ability to recognize a tacit feeling, assumption, or behavior and then immediately adjust his response to take this new awareness into account.[5]

As this new capacity developed, David was quick to recognize opportunities for joint problem solving. He also developed the ability to shift, on the spot, from unilateral to collaborative intent, pausing after key advocacy statements to inquire about others' views. With continued coaching and a few refresher workshops over the two years that followed, these skills gradually became a natural part of his repertoire, and his leadership agility began to restabilize at the Catalyst level.

During this period, David played a major role in transforming what had been a poorly functioning executive team into a collaborative leadership team that transformed FSS into a high-performing business.

TEAM LEADERSHIP AT
THE CATALYST LEVEL

Joan came to the front of the ballroom and looked out at sixty expectant faces. For the past year, she'd served as COO for the people sitting before her, a highly respected consulting firm called Pricing Strategy Solutions (PSS). Now in her mid-fifties, she had substantial experience in similar roles, including a stint as managing partner of a much larger firm.

Joan's first year at PSS had been a bad year for many consulting firms, but especially so for PSS. Some of its Fortune 1000 clients had taken their business to the full-service global consulting firms they used for other purposes. It was a challenging situation:

> As in many partnerships, whatever profits were made in the year before I arrived had been disbursed to the shareholders, so there was very little money in the bank. When we had this bad year, we were forced into salary deferrals, and we laid off eleven people. I've had experience with this sort of thing, but for PSS it was the first time. So it was a very tough year. The only upside was weeding out our low-performers.

The meeting was in a hotel about a mile from the firm's main offices near Research Triangle Park, the huge industrial park between Durham, Chapel Hill, and Raleigh, North Carolina. The meeting had started shortly before dinner, just as the group from their small San Francisco office arrived. Doug, the firm's pricing guru, primary owner, and nominal CEO, began the meeting with an important message:

> I'm not interested in surviving. I want us to thrive. As far as I'm concerned, everyone in this room is part of a team. I'm going to stick with this team. We're going to sink or swim together.

Now, as Joan came to the front of the room, people looked both concerned and curious. She and Doug had decided to speak before dinner to give everyone a chance to talk and think things over before the next day's meeting. Joan's remarks were brief:

I'm going to put what Doug just said in very concrete terms: There won't be any more layoffs. We've evaluated the business, and we've decided we want everyone in this room to be a part of the firm's future. Tomorrow's meeting will be an opportunity for all of us to participate in creating that future. I urge all of you to jump in and give us your best thinking.

Members of the firm spent most of the next morning in small groups, addressing key topics concerning their collective future. Each group had people from all different levels of the company, and one person in each group was assigned as a facilitator. During the late morning report-outs, the most commonly mentioned idea was to explore the possibility of being acquired by a larger consulting firm. Doug and Joan said this had already occurred to them as an option, but they'd postponed any serious discussion to see what emerged at this meeting. Now, seeing the groundswell of interest in the idea, Joan suggested that they spend the afternoon testing its viability by having subgroups flesh it out in more detail.

By the day's end, the groups had identified the pros and cons of being acquired, both on a business level and on a personal level. They also took a first pass at defining the desired characteristics of the larger firm. What emerged was a strong business case for pursuing an acquisition partner. Joan summed it up this way:

> The larger firms were beginning to get into pricing strategy. The work we'd been known for was on its way toward becoming a commodity. To retain leadership in this area, we needed to be part of a broader platform.
>
> Also, for PSS to grow the way we want it to, we need more marketing muscle and financial wherewithal. Doug is a genius, but he's an idea guy. I'm a strong strategic and operational person. But, unlike many successful small consulting firms, our top person isn't a sales and marketing type who can go out and make it rain.[6]

At the end of the all-hands meeting, Joan told everyone that the management team would devote their next few weekly meetings to serious consideration of the work they'd all done at the retreat. The management team decided they wanted to be acquired by a global consulting firm that shared their values and would honor their autonomy. Within the month they initiated serious conversations with several larger firms.

The trap in a small firm is to think that everyone already knows what's going on. So you really have to work at keeping people informed. You really can't communicate enough. It increases the trust quotient. I'm still amazed at what people make up about why certain things are happening if you don't tell them.

We have two meetings every Friday, an hour with the executive team and an hour before that with our go-to-market team, which is the executive team and about ten more people. This larger group talks about how the business is doing, the opportunities we're pursuing, what kind of help we need. So these meetings keep our core people informed. In addition, someone on the executive team sends a voicemail each week to everyone in the firm. We were especially conscious of this during the acquisition process. All the way along, we were very open with people about what we were doing and why.

When the executive team narrowed the options down to the top three firms, Joan got everyone's agreement to conduct interviews with the whole go-to-market team, about twenty people in all. Each of the three firms knew how important it was to make sure PSS's culture would mesh with their own. By using this interview process it also became very clear to the whole go-to-market team which firm they wanted to join.

When the deal was consummated, Joan called everyone in PSS together to celebrate. As part of a top-quality global consulting firm, they would now have access to a worldwide client base. At the same time, PSS would enjoy a high degree of autonomy. Pricing Strategy Solutions would keep its name, its management team, and its consulting staff. Given the larger firm's values and its acquisition track record, PSS felt confident that these commitments would be honored.

When PSS decided to be acquired, all its consultants were highly marketable. Some got offers to go elsewhere at higher salaries, but everyone stayed with the firm.

I think the retreat and the way we managed the acquisition process had everything to do with the end result. Because of the way we handled it, I think the crisis we faced turned out to be extremely fortuitous. It allows us to bring the mind-set we'd developed within the management team into the whole firm.

When Joan joined Pricing Strategy Solutions as its COO, she started holding weekly executive team meetings each Friday that focused primarily on operational issues and a monthly meeting that focused on strategic issues.

> Doug selected me because PSS had never been managed by anyone with experience growing a firm. He needed someone who would come in and do things differently. At the same time, he knew it wouldn't work to have someone come in and impose things on people. So he needed someone with a participative style, who would respect people's individuality and, at the same time, get them to work together as a real team.

Joan said she originally developed this style because team members wind up feeling greater ownership for decisions, which results in better, faster implementation. "When it's not just me pushing but everyone is pulling in the same direction, everything is much easier and a lot more likely to succeed."

> I usually ask for input. It's a genuine request. More often than not, I've had some ideas about a solution. So I often say, "Here's what I'm thinking—what do the rest of you think?" At other times I'll just say, "What do you think?" But either way, the key to making it work is that, even when I think I know the solution, I realize there could be more to the picture.
>
> Doing it this way, I get a lot of good ideas. Sometimes people agree with me, sometimes they make small modifications, and sometimes it results in dramatic changes. When people are engaged and feel some ownership, it's not at all unusual that we'll come out with a better solution.

It's important not to confuse Joan's participative approach to team leadership with an accommodative power style. She had honed a well-balanced power style by observing other leaders who were either too assertive or too accommodating. Her approach was to encourage a good team discussion that examines issues from multiple viewpoints:

> When we do that, it doesn't become me versus the team. Everyone is influencing everyone else. I'll certainly state my own views, but at

times, other people will express these same views in ways that are more persuasive for the team as a whole. In addition, when we talk something through from multiple perspectives, I wind up feeling more confident myself that we're doing the right thing.

There are also times, of course, when several team members take one position and several take an opposite position—or when Joan takes a position that's different from most of the team. In these situations, she is quite comfortable making the decision herself and moving on. She observed that when team members see their input considered and acted upon as frequently as they do, they have no problem supporting her decisions, even when they may disagree.

> But I don't always do it the same way. Occasionally, when I get strong resistance to my position, I back off a bit and go for a compromise that gets things moving in what I feel is the right direction. I may ask them to keep an open mind and revisit the issue at a later date. Later, I may come back to the issue from a different angle and persist in taking it where I think it needs to go.

When she's let the team have its way, she's often been pleasantly surprised with the outcome. For example, in addition to consulting services, PSS also provides educational seminars on pricing strategy. When Joan first arrived, the seminars weren't growing. She pulled together a team to look at the issue and endorsed their recommendation to grow educational services as a separate business line. The best way to do that, she said, was to hire someone from outside the firm with experience doing just that. However, the team felt very strongly that Nick, one of the firm's best presenters and educators, should run the business.

Joan didn't think so. Nick had no experience growing a line of business. But the team pointed to his passion for this line of services and said Nick would get great internal support because he lived the values of the firm. The team did not address Joan's concern about Nick's lack of business experience, but she decided to take the risk that the team was right. As it turned out, Nick and the business line he now heads have both flourished. As Joan put it:

> This wasn't about giving up my authority and making sure everyone else was happy. I couldn't do that. What I think is most important,

overall, is that people know they can influence me and they can influence each other. That creates a level of trust and cohesiveness that's really hard to beat.

LEADING ORGANIZATIONAL CHANGE AT THE CATALYST LEVEL

Robert had recently become president of a Canadian oil company. He was now seated across the table from Ian, a senior partner in one of the world's top strategy consulting firms. Robert had retained Ian and his team because he faced a monumental strategic challenge: He wanted to transform his rather lackluster company into the best regional in North America. In fact, his vision was to develop an organization whose business performance and innovative ways of operating would be benchmarked by companies from a wide variety of industries. At the same time, he needed to boost the company's stock price at least $5 a share right away.

In light of present circumstances, this was an extremely ambitious vision. Robert's company was an average player in a crowded, mature, margin-sensitive marketplace where long-range demand was projected to be flat. His predecessor had tried to improve the company's performance, but he'd come up short. Earnings were going steadily downhill, and morale was at an all-time low. As Robert described it later:

> People were frustrated and unhappy. My predecessor did everything he knew how to make the company more efficient, but he couldn't get any traction. There'd been a lot of reactive downsizing in response to the pressure to cut costs—without much communication, understanding, or participation in the process. The whole organization was in a state of fear. People didn't know what was going to happen next.

Now, a month into work on a new strategy, Robert and Ian were meeting because they both felt uneasy about how the work was progressing. Ian was a Catalyst in a consulting firm wedded to Achiever-level assumptions and methodologies. On one hand, he had great respect for the firm, its people, and their capabilities. On the other hand, he understood its limitations in a way that few other partners did. Sitting across the table from Robert, he felt he had to be frank:

> The people on my team are among the best in the world when it comes to assessing an oil company's strategic options. I'm sure we'll come up

with some very good ideas. But there won't be any silver bullet here. To realize your vision, you need a number of breakthrough strategies. For that, you'll need some really fresh ideas. Our methodology is very solid, but it's also very linear. Your team and my team both hold so many assumptions in common, I think we could miss some important opportunities.

This was exactly what Robert had been feeling. Ian said, "I think you need to find a boutique consulting firm that can come in, bring groups of employees and other stakeholders together, and have them think creatively about a wide range of possible strategies. We can feed the best ones into our strategic review." Ian hadn't done this before, but as a Catalyst he had a history of initiating experiments that expanded his repertoire. Robert approved the recommendation.

With Ian's help, Robert hired a small consulting firm that could work collaboratively with the company and with Ian's team. The new firm custom-designed and facilitated ten "Idea Factories"—creative strategic thinking sessions, each attended by fifteen to twenty people. They did one session with the executive team and their strategy consultants, two with a variety of external stakeholders, and seven others with a wide range of company employees.[7]

In the Idea Factories, trios of participants created metaphors that captured the company's strategic situation and listed its greatest challenges and opportunities. The entire group was then guided through a "creative leap"—a visualization of their industry as they imagined it seven years in the future, recorded on a large blank mural at the front of the room.[8] Still thinking seven years out, participants visualized their company as the leading regional in North America, then engaged in an energetic brainstorm of what the business and operational strategies of such a company would be.[9]

Robert and his team were so enthused by the Idea Factories that they had the new firm design and facilitate a one-day meeting to synthesize these ideas with those developed with the strategy firm. At that meeting the management team made creative connections between hundreds of "raw" strategy ideas and developed them into powerful strategic initiatives. Only after each initiative was strengthened as much as possible were they subjected to rigorous evaluation.[10]

Roughly a third of the new strategies approved came from the Idea Factories. About a third came from the strategy firm, and another third came from both sources. One strategy was a strong commitment to becoming a leader in the area of environmental responsibility. Another was a "people strategy" designed to catapult the company into the ranks of high-performing organizations.

This new "people strategy" included human resource policies and practices that gave priority to the development and retention of highly effective personnel. It also included a commitment to increase the frequency and quality of communications with company employees and to build an organizational culture that would foster greater teamwork, empowerment, and accountability.

The top team also decided they needed a smaller, more focused organizational structure, which immediately put the company's new "people strategy" to the test. When it was time to launch the new strategies, Robert and his team presented them to their employees before announcing them to the market. At the end of the presentation, even though some jobs would be changed and others eliminated, people applauded. As Robert later described it:

> This was not a slash-and-burn exercise. We were undertaking an organized, step-by-step three-year project. We wanted to treat everyone fairly. If someone's job was going to disappear, we gave them as much notice as possible. We tried to find homes in the organization for as many as possible of those who were displaced.

As implementation of the new strategies proceeded, Robert and his team opened the communication channels. They created opportunities to discuss the company's new direction and its organizational implications in forums ranging from one-on-one conversations to large group meetings. They used these forums to keep everyone informed about the company's business performance and the progress it was making in implementing its new strategies. In addition to holding quarterly company-wide meetings, Robert met personally with twenty different management teams each year to discuss issues and ensure alignment with vision and strategy.

Over the three years that followed, Robert and his team led the company through a remarkable transformation. The once-faltering company not only survived without selling any of its divisions (a move under serious consideration by the outgoing president), it entered a phase of aggressive growth. Annual earnings grew from $9 million to $40 million, and cash expenses were reduced by $40 million a year. The company became one of the most efficient and effective refiners in

North America and one of the top retailers in its marketplace. Once shunned by investors, the business press now pronounced it one of the darlings of the stock market.

Robert later said that, while developing the right strategies was an essential part of the turnaround, the participative process he used to arrive at these strategies was equally important. Why? Because it developed the trust, alignment, and commitment needed to implement the new strategies effectively. "We started to think with one brain. Instead of being at cross-purposes, we could understand and support each other's decisions."

Let's step back for a moment and compare Robert's post-heroic approach to the heroic approach used by Mark, the CEO described in Chapter Five. Everything Mark did proceeded from the assumption that, with some input and assistance from others, *he* should be able to figure out the right strategy for his company. He involved his boards and his management team in an exploration of the HMO's strategic options, not because he thought it might change his mind, but to increase stakeholder buy-in.

When Robert became president of the oil company, he established an ambitious, inspiring vision for the company, and he involved a wide variety of stakeholders in developing the strategies needed to achieve this vision. Although he remained the final decision maker, he did not feel, as Mark did, that it was his responsibility to figure out the new strategies and then sell them to others. Mark involved only those stakeholders whose buy-in was essential. Robert's central question was, "Who can we learn from?"

Mark designed his retreat so that no strategic decisions would be made during the meeting. This way, he didn't risk losing control of the decision-making process. By contrast, Robert's strategy retreat was the primary forum in which he and his team, together, developed the company's new strategies. Although Robert clearly articulated the *criteria* for good strategies prior to the retreat (consistency with the vision and with the need to raise share price), the specific strategies that emerged could only be partly predicted in advance.

CATALYST-LEVEL LEADERSHIP AGILITY COMPETENCIES

The development of Catalyst-level competencies is fueled by a shift in a leader's level of awareness and intent.

Catalyst Awareness and Intent

The new level of awareness that emerges at the Catalyst level begins with a heightened interest in the relationship between experience and reflection. At the Achiever level, you have a well-developed reflective capacity, but your reflections on your experience don't take place on the spot. Motivation to develop to the Catalyst level arises when you repeatedly experience the limitations of this after-the-fact awareness and begin to want something more immediate.

For example, when one of our clients made the transition from Achiever to Catalyst, she kept a journal of the process. A key early insight came when she realized that she reflected on her behavior every day but had trouble reflecting in action. For example, she'd go into a meeting with her direct reports intending to have a rich group discussion about important departmental issues, then realize afterwards that she'd once again dominated the meeting. The story of David, the software company EVP, illustrates how leaders can develop a level of awareness that allows them to adjust their behavior on the spot.

This level of awareness begins with direct, momentary attention to some aspect of current experience, followed immediately by a rapid reflective process that allows you to make sense out of the experience and adjust your response accordingly. Patrick, a fully developed Catalyst manager in a large consumer products company, provided a lucid description of this level of awareness:

> It starts with being aware of the situation I'm in. One part of this is my perception of what's going on around me, how other people are behaving. What does their body language say? What are their tones of voice? Another part is being aware of what I am feeling, how I'm reacting to what I see. If I'm in a foul mood, that's going to influence how I see things. Or maybe what's going on is a conflict between two people and maybe this scares me, or maybe I'm excited about the issue they're arguing about. But whatever I'm feeling, I need to be aware of that, so I can take that into account when I respond.[11] It's a process of being aware of my experience, interpreting my experience, then taking action.

As a fully developed Catalyst, you make it a practice to return frequently to this new level of awareness, but it's not as if you're constantly operating on this frequency. Rather, you've activated this level of awareness often enough that it's usually available to you when you want it to be. Meanwhile, you retain the after-the-fact reflective capacity you developed in the Achiever level.

The more you practice Catalyst-level awareness, the more you realize that your actions are governed by assumptions, feelings, and priorities of which you're often unaware. As you develop this facility, your agility increases because you can now make adjustments that, formerly, you wouldn't have made. For example, as you're talking, you might realize that you've just made a major assumption, then pause and find a way to check its validity. Or you might catch yourself as you're about to escalate a conflict and switch to a more constructive response.

At the Achiever level, you develop a strong sense of identity and a robust value and belief system. At the Catalyst level, you develop a compelling interest in discovering what lies beyond the boundaries of your known world. As you begin to recognize the tacit feelings and assumptions that shape your actions, you realize that your image of yourself isn't entirely accurate. You develop a keener interest in learning more about yourself and your impact on others.

You also see that your self-chosen values and beliefs are more profoundly conditioned by your life circumstances than you formerly realized. As a result, you may develop an interest in questions such as: What would it have been like to grow up in a family where your parents' backgrounds and expectations were entirely different from those of your actual parents? What if you'd grown up in a community somewhere else in the world, at a completely different level of economic development, or where you were treated quite differently and learned dramatically different lessons about life? What's it like to belong to another racial or ethnic group, have a different sexual preference, or grow up with a completely different religious background?

One way or another, you realize that the conditions governing people's early development and current life have a profound effect on their system of values and beliefs. You see that you harbor more unconscious biases and assumptions than you formerly imagined. The critical attitude you formerly held toward value and belief systems that differ from your own begins to shift: Your appreciation of diversity increases, and you develop an interest in understanding other ways of life from the inside out.

The Catalyst level of intent is clearly illustrated in Robert's story. While Mark focused on creating and implementing the right strategy for his organization, Robert had a broader aspiration: He created a *context* that fostered sustained organizational achievement. The creative strategy process was only the beginning. What he really established was an ongoing process of participative decision making that catalyzed his direct reports into becoming a true leadership team. Together, they created an organizational culture that emphasized increased employee involvement.

Catalyst Context-Setting Agility

We now turn to the leadership agility competencies that emerge at the Catalyst level.[12] The two capacities that affect your level of context-setting agility are your *situational awareness* and your *sense of purpose.*

SITUATIONAL AWARENESS. In Chapter Five, we likened the Achiever's situational awareness to an adjustable camera lens: You can zoom in to focus on a particular person, issue, or organizational unit, and you can zoom out to observe the dynamics of its surrounding environment. For example, we saw how Mark focused on the competitors, providers, and purchasers in his marketplace, identifying their motivations and anticipating their future moves.

Catalyst leaders have this same capacity, but they can also take a more wide-angle view. This capacity makes them more attentive to the larger context within which they and their stakeholders operate. As a result, leaders who reach the Catalyst level are more likely than they were at previous levels to be attuned to the health of the natural environment and the well-being of the larger society.[13] Brenda's environmental perspective is one clear example. Robert's decision to pursue a strategy of environmental leadership also reflects an enlarged situational awareness.

Within their teams and organizations, Catalysts know that everything they focused on as Achievers still requires attention. But their primary intention is to create contexts that will generate the sustained achievement of valued outcomes. Put differently, at the Catalyst level, leaders pay more attention to managing the "white spaces" in the organization chart: the working relationships within and between units and the organizational culture that shapes these relationships.[14]

SENSE OF PURPOSE. At the Achiever level, you develop a strategic orientation and a strong interest in achieving outcomes that lie two to five years in the future. Over the past two decades, as more and more leaders have been encouraged to articulate their "vision," this term has been increasingly applied to Achiever-level outcomes, whether or not they're truly visionary. For example, Mark wanted his HMO to become an organization that could offer a full range of health care provider models. This strategy was a new one for his organization, but it followed what other HMOs were doing.

By contrast, Catalyst leaders have the capacity to create visions that challenge commonly held assumptions.[15] This proclivity for visionary thinking is fueled, in part, by their desire to find greater meaning in their work. Brenda's vision, which held that environmental responsibility and long-term profitability are mutually compatible objectives, held great meaning for her personally. The same was true for Robert. He not only took a number of steps that made his company and its parent corporation more environmentally responsible, he also served as chairman of a leading environmental organization dedicated to protecting Canada's most threatened habitats.

Even if Catalysts don't have a strong personal commitment to social and environmental responsibility, they focus on creating environments within their organizations where people can find greater meaning in their work. For example, Joan was strongly committed to creating a participative management team and organizational culture. As David and his colleagues moved to the Catalyst level, they developed and delivered on a similar commitment.

As your visionary capacity expands at the Catalyst level, so does the time horizon that motivates your strategic thinking. Because you can more vividly envision long-term outcomes, you can be inspired by visions that take a decade or longer to fully realize. You also become a more agile strategic thinker, moving with greater ease through short, medium, and long-range time frames.

Catalyst Stakeholder Agility

The two capacities that influence your level of stakeholder agility are your *stakeholder understanding* and your *power style*.

STAKEHOLDER UNDERSTANDING. As we discuss later in this chapter, at the Catalyst level you begin to see that your image of yourself is just that—an image. You also begin to develop an attitude toward yourself that's more accepting of your faults and foibles. This attitude toward yourself is mirrored in your attitudes toward other people. You begin to see that behind everyone's socially conditioned persona is a totally unique person who, paradoxically, shares a common humanity.

In addition, your on-the-spot reflective capacity allows you to catch underlying assumptions you previously overlooked. The more you engage in this kind of reflection, the more you find that your value and belief system is biased by a variety of factors, including your family upbringing, socioeconomic class, and national culture. Through these discoveries, you see that your views and priorities, and those of everyone else, are irreducibly subjective.

Through these insights you begin to place real value on understanding views that differ from your own. At the Achiever level, "putting yourself in another's shoes" usually means realizing how *you* would react if you were faced with their circumstances. At the Catalyst level, this capacity deepens. It now becomes easier to imagine what it's like to be someone else, experiencing their circumstances as *they* experience them.[16] We saw the leaders of the software company put this level of stakeholder understanding into practice in their pivotal conversations, when they advocated their views and immediately invited others to express theirs. We also saw this capacity at work in Robert's insistence on involving a wide range of stakeholders in the company's strategic review process.

POWER STYLE. At the Achiever level, you realize that an organization is, in part, a political arena where multiple stakeholders exercise power and influence. However, you tend to equate the exercise of power with the unilateral pursuit of self-interest. From this perspective, organizational politics can never be more than a zero-sum game where you can either win, lose, or compromise. You think of empowerment as something that people with more power do for people with less power, and the primary methods you use to empower others are structural. For example, an Achiever-level executive might empower middle managers by giving them increased budget authority.

At the Catalyst level, you remain cognizant of personal and political power, but you become interested in two new forms of power: the power of vision and the power of participation. Of this pair, vision represents the more assertive side of power, while participation represents its receptive side. Because assertion and accommodation are most powerful when they work together, Catalysts are most effective when they use a leadership style that balances vision and participation.

Catalyst-level visionary leadership differs from the Achiever's approach in several important respects. First, as we've noted, the visions that Catalyst leaders are capable of creating tend to be more far-reaching. Second, Catalysts are more likely than Achievers to develop an inspired vision that has significant personal meaning. Third, because their visions spring from their desire to make a meaningful contribution, they can communicate them in a way that evokes the same intrinsic motivation in others.

Catalyst leaders also emphasize the power of participation. They don't abdicate their decision-making authority, but they enjoy creating teams and organizations where people feel empowered to contribute their own unique talents and ideas. While Achievers sometimes express frustration that their people don't take more initiative, Catalysts work to create environments where initiative is infectious.

Catalyst leaders are most effective when they articulate an inspiring vision and actively encourage others to participate in bringing it to life. Overly assertive Catalysts, who articulate a compelling vision but don't actively encourage participation, ultimately turn people off by stifling the very energy their vision arouses. Overly accommodative Catalysts, who develop participative environments but don't provide sufficient direction, generate a scattered energy that ultimately devolves into frustration.[17]

The four Catalyst leaders featured in this chapter all provide examples of balanced power styles. David and Joan both worked with their colleagues to create participative organizational cultures, but they also exercised the power of vision. Robert responded to his leadership challenge by creating a far-reaching vision and endorsing a process that allowed a wide range of stakeholders to engage in developing the strategies needed to realize it. Brenda used the same approach to mobilize change efforts that helped her company become simultaneously more profitable and more environmentally responsible.

Catalyst Creative Agility

To achieve results consistent with a far-reaching vision, you need to tackle and resolve complex, non-routine problems. Creative agility transforms these ill-structured problems into desired results. Your level of agility in this domain is supported by your capacity for *connective awareness* and *reflective judgment.*

CONNECTIVE AWARENESS. Connective awareness is the ability to hold different ideas and experiences in mind, compare and contrast them, and make meaningful connections between them. At the Catalyst level, your understanding of the relationship between intentions and results deepens, and you begin to appreciate the extent to which others' behavior isn't always consciously intended. You get interested in the fact that, even when you achieve your objectives, your actions can have unintended negative consequences—for yourself as well as for others. This realization is part of a more general insight that causality in human relationships can be circular as well as linear.[18]

As your capacity for connective awareness expands, you develop the ability to "try on" frames of reference that differ from your own. To understand how this new capacity goes beyond Achiever-level awareness, it's important to understand the role that underlying frames of reference play in giving meaning to ideas and experiences.

For example, when David and John discussed the EDR installation problem, both were operating at the Achiever level. Each had the ability to hold the other's solutions in mind and compare them with his own. However, neither had yet developed the capacity to ask and accurately answer the question: "What would it be like to be the other person in this situation, with his needs and priorities? How do my solution ideas sound from that frame of reference?"[19]

At the Catalyst level, you can "try on" frames that differ from or even conflict with your own by exercising a "willing suspension of disbelief."[20] You temporarily drop your own frame and adopt one with alternative assumptions and priorities long enough to understand what a situation looks like from a new perspective. You then return to your own frame of reference with a better understanding and greater appreciation of an alternative viewpoint. This capacity, which allows you to import ideas from other frames of reference into your own, also makes you a more creative thinker than you were at the Achiever level.[21]

As an Achiever, you see that diametrically opposed ideas are related to one another along a continuum with many shades of gray between them. Faced with conflicting alternatives, you can choose between them, but you can also envision various degrees of compromise between the two extremes. At the Catalyst level, your ability to move back and forth between opposing frames of reference opens you to a new understanding of paradox: Perspectives and priorities that seem to contradict one another may each be valid in their own way.[22]

The major limitation in Catalyst-level connective awareness is that you can try on only one frame of reference at a time. If your power style is primarily assertive, then even though you can perceive situations from other frames of reference, you'll have a strong tendency to default to your own frame. If your style is accommodative, you're more likely to side with nondominant frames of reference. It's not until the Co-Creator level that you develop the capacity to hold differing frames of reference in mind at the same time, compare and contrast them, and make meaningful connections and choices between them.

REFLECTIVE JUDGMENT. Reflective judgment refers to the way you determine what to believe and what to do about the problems you face— and how to justify these beliefs to yourself and to others. As an Achiever, you realized that any point of view is ultimately personal and subjective, but you assumed that biases in human thinking could be corrected through rational thinking supported by verifiable data. At the Catalyst level, you still believe that good data and rational thought are important and useful, but you also see that underlying frames of reference are much more powerful and pervasive than you'd formerly imagined.

As we noted earlier, the Catalyst level of awareness involves directly but momentarily attending to some aspect of current experience, followed immediately by a reflective process that makes sense out of the experience. Once it's a reliable part of your repertoire, this level of awareness allows you to recognize and reflect on a new whole array of assumptions, feelings, and priorities. Through these discoveries you gradually experience for yourself the famous insight recorded in the Talmud: "We don't see things as they are. We see things as we are."

Consequently, at the Catalyst level you see that virtually every problem you work on is ill-structured, simply because other people are involved. You know that any time two or more people work together to solve a problem—such as the software installation problem faced by David and John—the chances are extremely high that they'll each define the problem differently and have different solution criteria.

Further, your understanding that every problem statement is based on a particular frame of reference makes you much more likely to ask yourself, Is this the right problem to be working on? and What assumptions have we made in the way we've defined this problem?[23] As in David's story, you're also more likely to ask if you're getting to the underlying issues that generate problems on a regular basis.[24]

Catalyst Self-Leadership Agility

Your level of agility in developing as a leader is made possible by your level of *self-awareness* and *developmental motivation*.

SELF-AWARENESS. As an Achiever, your robust reflective capacity allows you to develop a strong sense of identity, including a clear image of your strengths and limitations as a leader. However, with the development of Catalyst-level self-awareness, you find that your image of yourself is based partly on accurate self-observation and partly on a combination of wishful thinking and overly negative self-evaluation. You discover that your self-image acts as an interpretive filter, screening out internal feelings and external feedback that would give you a more complete picture of yourself.

This realization fuels a desire to increase your level of self-knowledge. By detecting and letting go of your own defense mechanisms, you discover more about your "shadow side," those parts of yourself—both positive and negative—that lie beneath the rational persona of your Achiever self.

With this new level of self-awareness, you discover that you're motivated by feelings you thought you'd already transcended. For example, you find that you're more strongly motivated to seek others' approval than you thought you were. In Chapter Five you met Karen, an Achiever who became a Community Development Corporation administrator. At that time, she fulfilled her drive for independence by establishing a career and becoming financially self-sufficient. However, when we interviewed Karen, she'd developed to the Catalyst level, and she'd redefined independence as an emotional issue:

> The biggest conflict I feel now in my development is between emotional dependence and independence. Now that I'm aware of the extent to which I've been dependent on other people and their approval, I understand more clearly what it means to be emotionally independent.

Patrick, the Catalyst-level consumer products manager introduced earlier in this chapter, reported a similar discovery. In his work with a coach, he discovered that his need for control, so central to his Achiever-level persona, was often motivated by a desire for others to admire his abilities. For example, he discovered that he unconsciously manipulated group meetings and other situations so that he would look good. This discovery and his Catalyst level of self-awareness allowed Patrick to alter his behavior by changing his frame about what was at stake:

> When my desire to get others' approval gets mixed in with the need to get the job done, then if I don't get my way, I wind up feeling bad about myself. That's a really counterproductive set-up. But now I'm starting to separate those out. Sometimes I get my way, and sometimes I don't. But my feeling of self-worth isn't on the line.

A related discovery is the realization that your degree of dependence on others' approval is a direct function of your own level of self-acceptance. Further, you begin to realize that any feelings of inadequacy that lurk beneath the surface are created primarily by automatic and largely unconscious self-judgments. Consequently, you see that the best way to overcome these feelings is not to try to control others' perceptions but to develop a more affirming attitude toward yourself. As a result, you begin to discover the inner dimension of empowerment.[25]

Rather than automatically judging or rejecting thoughts, feelings, and behaviors that conflict with the way you "should" be, you learn to meet them with an attitude of curiosity and reflective acceptance. This posture gives you more choice and flexibility in responding to a whole range of different situations. It also makes it easier to accept the fact that you have mixed feelings and inner conflicts. For example, this is the first level where you can clearly appreciate the fact that assertion and accommodation are expressions of two different sides of yourself.

DEVELOPMENTAL MOTIVATION. Joyce was an extremely effective Catalyst-level organization development consultant who worked for a large computer company. When we interviewed her, she was the lead internal consultant helping to transform a traditionally managed plant into a flatter organization built around empowered work teams. She was so personally committed to this innovative vision that she drove herself very hard. One night, about a year into the assignment, she was up late again working in her office, when the janitor came by and poked his head in the door. As Joyce relates the experience:

I had stacks of paper around me and felt under tremendous pressure. I was totally stressed out and was actually close to tears. Victor is a sweet man, a simple man. He comes in, takes his headset off, and says, "Do you ever listen to Enya?" I say, "Yeah, sometimes, Victor, sometimes I do." He goes, "I think you should listen to her music, Joyce. I think you should get a stereo in here. It would change the energy in this room."

Then he says, "Come with me for a minute," and we walk outside the building onto a little knoll. He gestures to the facilities that surround us, and he says, "This is your community—all the people who work here, day and night. The people here trust you. They believe in you. They know you're working really hard to make this place the best it can be."

"So don't be so hard on yourself," he says. "You've already changed this place so much. You have no idea the power of the love that you've brought to this community. They love you for it in return. That's more important than anything else in the world. You gotta remember that, Joyce. It's all about people. It's all about caring for each other. That's what's changing this place. You gotta believe in yourself, because the rest of us do."

The *janitor* says this to me. What a gift![26]

If Joyce were still at the Achiever level, she probably wouldn't have been so receptive to Victor's message. At that level of agility, the time you spend working toward future outcomes seems like a commodity, a means to an end. Because it keeps you focused and produces results, this orientation can become subtly addictive.[27] As Joyce's story shows, Catalysts aren't immune to this syndrome. However, at the Catalyst level it's easier to catch it when it happens, step back, and shift to a larger perspective.

At the Achiever level, your primary motivation to develop as a leader is a desire to succeed in achieving your chosen outcomes. As a Catalyst, you're still motivated to achieve outcomes. In fact, as we've seen, you may be motivated by a very ambitious vision. But you also begin to focus on something deeper: You want the vision and the outcomes you pursue to have personal meaning, and you want your life between achievements to be meaningful and fulfilling as well.

When she reached the Catalyst level, Karen, the Community Development Corporation administrator, said she saw leadership development as being as much about personal growth as about learning new skills. And personal growth at this level isn't so much a goal to achieve as an ongoing, open-ended process:

> You never quite reach that place where you know yourself completely. I may never totally achieve my goal of freedom. I just feel that it's a continuing process. As I perceive it now, you have to work on it until you die.

CHAPTER SEVEN

Co-Creator Level
Realize Shared Purpose

T he New Year's party had ended, and Larry's guests had all gone home. He sat on his deck smoking a cigar, looking at the stars, thinking about his life. Here he was, thirty-nine years old, newly divorced, and it seemed like his whole life had emptied out before him. He didn't want to go into one of those after-divorce tailspins like some of his friends had. Instead, he'd use the divorce as an opportunity to do what he'd always wanted to do—if he could just figure out what that was.

In many ways, Larry's career had been very interesting and productive. During the early 1980s, he worked at Bell Labs and did some of the groundbreaking work that brought computerization to the desktop. After earning his MBA, he'd managed a number of different IT functions in both client and vendor IT companies.

Sitting on his deck, blowing smoke rings into the night air, Larry kept thinking about a book he'd just read called *The Experience of Insight*, by Joseph Goldstein. It was a clearly written guide for what is known in the West as insight meditation.[1] Learning to meditate was something he'd wanted to do for years. The next day he called a local meditation center and enrolled in a class. A week later he began a daily meditation practice.

Several years later, he joined a Fortune 100 financial services company based in New York City. Once there, he started going to some of the evening sessions at the insight meditation center in Manhattan, and he attended some of their weekend retreats in the heart of the city.

> After a couple of years in New York—about four years into my meditation practice—one of the teachers at the center, a retired businessman, started a group that meets once a quarter specifically to talk about mindfulness in business.[2] I've met some great people through that group. We meditate together and talk about what it means to apply Buddhist ethics in the workplace.[3]

WHAT LEADERSHIP
MEANS TO A CO-CREATOR

In the five years since he joined this group, Larry says, it's had more impact on his work as a leader than any other single thing he's done:

> Combining sitting meditation with deep conversations about ethics, I started seeing more subtleties—how everyone is connected with everyone else—how a company's policies and practices affect the human beings inside and outside the corporation—how the way you treat other people affects your own happiness. Being in this group brought me back to a question I'd had since my Bell Labs days about the relationship between personal growth and global issues. In one way or another it's a question everyone in the group is grappling with.

As an outgrowth of this experience, Larry began to volunteer his time with nonprofit organizations, and he got quite involved in the "resource groups" his corporation established to support employees from diverse backgrounds. He's now a participant in the Women in Technology group, the Asian American group, the African American group, and the Native Peoples group.

> If I wanted to work in a company that was fully living the values I believe in, a large financial services corporation wouldn't be the right place for me. But if everyone with my values reacted by leaving their

company, I think we'd have even more Enrons and Global Crossings. By staying here, I and others who feel the same way have an opportunity to help change things from the inside. For example, I've had some involvement in helping set the direction of our Environmental Affairs Council. I'd like our company to be doing more along these lines, but I feel I'm influencing things I wouldn't otherwise be able to influence.

I used to think that leadership was the charismatic side of being a manager—how to inspire and influence people to take action. But increasingly, I see leadership more as a form of service. Sometimes I've even chosen to move "down" a level, because this is how I could best be of service. But I kept getting promoted back up! So I decided, OK, I'm someone who's good at leading large organizations. Since this is the service I'm apparently able to offer, the main thing is to be conscious about how I do it.

For example, I have mentor relationships with about fifteen managers. I help them with management challenges, ethical quandaries, and career issues. I try not to focus just on how they can climb the ladder, but on how they live their lives. I ask them: What do you find fulfilling? Is your life in balance? Are you doing anything that gives back to the community? I see them as human beings who inhabit professional roles. I try to help them see that, if they approach work as an opportunity for self-development and serving others, it can be transforming for them and for the teams and organizations they work within.

For Larry, leadership also means being conscious of the behavior he's modeling and being able to acknowledge specific mistakes he's made and what he's learned from those mistakes.

I'm very committed to collaboration. But I found myself in a situation a few months ago where I was anything but that. I'd recently taken over a position leading a management group that had been fairly dysfunctional. Its relationships with other groups weren't very good.

I was in a meeting with my boss [the CIO] and his other direct reports. We were talking about how IT could be more responsive to the needs of the business, and I described a slightly different way to organize the IT function. Then, Craig—this guy who runs a unit my group has had problems with in the past—he completely blows up and rips into me, telling me in a very insulting way that I had no business trying to change his organization when my own unit was doing such a piss-poor job. Before I knew it I was yelling back at Craig at the top of my lungs.

In the midst of the shouting, Larry suddenly remembered sitting in meditation that morning. The discrepancy was so shocking, he immediately stopped. The meeting broke up shortly after that.

I'd never been attacked like that or reacted like that in a public forum. When I left the room, I was breathing hard and my hands were shaking. I went into the men's room, went into one of the stalls, and just stood there. I didn't try to shut down all the churning, but by being mindful of it I stopped feeding it, and it gradually subsided. It hit me that I've carefully lived my life to avoid getting upset—and I wondered what it's cost me to do that.

The next day Larry had a weeklong vacation scheduled. Rather than taking the hiking trip he'd planned, he decided to go to a meditation retreat and use some of his free time to reflect on his conflict with Craig.

After several days of meditation, I found it much easier to see how my group's behavior had affected Craig and his group. I also realized that I'd said things to my group that just reinforced their negative feelings about Craig's unit.

When I came back, I called him and set up a meeting, but I was nervous about how it would go. He came to the meeting with a book called *The Five Dysfunctions of a Team.* He said, "I read this, and I think it captures a lot of the problems that both of our teams have." I was amazed. I almost wondered if all the time I'd spent at the retreat empathizing with Craig had somehow affected his attitude. He suggested that I read the book. I did, and he was right.[4]

We sat down the next week and made a commitment to work on the problems within our own teams and to model the right behavior by publicly supporting each other and seeking common ground. We continued to meet once a week and talk about the good, the bad, and the ugly. It was a real breakthrough. It was also very striking how much our teams' behavior changed once Craig and I developed a more collaborative relationship.

When leaders grow into the Co-Creator level, they develop capacities that build on those that emerged at the Catalyst level. Their visions often take into account realities beyond their own industry, reflecting an evolving sense of life purpose aimed at enhancing the lives of other human beings. In fact, as you'll see, Co-Creators who establish new companies are often visionaries who pioneer new forms of organization with a firm commitment to social and environmental responsibility.

Co-Creator leaders are intent on developing organizations animated by shared purpose, where individual initiative and shared responsibility are both strong norms. Whenever possible, they prefer to develop stakeholder relationships characterized by mutual commitment, trust, and collaboration. Their ability to build these kinds of relationships is supported by a "centered" power style that allows them to enter deeply into others' frames of reference, as well as their own, balancing self-assertion with appropriate receptivity to others' needs.

This capacity to enter into multiple frames of reference gives Co-Creators a keen awareness of interdependence and a well-developed capacity for integrative thinking. Their ability to step back and see where different frames conflict and where they have common elements allows them to enter into creative problem-solving dialogues and discover true win-win solutions.

The level of self-awareness you develop at the Co-Creator level gives you the capacity to stay with difficult feelings longer than you would have at the Catalyst level. As you gradually become more aware of your own experience, you discover inner conflicts and begin to integrate parts of your "shadow side" into your conscious personality. As you become more attuned to your actual thoughts, feelings, and behaviors, you increase your capacity for experimenting with new perspectives and behaviors and for learning from your experience.

Meditation plays a part in several stories in this chapter, and you may wonder why. Through our research, we found that many of the leaders who develop Co-Creator-level awareness and intent do so by bringing the attentiveness they cultivate during meditation practice into their everyday lives. Meditation certainly isn't the only way to develop this level of awareness and intent. However, while only a few Catalysts in our sample practiced meditation, we found it noteworthy that 40 percent of our Co-Creators had a more-or-less daily meditation practice, with another 10 percent meditating on a less regular basis.

This chapter presents stories about three Co-Creator managers:[5] Ken, an entrepreneur who created an innovative health spa; Alison, an attorney who started a multidisciplinary firm dedicated to collaborative law; and Graham, a researcher and activist who organized several dozen global problem-solving networks into a "meta-network" dedicated to mutual support and action learning. One note of caution: By using these three examples, we might give the impression that the vast majority of Co-Creators work in very small organizations. A comparison of our Catalysts and Co-Creators does show that the latter are much more likely to start small organizations dedicated to operating in a socially and environmentally responsible manner. Yet just as many Co-Creators, like Larry, work in large organizations. We include several of these leaders toward the end of this chapter. Also note that most of the Synergists in Chapter Eight (all of whom are former Co-Creators) work in large organizations.

PIVOTAL CONVERSATIONS AT THE CO-CREATOR LEVEL

From the moment you enter the path that leads to the Deep Peace Day Spa, you begin to absorb its atmosphere. The walkway winds through a lush landscape of oriental grasses and Mediterranean flowers, takes you past a secluded meditation garden, and brings you to a clear, tranquil pond. Beyond the pond stands a low Japanese-style building where the spa's guests are welcomed. There, the subtle scents that waft through the air, the respectfully quiet voices that greet you, and the orderliness of robes artfully arranged in the changing rooms all speak of a single-minded intent: Relax, quiet down, and let go. You will be well cared for.

Guests arrive daily for facials, body wraps, massage therapy, and yoga classes. Ken, the majority owner of Deep Peace and its top executive, is justifiably proud. After only six years in existence his day spa is rated one of the best in the country. The grounds of the spa are a large part of its attraction. Guests are invited to remain after their appointments to sit or roam quietly through four acres of authentic Japanese gardens.

Ken, a Japanese American in his early forties, grew up and attended college in California. Although he majored in computer science, he spent much of his free time working in a landscaping business he started with some friends. After college he cut off his long ponytail and took a job in San Diego as a computer programmer for Sony Electronics. Just before his thirtieth birthday, the company offered him a job in Kyoto, the city where his great-grandfather had lived and died. Still single and bored with his life in San Diego, he decided to take the leap.

In Japan, Ken was surprised to find himself drawn to the traditional Japanese arts. He was especially moved by the quiet dignity of the tea ceremony, the elegant simplicity of Japanese flower arrangement, and the spare beauty of Kyoto's historic Zen gardens. One cold winter afternoon, he was walking slowly and appreciatively through one of those centuries-old gardens. The trees were bare, and no one else was in sight. As he stopped and surveyed the scene, all his thoughts dropped away. At that moment it seemed as if everything around him had been purposefully designed to bring him to a deep, peaceful, intensely present state of mind.

Shortly after this experience, he met a traditional Japanese gardener who invited him to become his student. Without knowing where this might lead, Ken quit his job at Sony and accepted the gardener's invitation. During this period, he developed many new friendships and experienced a sense of community that had been sorely lacking during his years in San Diego.

Ken's new friends included a number of hip young professionals who were starting their own businesses. Maro and Yoshimi, a couple he was especially fond of, were about to start a day spa just outside Kyoto. One night over a long dinner, they asked him if he'd turn the day spa's grounds into a Zen garden. If he'd do that, invest some money, and work with them to make it a success, they'd make him an equal partner. Ken jumped at the offer. He later said that learning to run a business and to deal with all the conflicts that arose among the three of them matured him much more rapidly than any previous experience.

About four years after they started the spa in Kyoto, Ken met a young woman named Stacie who was in Japan visiting her cousin. They fell in love, and within a year they were married and back in southern California with a baby on the way. Through Stacie, Ken met Carlyene, a woman who'd managed a successful day spa in Los Angeles and wanted to make a fresh start. As they talked, a vision grew: They'd create a day spa outside Los Angeles, a true oasis from city living. The grounds of the spa would be an expanded version of the Zen garden he'd created in Kyoto. Ken, who made the largest investment, would be the spa's executive director. Carlyene would be spa director, hiring and supervising all personnel involved in guest services.

Soon they were having long phone conversations with Tomo, a younger student of the Zen gardener Ken had worked with in Kyoto. Because of Tomo's love of adventure and his great respect for Ken, he was persuaded to move to California and become a third partner. Ken and Tomo would design the gardens together, and Tomo would supervise the maintenance of the spa's grounds and facilities. They hired a woman named Luisa to oversee the financial aspects of the business.

Two years into the business, they created an explicit shared vision: Everything about the spa would create a palpable atmosphere of deep peace. Guests would leave feeling rejuvenated in body and spirit. Deep Peace would be an environmentally responsible business and would make modest contributions to local nonprofits. They would create a working environment where communication, collaboration, shared understanding, and organizational learning were the norm.

Now six years old, Deep Peace has more than a hundred employees and almost two dozen massage therapists and yoga instructors on contract. Many employees are part-timers who often work for the company only for short periods before moving on. Ken and his management team originally envisioned a profit-sharing plan for employees, but they discovered it was more practical and effective to offer fun, attainable monthly incentives.

Once a month, Ken and his three-person management team meet as a "vision circle" to discuss their vision, their current action plans, and how well they're doing. Ken's aim is for everyone to feel a sense of personal responsibility for the business as a whole—something that's just now starting to jell.

When we interviewed Ken, we asked him to describe a conversation that had been pivotal for the organization. He related the following story:

> Something like that actually happened earlier today. It involved an employee named Jim, a big, strong guy who came to work on our maintenance crew about a year or so ago. He was exceptional—the best we've ever had in that role. Very tuned in to the values of our company. Took on additional things without being asked—that kind of thing.
>
> One day I was helping Tomo get things ready for some major maintenance and repair work on the pond. I ran into Jim and asked him to

do some heavy lifting. I didn't know it, but he'd just injured his shoulder. He was offended by my request, and we had an unfortunate interaction that left him angry and me confused. I finally told him I was sorry if I'd offended him and went on about my work.

The next day he came to me, very steamed, and said he was resigning. He said he had some hard truths he needed to tell me and, since this was supposed to be a community, he wanted to say these things to me in front of the management team.

I thought it over for a moment. I was raised in a very conflict-averse family, and for years conflict was very hard for me to deal with. But I'm quite a bit better now dealing with emotionally charged situations. Besides, he was right. I do want our communications to be open and above board. So I agreed.

When I walked into the meeting room, Jim and everyone else looked very uncomfortable. I was nervous but I was also confident I'd be able to handle whatever might come up. I thought, if I can be comfortable with this discomfort, maybe I can provide some comfort to others.

Jim quickly got up a head of steam and blasted me with a long list of criticisms: I don't walk the talk. I'm too tight with money. I don't express appreciation for people's hard work—things like that. I could see that the others were sort of in shock. It was very intense, but I didn't interrupt him. More than a few of the things he said were based on misinformation or misunderstanding. But some were at least partly related to shortcomings I've been aware of and trying to work on.

When I was sure he'd finished, I asked him if he'd be interested in having some conversation. He'd built up such a case in his own mind that I didn't expect him to change his position. But I thought maybe we could end with some level of mutual respect and understanding. He thought about it for a minute, then he said, yeah, he was willing to hear what I had to say.

I told him he was right—a lot of what he'd said was hard to hear. I said I have great respect for him—for being the best maintenance worker we've ever had and for his strong commitment to the values we stand for.

He said the whole problem was that I treated those values like they were just words. He spoke with passion, but I noticed that his tone and demeanor had softened. I acknowledged that some things he said about me are things I need to work on. I also went on to clear up some things he'd been misinformed about. In response to his rant about money, I said I'd learned in Japan that you can be successful in business and still care about other people—that the fusion of the two is what I want Deep Peace to be.

As we talked, it turned out there were some other reasons why he needed to leave besides how he felt about me. I don't know how much he changed his mind, but it felt like we resolved things on some level. I thanked him for having the courage to share his truth, and the others did too. He does some kind of sculpture in his spare time. Before he left, he invited me to come to his studio to see his work, and I accepted his invitation.

We asked Ken what allowed him to sit there in the face of all that negative energy and take in what Jim had to say.[6]

It's a carryover from my meditation practice. While I was working with the Zen gardener in Kyoto, he offered to teach me how to meditate. My practice hasn't always been as consistent as I'd like, but I've continued here with what I learned in Japan.

There were many times back when I was in business with Maro and Yoshimi that I'd sit down to meditate and all kinds of strong, painful emotions would come up. It still happens from time to time. When it does, I've learned to let go of my tendency to either shut off the feelings or keep feeding them with my thoughts. When I just let them be and they just play themselves out, it's like silt settling to the bottom of a pond. When this happens it increases your reflective capacity and gives you a greater sense of inner peace.

While I was listening to Jim this morning, I was able, to a certain degree, to let my feelings just play out internally without adding additional negative reactions. By the time he'd finished blasting me, I didn't have any desire to blast him back. I just wanted to stay with the process. That's why I asked him if he wanted to have a conversation.

We then asked Ken how his management team reacted to this conversation and what he felt he'd learned from the experience:

After Jim left, Carlyene, Tomo, and Luisa asked me how I was doing. I said I was feeling moved by the experience and very good about where we got to. Although I don't want us to go around blasting each other, I said it was good for me to hear how someone like Jim perceives me.

I have to sort out what I think is and isn't valid, but I think it may help me be a better person and a better leader.

Even though they were quick to say they didn't agree with Jim, I said I hoped this little encounter would make it easier for the four of us to talk about issues that could be hard to discuss. Like: Do our employees feel as appreciated as we think they do? Are there, in fact, some issues about money or incentives or recognition that we need to understand?[7]

Finally, we asked Ken what was the most important thing this experience had taught him about leadership.

When you're the top person in an organization—even when you're trying like I am to be a nontraditional, low-profile leader—you're much more visible to people than you think. Like everybody, I have flaws, but in a position like this everything about me becomes more visible. And you don't really have much control over how you're seen. Like with Jim. I'm just starting to come to terms with some of the exaggerated expectations and projections that people can put onto someone in this kind of position.

TEAM LEADERSHIP AT THE CO-CREATOR LEVEL

Alison sat across from her husband in a Manhattan restaurant talking about a crossroads she'd reached in her career. It was the end of the millennium, and they'd been through a lot together. Back in the late 1960s, they'd both attended the University of Wisconsin, where they were active in the civil rights and anti-war movements. When they graduated, they got married, settled in Madison, and had two children. By the end of the 1970s, Alison's husband had established himself as a documentary filmmaker, and she had entered social work school.

After studying social work for a year, Alison decided she could better pursue her passion for social justice by going into public interest law. When her application was accepted at the NYU law school, the family relocated to New York. When Alison graduated in 1984, she joined a Manhattan law firm.

During my first six or seven years as a litigator, I began to see how litigation, even for good causes, isn't a very effective way to resolve conflict.

In family disputes it actually tends to exacerbate the conflict. I felt there had to be a better way.

Some of my colleagues in the firm had become interested in alternative dispute resolution. They asked me to join a committee to see if it made sense for the firm to create a subsidiary with this as its focus. We decided it didn't, but it piqued my interest. I decided to get trained in arbitration and mediation. By the end of the 1990s, about two-thirds of my practice was a combination of mediation, arbitration, and collaborative law. Collaborative law is a process where the parties to a dispute are represented by legal counsel, with a written agreement that they'll attempt to settle without litigation or the threat of litigation.

Alison's career conversation with her husband grew out of a lunch meeting with Cliff, a colleague at the firm. Like Alison, he'd grown up in Madison, gone to law school in the East, and developed a strong interest in collaborative law. They had a good deal of respect for one another's work. Over lunch, Cliff told her he'd decided to move back to Madison to start his own collaborative law firm. When Alison told him how much she envied his decision, Cliff asked if she'd consider moving back to Madison and joining his firm. Alison said she'd give his offer some serious thought.

The more Alison and her husband discussed it, the more they warmed up to the idea. Their children had both graduated from college and were living their own lives. Her husband didn't need to be based in New York, and they both felt their quality of life would be better in Madison. They moved within the year, and Alison became the fifth partner in the Madison Collaborative Law Group.

Alison's practice prospered, and she became increasingly interested in adding multidisciplinary affiliates to the firm.

I read an article in the *ABA Family Law Journal* about a firm that had a clinical social worker on staff. Having been to social work school myself, I could see how helpful someone from that discipline could be to clients. Also, if you believe in deep conflict resolution and in looking at people in a holistic way, an interdisciplinary approach makes sense. More than 90 percent of divorces involve financial issues, so I could see some real value in adding a financial planner. And, in divorces where children are involved, I felt a family therapist would be very helpful.

Alison was rather surprised when Cliff and her other colleagues strongly opposed the idea of developing a multidisciplinary practice. They felt it would dilute the firm's focus. Ultimately, Alison found that she felt so strongly about working in an interdisciplinary manner that she made the difficult decision to leave the firm, hire an assistant, and put out her own shingle.

Later that year, she began to refer some of her clients to Tim, another Madison attorney who practiced collaborative law. Tim shared Alison's vision of creating a multidisciplinary firm and soon joined her as a minority owner of the practice. Their firm blossomed: Over the next several years, they added five more attorneys, an office manager, four paralegals, and three affiliate members in the disciplines she'd earlier envisioned: a clinical social worker, a financial planner, and a family therapist.

> In bringing people into the firm, I've tried to present it as work in process, so that they can participate not only in doing the work but in creating and shaping the firm and making it better.
>
> We have weekly staff meetings. They start at noon with lunch. Then we go into a business meeting that usually lasts until two or two-thirty. Everyone in the firm is invited, including the paralegals and support staff. Attendance usually ranges from ten to twelve people. Many law firms do something like this, but only the lawyers are invited. We wanted to depart from that for several reasons: To avoid creating a caste system within the firm and to foster communication and teamwork across different levels of responsibility.
>
> In the business meeting portion, we either talk about cases or about marketing, ethical issues, or other issues associated with the complexities of running a multidisciplinary practice.[8] Other than the retreat we do twice a year, this is our firm's forum for team problem solving and decision making.

Alison and Tim run the firm in a highly collaborative manner with a great deal of emphasis on consensus decision making. They use their semi-annual retreats as a way to address big issues that need to be discussed by the firm as a whole. One of the affiliate members interviews everyone in the firm. At the retreat, without identifying individual comments, the affiliate highlights the most frequently voiced issues and facilitates the discussion. At one retreat a suggested enhancement in employee benefits led to a wellness initiative that now includes a Weight Watchers program, a runners club, and a Tuesday morning meditation session for those who are interested.

At another retreat, Alison and Tim learned that people thought they were placing too much emphasis on consensus decision making. Certain decisions, the group felt, should come from Alison and Tim.

> Part of my commitment to consensus decision making comes out of my commitment to social justice. If you're young or a woman or a person of color or you don't have a law degree, everything about our legal culture tells you that your views, your energies, are not as important as those of the white male, the highly educated, highly experienced lawyer. On paper, the structure of most law firms, including the more progressive firm I joined in New York, is supposed to be a true democracy of the partners. In fact, it rarely is. It can even feel quite alienating at times. Tim and I had each experienced that, so we didn't want to duplicate the traditional structure. We both feel that a consensus-based firm is both more respectful and more productive than a traditional hierarchical firm.
>
> However, when we got that feedback at the retreat, we took it to heart. We realized that we were probably overreacting to our experiences with traditional firms and that we needed to modify the process somewhat to take into account that Tim and I are, in fact, the two owners of the firm.

Since that time, Alison and Tim have been much clearer in the weekly meetings about how specific decisions will be made. They listen to each issue to determine whether it's something the group can decide on the spot, something a subgroup needs to discuss or flesh out for a future meeting, or something the two of them need to go off and decide based on the group's input.

> The decisions that Tim and I make together tend to be strategic rather than operational. Fortunately, we have a common vision for the firm and a great deal of respect for each other's judgment, so these decisions have been fairly easy to make. Also, whenever we bring our decision back to the group, we always ask for their feedback. So far, no one has pointed out any problems with what we've proposed. If they did, I think we'd want to at least consider their comments before making a final decision.

Alison and Tim have also elevated Nora, a lawyer in the firm who initially served as its administrative director, to executive director. Nora now meets regularly with Alison and Tim, has some influence on their decisions, and manages the operational aspects of the firm.

Above all, it's been Alison and Tim's intention to create a firm where everyone feels the same sense of responsibility the two owners feel for upholding the firm's mission and values and for sustaining its success. For example, the weekly staff meeting isn't the only opportunity for staff to have input into key firm decisions. Whenever someone interviews to join the firm, they meet with paralegals, administrative staff, and staff attorneys as well as Tim and Alison. The firm has also initiated an annual 360-degree feedback process for partners, staff attorneys, and administrative staff that includes input from paralegals.

When someone comes in new, it doesn't take them long to catch the spirit of the place. Nora likes to tell the story that when she first interviewed with us, Jonas, one of our paralegals, told her, "You'll never work for a firm that you'll want to succeed as much as this one." Another lawyer has frequently said to me, "Working here is my dream job." A third attorney, who does wonderful work for us, said in her annual salary review, "I love working here. I want to work here for the rest of my life, whether you give me a raise or not."

I'm also thinking about one of the paralegals, someone who works closely with me, who's a wonderful example of this kind of commitment. She cares about every aspect of what we do—how our clients are cared for, how people out in the world see us, how our mission is viewed and understood. She comes to me frequently with very good improvement ideas, including ideas that won't benefit her directly but will benefit the firm as a whole.

A lot of the best ideas we've had come from this keen sense of responsibility that people feel for maintaining our unique culture and for ensuring the firm's success. I'm impressed that people are willing to give up their time to go to retreats and to go out and give talks about what we're doing. It's really very moving, having planted the seed and nurtured the sapling, to see that we're now a group that cares very much about what we've created together. Perhaps that's the key: We feel that we're in this together and that you don't have to be one of the owners to have a serious influence on the firm's direction and how it operates.

This sense of shared responsibility stems partly from a common commitment to the firm's mission (resolving conflict) and to the values it stands for: multidisciplinary client service, integrity, work-family balance, and service to the community. Over the past three years, the firm's attorneys have provided charitable donations and pro bono services for more than two dozen local and national organizations.

I think it helps people, myself included, when they go to work each day and feel they're doing some real good in the world. Coming home each day feeling they helped carry forward this mission to change the way law is practiced—to change the way people resolve conflict.

Before I started this firm, I never really thought of myself as a leader. But now I'd say that the leadership role I play is one of the most meaningful aspects of my work. Especially the more intangible aspects of leadership. Back in the 1970s, I learned this technique called Transcendental Meditation.[9] I haven't done it all that consistently, but I've kept it up over the years. It's helped me to experience a certain degree of centeredness. On my better days, I try to bring that sense of being centered into my work. My hope is that this energy somehow resonates with others and helps create a space where they too can feel centered and self-aware. This part of leadership isn't so much about what you do. It's more about the quality of being that you bring into every interaction.

I think this is why I so much enjoy what I'm doing now. It allows me to reach toward being my best self and at the same time toward being of real service to others.

LEADING ORGANIZATIONAL CHANGE AT THE CO-CREATOR LEVEL

During the 1990s, Graham served as program director for a small organization in Washington, D.C. The firm used action research methods to improve working relationships between business, governmental, and civil society organizations that addressed global problems like poverty, hunger, malnutrition, disease, and environmental degradation.[10] A native of Australia, Graham had worked there during his twenties on projects that brought companies and government agencies together to work on various social and economic issues. In his early thirties, he moved to the United States, where he entered a dual degree program, emerging with an MBA and a Ph.D. During this period he also attended a series of personal growth workshops and began what has become a lifelong meditation practice.[11]

After moving to Washington, Graham spent a good part of the 1990s researching and consulting to projects addressing global problems in various parts of Asia, Africa, and South America. For example, when South Africa's post-apartheid government came to power, they wanted to create an alternative to traditional approaches to installing water facilities in poor areas, because those approaches had resulted in rapid breakdowns.[12] To address the problem, the government formed a consortium that included local communities, NGOs (nongovernmental organizations),[13] and water companies like the global giant Vivendi.

The consortium's members used a collaborative approach to define their roles and coordinate their activities. The NGOs helped organize the communities so they could participate fully in the planning and construction process. The corporations changed their role from that of conventional construction companies to developers of sustainable water systems. The communities took responsibility for ensuring they could maintain and pay for a reliable water system infrastructure once it was built. Based on his experience with this project and others like it, Graham discovered that these collaborations work when each sector contributes a unique set of competencies and resources that compensates for the limitations of the other sectors.

At the end of the 1990s, Graham was asked to contribute to a UN report on the future of global governance.[14] His work on this project drew his attention to a new type of network organization dedicated to solving global problems. Like the South African water consortium, these networks brought together business, government, and civil society organizations to work on a shared issue. However, unlike that consortium, these networks operated simultaneously on the local, national, and global levels.

For example, in 1993, stimulated in part by the Earth Summit and the failure of an intergovernmental process to agree on a global forest compact, 130 people from around the world came together to found the Forest Stewardship Council. FSC is a network that now includes members from more than six hundred logging companies, forest product manufacturers, forestry organizations, and environmental and human rights groups. Its mission is to promote sustainable forestry worldwide.

Committed to operating in a manner that is both democratic and transparent, FSC's members examined the existing international forestry product supply chain and its environmental, social, and economic impacts. They then developed a set of standards to transform this supply chain into a process that is environmentally appropriate, socially beneficial, and economically viable. Establishing these standards has allowed FSC to accredit independent third-party organizations to certify forest managers and forest product producers who operate according to sustainable forestry principles.[15]

Graham eventually came to call organizations like FSC "Global Transformation Networks," or GT-Nets. What he found most intriguing about these networks was the fact that they'd developed ways to overcome the key limitations of the dominant approach to global problem solving. A good example of the dominant approach can be found in a series of UN conferences on environmental degradation and world poverty. The first UN conference on the environment, held in Stockholm in 1972, produced an agreement to integrate environmental concerns into national economic planning and decision making. But years went by, and global warming, ozone depletion, and water pollution all became more serious problems, and the destruction of the Earth's natural resources accelerated at an alarming rate.[16]

Finally, in 1987, the UN's World Commission on Environment and Development produced the Brundtland report, which advocated a global commitment to sustainable development, a new approach to socioeconomic development designed to "meet the needs of the present without compromising the ability of future generations to meet their own needs." To mobilize commitment to sustainable development on a global scale, the UN General Assembly called for an Earth Summit to be held in Rio de Janeiro in 1992.

At the Earth Summit, 108 national governments signed Agenda 21, an agreement hailed as a blueprint for combating poverty and achieving sustainable development worldwide. Following Rio, the UN held additional conferences on specific environmental issues, forged additional agreements, and integrated the concept of sustainable development into its own policies and programs. However, at the end of the millennium, no one disputed the fact that progress on sustainable development had been extremely disappointing. World poverty was deepening, and the global environment continued to deteriorate.[17]

This approach and others like it, by themselves, clearly aren't agile enough to be effective in addressing the complexity of global problems—or the rate at which they're growing and changing. More specifically, Graham's analysis is that the dominant approach to global problem solving is hampered by two primary limitations.[18]

First, the dominant approach is a bureaucratic one, where each step is carried out by a different set of specialized actors. In the example just cited, specialists in socioeconomic and environmental issues collected data and analyzed problems. Representatives of national governments drafted and signed agreements. Then a much larger set of actors from multiple sectors within each nation state was expected to implement the agreements.

Second, the dominant global problem-solving process relies on agreements between national governments. For the most part, the negotiators for each nation state hold the implicit assumption that they must maximize the economic and political self-interest of their country's elites.[19] Even when they sign agreements like the ones in Stockholm and Rio, this mind-set has an extremely strong influence on their subsequent actions.

The result is a long, drawn-out process that's unable to forge alignment between the many organizations that need to work together to address complex, rapidly growing global issues.[20] GT-Nets are faster and more effective, because they work at a more advanced level of agility.[21]

Rather than relying on negotiations between nation states, a GT-Net spans global, national, and local action arenas and brings together those organizations from the business, government, and civil society sectors needed to solve a particular global problem. In so doing, it connects people from rich and poor countries and from different cultures and professional disciplines. By establishing a shared mission and a collaborative operating style, each GT-Net creates a "container" that allows all its participants to see their individual self-interest in a larger context.[22] Richard Barrett, now a fellow of the World Business Academy, describes this broader understanding of self-interest as follows:

> All human motivations are based on self-interest. We are only motivated to do something when it benefits us in some way. What about the common good? Are actions that support the common good also based on self-interest? Yes, but . . . it is a self with an enlarged sense of identity. . . . It is a self that recognizes that it is part of a web of interconnectedness that links all humanity and living systems.[23]

In addition, when GT-Nets are operating at their best, initiatives are treated as action experiments where multiple stakeholders are involved in each step of the process: diagnosing issues, developing solutions, and taking action. Regular collaborative progress reviews provide a way to maintain a reasonable degree of stakeholder alignment, while achieving results in a timely manner.[24]

When Graham learned that the UN and the World Bank had no plans to support the emergence of GT-Nets, he decided to embark on his own initiative. As a first step, he wanted to further clarify the features that make GT-Nets different from hundreds of other global networks. To do this, he put together an advisory group and raised enough money to do detailed case studies of four GT-Nets. To test his conclusions and start making the people engaged in these efforts more aware of one another, he invited members of each network to a small conference to discuss the case studies.

The success of this initial step led to action research projects with two additional GT-Nets. During this period, the vision implicit in Graham's initiative began to take shape: He would facilitate the formation of a GT-Net network that would support the development of member networks and help them learn from one another's experiences. He teamed up with a U.S. activist and philanthropist named Alan and put together a budget for the initiative.

As Graham met with members from a wider variety of GT-Nets, sharing what similar networks were doing, interest started to build. He and Alan then held a second annual conference that drew twenty-four people, including several key GT-Net funders. It was at this conference that the concept of Global Transformation Networks and the value of bringing them together really took hold. This meeting was followed by a series of teleconferences that began to build relationships among GT-Nets. When Graham and Alan held the third annual conference, they had no trouble attracting participants. Thirty-five people attended, representing twenty-one GT-Nets in various stages of development as well as six additional organizations.

The third annual conference had two primary purposes. The first was to reaffirm the shared vision of a "meta-network" of GT-Nets that had already emerged over the past several years. The other was to launch a set of initiatives that would support this vision. The conference consisted almost entirely of working sessions on topics including funding strategies, leadership development, strategic planning, new communication technologies, and multi-stakeholder dialogue methods. By the end of the conference, Graham's dream had become a shared vision.

In the months that followed, GT-Meta-Net launched a variety of collaborative initiatives. One project, designed to develop the meta-network into a "community of practice," helps GT-Nets share experiences, develop new tools and practices more quickly, and avoid pitfalls encountered by other networks.[25] Other initiatives include identifying measurement criteria tailored to network structures and establishing e-conferencing relationships among GT-Nets. GT-Meta-Net is also supporting a group of Global Transformation Networks committed to complementing one another's efforts in Central America.

In addition, the meta-network will convene GT-Net CEOs to develop a shared long-term vision for their organizations based on a twenty-year time frame. Asked about his vision of GT-Meta-Net's future and his role as a leader in the network, Graham said:

> For the meta-network to be successful in the long run, there clearly has to be a strong sense of collective ownership, and I think we're on that track. I see myself right now as a steward of GT-Meta-Net's development phase. In the future I definitely want to be an integral part of the network, but I don't want to be its executive director. Raising money and doing budgets isn't where my passion and talents lie. I'm not even sure it needs an executive director.
>
> The leadership role I want to play as the meta-network matures is to continue to contribute to the development of a learning community—so it becomes something like a learning organization, only tailored to its unique purpose and structure.
>
> My personal vision is that GT-Meta-Net becomes a very broadly owned global community that transcends and includes the concept of citizenship. There's something at the heart of this that's about relationships—helping people connect in meaningful ways so they feel powerful in their lives. Ultimately, although it's very much about creating new collaborative structures, it's also about fundamental change at the personal level, improving our relationships with one another through ongoing action learning.

THE CAPACITIES OF CO-CREATOR LEADERS

What changes take place in the four leadership agility competencies when you grow into the Co-Creator level of leadership agility?

Co-Creator Awareness and Intent

To clarify the Co-Creator level of awareness, it's useful to briefly review the kind of awareness that emerges at the Achiever and Catalyst levels. At the Achiever level your reflective capabilities are typically limited to your conscious mind. As a Catalyst, you develop a more immediate reflective capacity that allows you to attend directly but momentarily to some aspect of current experience—a tacit assumption, an unconscious feeling, or a behavior pattern—that would otherwise escape your conscious awareness.[26] This momentary realization is followed immediately by a quick reflective process that allows you to make sense of the experience and adjust your response accordingly.

The level of awareness that emerges at the Co-Creator level can be described as the capacity to enter intentionally (though temporarily) into a state of effortless attention that psychologist Mihaly Csikszentmihalyi calls "flow."[27] You've probably had experiences of concentrating so intently on what you're doing that you become completely absorbed as one moment flows into the next. You're not distracted by extraneous thoughts and judgments, and you may lose track of time.

People at all stages of development have experienced flow at one time or another. It's easiest to enter into this state when you're engaged in an entertaining activity that requires little active participation on your part, like watching a good movie or reading an absorbing book. Csikszentmihalyi, however, has focused on the experience of flow amid goal-directed activities like sports, chess, and musical performance. He notes that people are most likely to enter the flow state when they're engaged in a relatively well-structured activity. This structure frees the mind to concentrate totally on the task at hand.

What's new about the Co-Creator's level of awareness is the ability to enter intentionally into the flow state while engaged in ill-structured leadership challenges that are mentally complex and often emotionally charged. Take, for example, Ken's ability to experience Jim's highly emotional attack on his integrity without reacting defensively. This clearly is not just "going with the flow," in the sense of doing whatever feels good at the moment. It's one thing to enjoy a good dance party, where the environment is designed to bring you into a pleasurable flow, and it's something again to enter intentionally into the flow of unpleasant emotional reactions.

Co-Creator awareness gives you the ability to stay a bit longer with direct attention to disconcerting feelings than was possible in the Catalyst level. However, at this level it still feels quite important to use your reflective capacity to resolve emotional turmoil. As with both Larry and Ken, Co-Creator leaders usually feel it's important to make meaning out of these experiences in ways that are nonblaming and lead to deeper understanding.[28]

At the Co-Creator level, your increased ability to understand what's behind surface-level thoughts and feelings extends to your relationships with others and the world around you. As a result, you can now enter more deeply into different frames of reference. This allows you to step back from multiple frames (including your own) and identify where they conflict and where they have common elements. You develop a keen awareness of interdependence and a capacity for integrative thinking that allows you to see how multiple frames of reference can work together to address ill-structured problems.

The Co-Creator level of intent is rooted in an evolving sense of life purpose that allows you to express your deeper talents and interests while enhancing the lives of other human beings. At the same time, following this sense of purpose frequently requires the courage to take significant risks. Larry decided not to leave a large corporation in search of more like-minded colleagues but to work for change within it. To pursue her vision, Alison had to undergo a painful separation from otherwise like-minded colleagues. To pursue his vision of a Global Transformation Meta-Network, Graham had to operate on a shoestring budget from a one-person office.

The risks entailed in pursuing a deep sense of life purpose often provide significant opportunities for personal and professional growth. Engaging in these challenging opportunities with the Co-Creator level of awareness and intent, a leader's personality becomes more integrated than it was at previous levels of development. For this reason, you'll see that the capacities that emerge at this level of agility are more closely related to one another than they were at earlier levels.

Co-Creator Context-Setting Agility

We now turn to an overview of the four competencies that emerge at the Co-Creator level, beginning with the two capacities responsible for context-setting agility: *situational awareness* and *sense of purpose.*

SITUATIONAL AWARENESS. As we've traced the development of situational awareness through previous levels, we've described Achievers' ability to analyze the motivations and behavior of the key players in their immediate environment and Catalysts' ability to take into account the larger context within which their industry and its key stakeholders operate. As a result, we noted, a business leader who's reached the Catalyst level is more likely than a heroic leader to demonstrate a proactive concern about the organization's social and environmental impact.

At the Co-Creator level, your situational awareness is likely to expand to a global scope, if it hasn't already done so. Even more significantly, this awareness changes in its quality and depth: You become more deeply aware of the experience of other human beings around the globe, your relatedness to them, and the interdependence between the human family and the natural environment.[29] As with Ken and Alison, when Co-Creator leaders start new businesses, it's very likely that they'll make a commitment to social and environmental well-being integral to the way they operate.[30] However, while some Co-Creators try to address issues on a global scale, others "think globally and act locally." [31]

At the Co-Creator level, the Catalyst's awareness of the "white spaces" in the organization chart deepens to include a keen appreciation of the interdependent nature of organizational life. For example, Co-Creator leaders see their organizations both from a macro perspective and a micro perspective: While organizational structure and culture shape individual behavior, it's equally true that structure and culture are co-created every day by the attitudes and actions of an organization's members. This perspective is reflected in Graham's earlier comment about GT-Meta-Net:

> Ultimately, although it's very much about creating new collaborative structures, it's also about fundamental change at the personal level, improving our relationships with one another through ongoing action learning.

SENSE OF PURPOSE. As leaders move through the post-heroic levels of context-setting agility, they develop the capacity to create visions with increasingly extended time frames.[32] However, while these visions are often long range, or have long-term implications, their time horizons can vary a good deal simply because of circumstantial factors. What most differentiates a Co-Creator's vision isn't so much its time frame as the depth of purpose behind it. At this level, your sense of purpose grows out of a desire for greater personal fulfillment that's fueled by an increased appreciation of present experience as the qualitative dimension of time.[33]

Denise, a VP of Human Resources for a growing adventure travel company based in Portland, Maine, puts it this way:

What's most important to me is that my life has meaning and purpose. A real sense of purpose isn't something you just think through and decide about. It's a lot more intuitive and intangible than that. I suppose you could also call it a sense of direction. It's not something you're always aware of. It's not something you figure out once and for all. It's not a destination you ever get to. Until you die, it's something that keeps evolving as you keep discovering it.

What I feel really gives life meaning is the process of intuiting that sense of purpose and moving to align your life with that. When my mind and my feelings can be aligned with what my deeper self is calling me to do, then I can act with real authenticity and integrity. To me, this is creative expression.

The sense of life purpose that emerges at the Co-Creator level is always unique, yet it has some universal qualities. For example, it usually involves doing something you find particularly fulfilling that enhances others' lives in a meaningful way. We see this with all the leaders featured in this chapter. While some Co-Creators pioneer new forms of organization firmly rooted in human values,[34] those who work within established organizations often adopt what might be called an ownership mind-set. Srini, a long-time individual contributor in a Fortune 500 computer company, describes this mind-set as follows:

Managing large organizations isn't one of my skill-sets. Fortunately, I've always been able to find or create an environment that feels like a start-up. I get involved in creating these little subcultures, where we're building a complete business model, working on something new and different, and there's a lot of room for creativity.

If I start thinking about all the bureaucracy, it really bogs down my creativity. So instead I think, "What if this new business model was my own start-up?" I imagine I'm totally in charge of my own destiny. If I had to write a one-page business plan for a venture capitalist, what would I want to put in it?

Empowering myself in this way is extremely motivating. It allows me to come up with creative ideas, which I then test with customers or whoever will benefit from them. Creating things that are both original and useful gives me the energy I need to mobilize other people and get them excited. What I've developed gets further refined by others, and then it gets implemented so that it changes people's lives for the better. It's like the circuit gets completed.

Like Catalysts, Co-Creators want to create teams and organizations characterized by open communication, increased autonomy, and participative decision making. However, they are particularly intent on developing work environments where high levels of collaboration, rooted in an ethos of shared responsibility, are the norm. For example, although Ken, Alison, and Graham were the primary visionaries for their organizations, they developed their visions in collaboration with other leaders. They also developed teams and organizations where status hierarchies are diminished and positional authority is used on an as-needed basis.

Finally, Co-Creator leaders often place a strong emphasis on organizational learning. Whatever the size of their organization, they establish forums that serve the purpose of the law firm's retreats and the day spa's "vision circle": People enter into honest dialogue about the extent to which they're living their mission, vision, and values, and they take responsibility for making needed changes.[35]

Co-Creator Stakeholder Agility

The two capacities that support your level of stakeholder agility are your *stakeholder understanding* and your *power style*.

STAKEHOLDER UNDERSTANDING. At the Catalyst level you realize that value and belief systems are strongly conditioned by factors such as family upbringing, socioeconomic class, cultural assumptions, and so on. As a result, you develop a greater tolerance for, and a greater interest in, frames of reference that differ from your own. You also develop a level of empathy that allows you to imagine what it might be like to be another person, experiencing life as *they* experience it.

In the Co-Creator level, this capacity for empathy grows, allowing you to enter more fully into frames of reference that may differ markedly from your own. For this reason, Co-Creators often develop a deeper capacity for understanding other cultures, subcultures, and ethnic groups. For example, although Ken is a Japanese American, he grew up with very little exposure to traditional Japanese culture. However, by the time he developed into the Co-Creator level, he could move fluidly between traditional Japanese culture, contemporary Japanese culture, and American culture. He was also at ease working closely with a management team that included an African American woman, a Mexican American woman, and a Japanese man. Similarly, Larry chose to get deeply involved in issues faced by a wide range of minority groups within his corporation.

The full extent of the Co-Creator's emotional capacity for stakeholder understanding is illustrated by Larry's response to Craig's attack and by Ken's response to Jim's attack. Larry and Ken both demonstrated a remarkable capacity for understanding and empathizing with what it felt like to be the person who'd attacked them.[36] This capacity enabled each Co-Creator to respond in an unusually constructive manner.

POWER STYLE. When you develop into the Co-Creator level of stakeholder agility, you have a solid appreciation for many kinds of power: the power of expertise and position (at the Expert level), the power of personality and political positioning (at the Achiever level), and the power of vision and participation (at the Catalyst level). As a Co-Creator, you retain the ability to function on all these levels. However, your growth into this level of agility brings with it a preference for the power of life purpose and deep collaboration.

Because the Co-Creator's sense of life purpose brings about personal fulfillment through the meaningful enhancement of other people's lives, it enables you to develop a power style that allows you to assert yourself and help meet others' needs at the same time. For example, Ken responded to Jim's feelings in a remarkably centered manner: he could put himself inside Jim's frame of reference, and he could also maintain his own frame. This ability to hold both frames allowed Ken to respond in a way that extracted valid points of feedback while taking both of their situations into account.

To understand what collaboration means to the Co-Creator, it's useful to review how it's understood at previous levels. At the Achiever level, you're likely to see collaboration as a process of working out compromises so your stakeholders will be more motivated to support the decisions you make. For Catalysts, collaboration is meaningful participation in decision making, initiated with the conviction that this leads not only to greater commitment but also to better decisions. At the Co-Creator level

> [Collaborative relationships] are characterized by authentic, open self-expression and the constructive clarification and working-through of differences honestly faced. Collaboration means a relationship in

which there is both individual integrity and shared vision and purpose. This is one of the reasons why truly collaborative relationships are so rare.[37]

Co-Creator leaders realize that everyone in their team or organization, even those who may see themselves as passive victims, plays some role in creating its overall power dynamic. Therefore, while those who hold the greatest positional and political power in an organization have a crucial role to play in creating a culture of empowerment and collaboration, leaders at this agility level realize that culture is ultimately co-created. As a result, they go out of their way to encourage others to join with them in developing teams and organizations characterized by mutual empowerment and shared responsibility.[38]

Co-Creator Creative Agility

Your creative agility is made possible by your level of *connective awareness* and *reflective judgment.*

CONNECTIVE AWARENESS. As noted earlier, at the Co-Creator level you develop a level of connective awareness that allows you to step back from several frames of reference, compare and contrast them, and make meaningful connections between them. In situations that involve conflicting frames of reference, this capacity allows you to identify what the frames are, where they conflict, and where they have common elements, enabling you to discover true win-win solutions.[39] For example, this capacity for integrative thinking underlies Graham's robust understanding of the differing mind-sets and operating styles of the business, government, and civil society sectors—and his deep appreciation of their interdependence and collaborative potential. We also see this capacity for integrative thinking at work in Alison's understanding of the ways each discipline housed in her current law firm can contribute to meeting the needs of the "whole client."

As your connective awareness evolves through each level, you develop a more complex understanding of causality in human interaction. At the Expert level, you have a simple, linear understanding: "If you want to accomplish X, do Y." At the Achiever level, you can work toward multiple outcomes, realizing that multiple pathways lead to these outcomes and that specific tactics may need to change to take changing circumstances into account. You also understand that human interaction is reciprocal: Each action you take affects what others do next, and vice versa.

At the Catalyst level you see that even your successful actions can have negative unintended side effects that can come back to haunt you. In other words, human interaction can be circular as well as linear. At the Co-Creator level you understand that human interaction involves mutual causality: All organizational processes and results are created by many people working together *simultaneously*. This understanding of mutual causality underlies the Co-Creator's interest in creating work environments that emphasize shared responsibility.

REFLECTIVE JUDGMENT. As we've noted, at the Co-Creator level you gain deeper insight into the extent to which value and belief systems are shaped by largely unconscious factors such as family upbringing, temperament, character structure, social class, ethnic background, religious and political conditioning, and so on. You also develop an increased ability to identify and understand the assumptions that underlie different interpretive frameworks, including your own.

Whenever you engage with others in solving business or organizational problems, you can readily see that these problems are ill-structured. Even before you enter into conversations about them, you know it's extremely likely that each person will define problems and evaluate solution ideas using differing assumptions and criteria. This perspective, combined with your preference for mutually satisfying outcomes, leads naturally to an interest in meaningful dialogue: collaborative conversation that explores differing perspectives in order to enhance shared understanding and develop mutually beneficial solutions.

Co-Creator Self-Leadership Agility

Your self-leadership agility is made possible by the depth of your *self-awareness* and *developmental motivation*.

SELF-AWARENESS. Catalyst-level self-awareness is the ability to attend directly to a behavior, feeling, or assumption you'd normally miss, followed immediately by a reflective process that puts your observation into thoughts or words. Applied repeatedly in a wide variety of situations, this level of self-awareness allows you to develop an understanding of yourself that's more accurate and complex than the one you developed at the Achiever level.

Yet some fully developed Catalysts sense that this level of self-awareness still limits their experience of underlying feelings and assumptions. For example, consider this statement by Patrick, the consumer products manager cited in Chapter Six:

> I go through periods of relative complacency, where everything seems fine. But sometimes I get into real emotional turmoil, usually triggered by some sort of unpleasant interaction. If I can't work it out with the other person in a way that leaves me feeling better, the turmoil keeps going. At those times, I try to talk it through with someone I trust. But even then, I mainly "head trip." I haven't been willing to experience these uncomfortable emotions in a really direct way just yet. If I tried to envision the next stage in my development, I would have much more direct and sustained access to a much broader range of feelings.

We asked Patrick if he knew anyone who he felt had developed this capacity, and he immediately thought of Marilyn, a senior product development manager in a biotech company. Patrick and Marilyn went to the same church and were both on the social action committee. When we interviewed Marilyn, we discovered that her transition to Co-Creator self-awareness began when she decided to see a psychotherapist. She entered therapy because she wanted to overcome an aversion to conflict that was limiting her effectiveness as a leader and creating problems in her relationship with her daughter.

After spending a number of months in face-to-face "talk therapy," Marilyn and her therapist decided to switch to a format that would help her experience a wider range of feelings more directly. As Marilyn put it:

> The therapist provides some gentle guidance, but she's not very directive. I lie down on a couch, close my eyes, and just tune in to whatever feelings are there—just let them come up and give voice to them. It's not so much that I'm analyzing different feelings and events. It's more just letting them flow through me by giving them voice and then just following that process wherever it takes me.

We've found that most people who've developed Co-Creator self-awareness do so either through a therapeutic process similar to Marilyn's, or through a meditation practice similar to the one that Ken described. Although these approaches have different long-range aims, they both allow thoughts and feelings to flow through conscious awareness without judgment or fixation.[40]

As with earlier agility levels, being at the Co-Creator level doesn't mean that you function continually at this level of self-awareness. However, when you do activate this level of awareness, it allows you to stay a bit longer with direct attention to painful and disconcerting feelings. You also find it easier to cycle back and forth between direct awareness of these feelings and the meaning you make of them.[41]

Marilyn told us a story similar to Larry's, which showed how this level of self-awareness made her a more effective leader by dramatically improving her ability to deal constructively with conflict. She said it had also improved her relationship with her daughter. "It's been a wonderful process, really," she said, "of reclaiming parts of myself that I'd somehow walled off." In other words, when you enter into the flow of thoughts and feelings once previously walled off from consciousness, this gradually and spontaneously integrates aspects of your "shadow side" (parts of yourself you normally avoid experiencing) into your everyday personality.

While Co-Creator self-awareness doesn't yet have the depth and subtle power needed to fully balance and integrate all your internal conflicts, it does make it possible to experience them with greater ease and clarity than you would have at previous levels. Perhaps the two most common internal conflicts you experience at the Co-Creator level are the one between your assertive and receptive sides and the one between an internal critic and the part of yourself that reacts to that internal voice with hurt or anger, conformity or rebellion.[42]

If you're like most managers, you won't be aware of this second basic conflict until you enter the Catalyst level. You then begin to discover how you unconsciously depend on others to bolster your self-esteem (for example, when Patrick realized that his need to be seen as a high-achiever was a form of emotional dependency). To overcome these dependences, you cultivate a more affirming attitude toward yourself, particularly in situations that may challenge your self-confidence and self-esteem.

At the Co-Creator level, you find that opening yourself more fully to your present experience provides a level of self-acceptance that's more direct and powerful than retrospective self-affirmation. You also become more accepting of the fact that all significant relationships entail some level of mutual emotional dependency. Paradoxically, the more fully you experience vulnerable feelings, the more you free your-self from these feelings and the reactive behaviors they lead to.

DEVELOPMENTAL MOTIVATION. As you become a Co-Creator your Cat-alyst-level interest in overcoming your defenses and living a more mean-ingful life evolves into a strong commitment to authenticity. And as you seek to live your life in a manner that expresses your deepest values and potentials, you become more attuned to a felt sense of life purpose. It's not a matter of feeling you *should* do this or that. Your motivation for development is fueled instead by a deep interest in self-fulfillment.

As a leader, pursuing an evolving sense of life purpose gives you the opportunity to employ your greatest talents. Almost inevitably, however, it also challenges you to overcome your personal limitations. In fact, you see more clearly than ever before that leadership development requires personal growth. But your interest in personal development isn't limited to how it will affect your leadership competencies. The central motiva-tion is a desire to bring about greater fulfillment in all aspects of your life. As Marilyn put it:

> Why live life only halfway? Why not experience the whole thing? If you don't try to develop as a person, you cut off so many experiences and emotions. If you're aware of yourself and you're constantly growing as a person, that leads to more satisfying relationships with other people, which is something I find very important, not just as a leader but as a person.

This stance makes Co-Creator leaders more honest with themselves about their real thoughts, feelings, and behaviors; better able to ex-periment with new attitudes and behaviors; and more proactive in learning from experience.

CHAPTER EIGHT

Synergist Level

Evoke Unexpected Possibilities

~~~

*C*hristine grew up in the South and went to Emory University in Atlanta, where she became very active in the civil rights and peace movements. After college, she earned a master's in theology and became a vocal member of the women's movement. During the mid-1970s, she became director of a center for women and religion that was funded by a consortium of theology schools. She and her colleagues singled out those seminaries in the consortium whose policies and practices were most sexist and racist. They confronted their presidents, publicized their shortcomings, organized protests, and tried to embarrass them into doing the right thing.

The confrontational strategies didn't work. In fact, they only made the schools they targeted angry and determined not to give in. The consortium's budget for the center began to shrink, and some schools threatened to cut off funding altogether. The experience was a turning point in Christine's development as a leader. Seeing that she and her colleagues were fueling resistance rather than change, she changed the center's strategy: They shifted their focus to those schools that were doing the most for women and minorities. They publicized the positive steps these schools had taken, and they championed their presidents, inviting them to speak to others about their visions and their values.

The new approach worked wonders.[1] Rather than increasing negativity, it amplified positive energy. They even found ways to use it with the schools they'd previously confronted. When they discovered that the least progressive school had taken one positive step to remove bias, they highlighted that step. The president of that school eventually became a big supporter of the center and praised it publicly for its work.[2]

Between the mid-1970s and mid-1980s, Christine held several other nonprofit leadership positions, and she became increasingly concerned about the impact of global corporations on the future well-being of the Earth and its people.[3] She also became convinced that her purpose in life lay inside the business sector, helping to reform corporations from the inside out. She began her new life humbly enough as a local staffing manager for a Fortune 50 high-tech corporation.

Early on, Christine had an encounter with one of the managers she supported, confronting him for abusive behavior toward an administrative assistant. By now, however, she'd developed a highly balanced power style. Through a series of firm but gentle encounters, Christine transformed a potential enemy into a long-term friend. When she suggested that he have a more open mind about hiring minorities as summer interns, he was skeptical, but he gave it a try. His experience was so positive that he agreed to hold his regular employee recruiting interviews at a minority college as well as the usual Ivy League colleges.

The manager came back astounded. He said the minority students were much more mature than the Ivy League kids he interviewed. He reported that they had already proven themselves to be exceptional managers, people who supported their parents and their children by holding down two or three jobs in addition to their full-time courses. He said they were just as smart and capable as the Ivy League students. "They just don't have the financial support the rich kids are getting." Together, he and Christine figured out how to bring many of these minority students into their division. Three years later, the division had far exceeded its affirmative action goals, and Christine became head recruiter for the whole corporation.

In the years that followed, Christine had many remarkable accomplishments. Each was consistent with her own sense of purpose, and each contributed to the success and well-being of the corporation. Whenever she reached a crossroads or felt conflicted or intimidated, she consulted a "still, small voice within, a deep knowing that's a part of myself and yet apart from myself." These inner promptings guided her to take initiatives that were aligned with her sense of life purpose, although she often initially had no idea how to proceed. Yet she succeeded each time by drawing on her strengths: Time after time, she collaborated with colleagues, amplified the positive, and turned potential adversaries into friends and allies.

After six years with the company, she became head of HR for one of its most important business units. In that role, she was tapped by the unit's EVP to lead a change initiative to transform it into the best organization of its kind in the world. Rather than ask the EVP to envision what that might look like, Christine advised him to pose a set of vision questions. People at all levels were asked what they could do differently to make the organization "the world's best."

Christine launched an employee survey that generated reams of ideas. Rather than distill all these ideas into a massive set of overhead slides, she used a process called Readers Theater, which she'd last used fifteen years earlier: She selected key quotes from the surveys and wove them into a play about the organization.[4] She then recruited six managers to speak the views expressed by engineers and administrative assistants, and six engineers and administrators to convey the managers' perspective. The play was then performed for the organization's top thirty managers. The response was silence followed by thunderous applause. They said they "got it" at a level that slide presentations can never reach.

The top management team's usual response to employee surveys was to delegate responsibility for change to people at lower levels. This time, they took responsibility for initiating change at their own level, and they encouraged and empowered people at all levels to contribute to the change process in any way they could.[5] Over the next several years, the intention to become the world's best found its way into a wide range of organizational improvement projects. Christine developed an incredible network of colleagues inside and outside the organization, all supporting her and the collective change effort.

Eleven years after she joined the company, she was asked to keynote its annual women's conference, an event she'd helped initiate several years earlier. After much trepidation, she decided to speak her own truth: She said that asking what they could do for the company was a necessary question, but it wasn't sufficient. Why? Because it confined them to the company as they'd always known it. The real question was: What contributions can our company make, through us, to our beautiful, fragile world and its precious, suffering people?

Christine touched a nerve. She was flooded with positive responses from men and women throughout the corporation. Before she knew it, her business unit's vision was no longer simply to be the best *in* the world, but to be the best *for* the world. Many adventures later, six years after the original initiative began, it could legitimately lay claim to being one of the best organizations of its kind in the world.

Meanwhile, Christine learned about the Grameen Bank and the microlending revolution it had sparked.[6] Twenty-seven years after its founding, the bank was lending $500 million a year to two million of the most destitute people on Earth and getting a remarkable 96 percent return rate. Inspired by this model's success in bringing people out of poverty, Christine initiated countless conversations about what her corporation could do along the same lines. In addition to old and new co-conspirators inside the company, she made contact with dozens of people around the world who had knowledge, expertise, and contacts in this area.

After three years of serious exploration and experimentation and with the support of her CEO, Christine co-founded a start-up within the company. The start-up, which is now five years old, collaborates with governments and the international development community to provide the world's poor with access to technologies that accelerate socioeconomic development at the grassroots level. This innovative organization not only empowers people in impoverished communities, it also makes the larger corporation more competitive through access to new talent and the discovery of new business models to serve emerging markets.

Christine is now a sought-after speaker and has a role in the company that allows her to focus full time on transformative projects. Her well-developed capacities for appreciative listening and creative collaboration have made her part of a vibrant network of global change agents, all dedicated to using their intelligence and good will to make the world a better place for everyone. Whenever she meets a kindred spirit, she invariably connects them with several people who can help them reach their goals.

WHAT LEADERSHIP MEANS
AT THE SYNERGIST LEVEL

When Christine was young, she thought great leaders were people born with special gifts. Maybe she'd find a real leader to follow, but she'd never be one herself. As she now sees it, leaders who make the world a better place are people who've chosen to live their lives in the context of a larger story that has deep meaning and purpose. First, she said, you need to search for a story that's worth your life—or invent one from those you find compelling.[7]

To help explain what she means, Christine described the story she holds: A vision that a critical mass of the world's corporations must become stewards for the planet. She acknowledges that there's plenty of evidence to justify despair rather than hope. Yet she still finds the story she's chosen consistently hopeful and compelling. By working with others to build on strengths and amplify positive movement, a leader can make a pragmatic commitment to hope into a self-fulfilling prophecy. If you commit yourself to a deep and meaningful story, she believes, great people will be attracted to you, and things will fall into place that you'd never expect.

As Christine's example shows, Synergist leaders have an evolving sense of life purpose that often expresses itself as a robust concern about human issues on a global scale. They are very strongly inclined to align their leadership initiatives with this sense of purpose, even when they work in organizations that have narrower objectives. They often experience heartfelt moments of purposefulness. At these moments, they may feel a remarkable sense of being the right person at the right place at the right time. Or they may have a strong intuition about a next step that will keep them "on purpose."

Playfully familiar with many forms of power, Synergists cultivate the "power of presence," a subtle form of stakeholder agility centered in the present moment. This orientation gives Synergists the capacity to deeply attune themselves to people, groups, and organizations. At times, they can sense subtle energetic dynamics that would have escaped their awareness at earlier levels. The power of presence also allows them to remain focused on the common good while holding in mind, in an accurate and empathetic way, multiple and conflicting stakeholder views and interests, including their own.

When they work with others to solve ill-structured problems, the Synergists' ability to hold mental and emotional complexity in awareness can result in "synergistic intuitions" that resolve apparently irreconcilable conflicts in ways that are beneficial for all parties involved. Yet, even when these intuitive breakthroughs seem to do just that, Synergists usually feel compelled to double-check the practical validity of their insights, either through feedback or by testing their ideas in action.

The Synergists' motivation for personal and professional development grows from a wish to engage with life in all its fullness and to be of real benefit to others. As Synergists cultivate a direct, present-centered awareness of their five senses, their physical presence, their thought processes, and their emotional responses, self-awareness takes on a fresh and immediate quality. As a result, Synergists not only develop greater awareness of their habitual reactions, they also experience the joy and wonder of being alive.

Even though this is the final level we describe in this book, it's important not to overidealize what leaders "must be like" who've grown into this level of agility. For one thing, the Synergist stage is not the final stage of human development.[8] For another, the process of developing as a human being is not a march toward perfection but a journey toward wholeness.

The remaining stories in this chapter illustrate the remarkable agility of which leaders at this level are capable, while also conveying their humanness and their diversity. You'll meet Jeff, the owner of a very successful wealth management firm and a master at the productive resolution of conflict. You'll find out why Don, a foundation CEO, is noted for his ability to solve difficult problems in ways that create mutually beneficial opportunities. You'll see how Stan, the senior VP of corporate governance for a Fortune 50 company, mobilized an IT organization that was an obstacle to corporate agility. Finally, you'll discover how Laura resolved a nightmare of stakeholder conflict over a health education program at a leading university.

PIVOTAL CONVERSATIONS AT THE SYNERGIST LEVEL

Jeff is the CEO of Generativity, a unique, highly successful wealth management firm headquartered in London, with branch offices in New York, Paris, and Frankfurt. *Generativity,* a concept that comes from the work of developmental psychologist Erik Erikson, is somewhat akin to creativity, but it refers specifically to the mature adult's contribution to the well-being of future generations.[9] The firm's motto is the often-quoted African proverb: "The world was not left to us by our parents. It was lent to us by our children."

Generativity's approach to financial planning goes beyond conventional methods, which are typically confined to easily quantified factors such as a client's financial goals and tolerance for risk. Generativity's advisers build high-trust client relationships and help clients clarify their core values and most heartfelt aspirations. Working collaboratively with each client, they then develop a sound financial plan designed to fulfill these aspirations. This approach has earned the firm an appreciative client base and kudos in the business press.

Generativity operates independently. It accepts no commissions or finder's fees and sells no services beyond its own. The firm works exclusively with high-net-worth clients and has a strategy of contained growth, selecting a limited number of new clients each year. Not surprisingly, most of its clients want to make contributions of lasting value to the larger world in which they live.

The partners have worked to develop an organization where the values of respect and generosity govern client relationships, internal working relationships, and the firm's relationship with the world around it. As an expression of these values, Generativity operates in a socially and environmentally responsible manner. The firm uses these criteria to screen its own investments, donates a percentage of its profits to charities, and has a profit-sharing plan for its employees.

Decision making among the partners is highly collaborative, and open communication and participation is the norm at the weekly all-hands meetings held in each office. Jeff and his partners also have a strong commitment to personal growth. Each partner has practiced meditation or some related discipline, such as yoga, tai chi, or chi gung, for several decades.[10] They also make it a priority to hire people who are committed not only to social and environmental responsibility but also to personal development.

Jeff has a reputation for being exceptionally effective in resolving interpersonal conflict. The awards he's won as a financial adviser are due partly to his fiscal acumen and partly to his ability to deal with difficult issues. For example, one of his specialties is helping couples work through conflicts regarding their money. Employees emphasize his masterful responses to client complaints. Even his wife says he's extremely good at dealing with conflict! Asked why he thought he was perceived this way, Jeff said:

I think it's rooted in feeling more and more at ease in "uncomfortable" situations. It's developed in a gradual way, mainly from my meditation practice. I took up meditation many years ago. Early on, my motivations were rather mundane: Wanting to be mentally sharper so I'd do better on exams. Then I found it gave me more confidence socially, which helped me get into some leadership positions while I was at university.

It's only the past seven years or so that I've been working with a genuine meditation teacher and sitting on a daily basis. The main practice is being present to my experience, just being aware of whatever comes up without judgment. Learning not to push any thoughts or feelings away, but to welcome whatever comes up.

Also, in recent years, much of the emphasis has been on bringing this kind of awareness into everyday life situations—first very simple situations like walking down the street, but gradually more complex situations like conversations with other people.

Developing this capacity to experience all kinds of emotions in sitting meditation—then bringing it into everyday life at home and at work—this is what's behind this ability to deal with conflict that you mention.

We asked Jeff to describe a situation where this capacity was at work, specifically a situation where at least part of the tension was between himself and another person. He related the following story:

When our London office manager departed about four months ago, I promoted a man named Tom to replace him. Initially, I thought he was quite good. But after a few months a whole stream of people began to troop into my office saying he was very hard to work with.

So, of course, I was concerned. I went round and in various ways talked with everyone who worked with Tom, and I had opportunities to see him in action. The people who worked for him directly felt he constantly criticized them and tried to control their every move. They felt quite resentful. Others were simply frustrated. They said he was difficult to work with, that he went on at length talking about himself, that sort of thing.

I used these conversations to coach these people about ways they might deal with some of Tom's quirks. But to get to the root of the problem I knew I needed to have a heart-to-heart with Tom. So I invited him to dinner.

At this point, we asked Jeff to go back and re-live what happened next, describing it in the present tense:

> I prepare for the meeting not by trying to figure things out but by going into a sort of meditation on Tom. I notice feelings of confusion and fear in my belly and some sadness around my heart. Tom has worked so hard for us, and in many ways he's doing a great job. Yet he's getting in his own way and not really enjoying what he's doing. I see images of Tom, and I see his up-tightness. I sense that Tom has the capacity for growth, but he can also be closed and defensive. As I stay with this uncomfortable stew, I feel a sense of empathy for Tom and a determination to do what I can to help him rise to the occasion.

We then asked Jeff to tell us what happened over dinner, keeping his description in the present tense:

> We've just ordered, and I'm bringing my attention back into my body, sitting across from Tom. I let go of what I planned to say and just tune in to him. He's already launched into a list of things he's accomplished over the past two months. His tone is ill at ease and defensive. For a moment, I wonder if he'll be at all receptive to feedback. Then I'm completely present with Tom. Taking in his words and his energy at the same time, I get this very visceral sense of what it must feel like to be him right now.
>
> I say, and it's quite genuine, "Tom, even without those particular accomplishments, you're a great asset to our firm. You've been extremely productive, and you've made a visible contribution in every role you've played." I see him take this in, let out a breath, and relax. His defensiveness melts and his whole demeanor shifts. I'm amazed and not amazed at the same time. I don't want to disturb what's happened, so I just hold the space that's opened up between us.
>
> Tom asks me if he can tell me something in confidence about a big crisis in his personal life. I say, "Of course. Whatever you feel comfortable sharing." He tells me about something quite painful—something very difficult for anyone to go through. Because of what's happened, he's lost a good deal of confidence in himself. As a result, he says, he often isolates himself at work—and he basically acknowledges all the things he does that the others complained about.
>
> He says, "It's strange. I was looking forward to this dinner, because I hoped you'd tell me how well I'm doing. But when you did, I realized

that hearing it from someone else doesn't make up for how I feel about myself. I'm going in circles. I don't feel good about myself, so I do things others don't like, which makes me feel bad about myself, and on and on."

At this point, I say that, if he's really willing to do some work on this, the company will pay for a coach. He says, "Yes, I could use some help. I'd really like to do that." What amazed me was that I didn't need to lay out all the feedback. He did that on his own. He started working with a coach about three months ago, and there's already been a very noticeable change.

Our interest in Synergist-level pivotal conversations also led us to Don, the president and CEO of a foundation headquartered in Seattle. A dedicated, unassuming leader, he is very adept at solving difficult problems and creating mutually beneficial opportunities. His office is tastefully decorated with artwork from Asia, Latin America, and other world cultures. He collected most of these objects earlier in his career while leading trips abroad for various educational and humanitarian purposes. One wall was filled with group photographs taken during these trips and on more recent visits to organizations supported by the foundation.

Don's foundation, only about twenty years old, operates on a fee-based model. It raises funds through donations and investments, then provides grants and loans for organizations around the world that promote sustainable economic development, political equality, and cultural autonomy. The foundation provides additional assistance in the form of philanthropic management, community investment, consulting services, and educational programs.

When we asked Don about his reputation as a creative thinker, he responded:

I would have to agree with that. I did receive a good deal of feedback to that effect last summer, when I attended a leadership program at the NTL Institute.[11] One person told me they felt I lead from my heart. Meaning that I often connect with a situation first through my heart and then with my brain. It's something that happens very quickly, but I've noticed that this is what generates some of the most interesting and useful ideas.

We asked if he could describe this process as if it were happening in slow motion:

It begins with an intention that I've been cultivating for many years. Whenever a person walks in the door, my inner question is always, "How can I help you?" This question takes me to a very, very deep place. It's almost as if the molecular structure of my body slows down and I'm in a semi-meditative state. I become so present that I actually feel the other person's emotions.

This is not about projecting my own feelings onto the other person, and I'm not thinking, "He must be feeling this or that." The best I can describe it, it's a direct, visceral experience of the other person's emotional state. Then it's like a spark suddenly goes from this feeling to my brain, and ideas just start popping.

We asked Don if he could describe an example of something recent where this had happened:

A few months ago, a man was sitting across from me, just where you're sitting now. He represents a nonprofit organization that certifies organic products. We'd given them a large grant, and they'd become a big success story. They were growing 20 percent a year.

But they were concerned about the results of customer surveys. There's a small group of consumers who started buying organic years ago. Much of their growth has come from people who are trying these products because they're something new. Their understanding of the real benefits seems shallow. With the greater expense of organic products, our grantee was concerned that interest would spike and then diminish.

They felt that the answer was better consumer education. But, because the majority of their revenue comes from licensing, they felt it would be a conflict of interest for them to receive donations to promote consumer education.

Many times what a person brings along with a problem like this is a good deal of pain and anxiety. These problems have to do with their ability to fulfill their mission, and they feel a lot is at stake. In this case I could feel that pain right here in the area just below my heart—in my solar plexus. I was feeling this knot of emotions in this man's solar plexus.

As I think of it, between what you might call "feeling the problem" and getting ideas to solve it I experience a space of "not knowing." It's like a feeling of acceptant anticipation—if there is such a word! It can be a very short space, or it can be longer. This is something I need to

pay more attention to. It's usually when I stay with not knowing a little longer that ideas come that address all aspects of a problem.

Then, as I said, I felt something like an electric spark. My brain was
turned on and ideas started coming. The main idea was that our foundation could establish a fund dedicated to promoting consumer education about organic products. Then their licensees and anyone else
concerned about this issue could contribute to the fund.

This was an edgy idea, because it required a high level of trust and
transparency between the foundation and the grantee organization.
By bringing its licensees into direct contact with the foundation, the
organization ran the risk that the foundation might mishandle these
relationships or hear negative things about the licensing program. But
the trust level was there, and the grantee organization embraced the
idea. Don added:

> When the ideas flow into dialogue, and I can see that something really
> needed is being created, a feeling of joy and gratitude comes over me.
> So the process ends up back in my heart, though I also feel it through-
> out my whole body.
>
> Sometimes it seems that something bigger is at work. Shortly after
> this meeting I've just described, I flew to L.A. to visit our office there.
> I had just come out of my hotel to find a place for lunch, when I ran
> into a woman who's one of our larger clients. We had lunch together,
> and a great deal happened. Potential new businesses were spawned.
> Later in the conversation, I mentioned the new fund for consumer ed-
> ucation on organic products, and she suddenly thought of a high-net-
> worth individual who'd want to help establish it.
>
> Things like this happen. It's amazing. When you get the sense that
> something bigger is at work, you've got to follow it. You get so much
> back when you do.

TEAM LEADERSHIP
AT THE SYNERGIST LEVEL

Stan powered down his laptop as Frank was shown into his office.
Looking spry for his sixty years, Stan had long ago developed the practice of "sensing" people. Nothing fancy, just a heightened attention to
his own physical presence and that of the other person. In a few sec-

onds, he could reliably sense Frank's comfort level and his readiness for open conversation.

Frank was nervous, and understandably so. Stan had just been assigned as interim CIO for a Fortune 50 manufacturing corporation, and Frank was one of his direct reports. For the past five years, the IT function had suffered from inadequate leadership. The last CIO used a hands-off, hub-and-spoke management style. His direct reports focused so much on their internal clients that the organization fragmented.

The corporation now had a new, IT-savvy CEO. After six months, he declared his intention to develop an IT function that would help differentiate the company from its competitors. To begin this transformation, he appointed Stan interim CIO and gave him from January to July to accomplish two major tasks: Get the 2,000-person organization moving in the right direction, and install a new CIO who could deliver on the CEO's vision.

Stan had begun his twenty-five-year tenure as an internal organization development consultant, but during the 1990s, he was tapped for a series of line management positions, creating the strategies and structures needed for emerging markets in Europe, Africa, and Asia. His formal title was senior VP of corporate governance, reporting directly to the CEO and the chairman of the board. He'd advised the board on four CEO successions and was still consulting to the CEO and the board—a rather unusual distinction.[12] Just before his CIO assignment, he'd completed an interim stint as head of Human Resources, where he'd changed HR strategy, made major personnel decisions, mobilized needed change, and found a new executive to take over the function—all in a very few months.

Although he was extremely bright and articulate, Stan had a way of engaging with others that put them at ease. In no time, Frank was telling him how much he wanted the CIO position and why he thought he was qualified. Stan said he appreciated Frank's forthrightness. But he steered the conversation to the question most on his mind: How prepared were Frank and his peers to transform their function into one that would help differentiate the company from its competitors?

Several months earlier, the corporation's senior leadership team approved a plan to create a consolidated Supply Chain function that would serve all five businesses, just like Finance and HR. The new structure would save the corporation billions of dollars over the next several years. In assessing the company's readiness to implement this change, the senior team looked at all the support organizations. Strategy and Law were ready. HR could help facilitate the change. Finance needed to learn to account for things differently, but that wouldn't be a problem. The only function that stood in the way was IT. Unless IT changed how it was managed and organized, the corporate change effort would be stymied.

Stan immediately reversed his predecessor's hub-and-spoke style of operating. The previous CIO brought the group together once every three months. Stan held day-long meetings on a monthly basis, with dinner together the evening before. During each intervening week, he held a half-hour phone conference where he got his own points out quickly, followed by a brief go-round. He also had monthly "net meetings" to communicate the latest developments to everyone in the global IT organization.

In his first two face-to-face meetings, Stan reiterated the CEO's high-level vision for IT and tried to focus the group on aligning with it. Because he had relatively little IT expertise, he relied heavily on the facilitative skills he'd developed as an OD professional. However, the first two meetings showed him just how fragmented the group had become:

> Marty was the strategy and architecture guy. Whenever he spoke, two of the five business guys—Frank and Gary—would each rebut whatever Marty said. But if Frank took the initiative and advocated his point of view, Gary would immediately rebut him. And vice versa. Classic bad group dynamics. I stopped the action several times and described what I saw. They acknowledged that what they were doing was counterproductive, but they kept doing it.
>
> Right after that second meeting, it hit me: Intentionally or not, I was being treated like a substitute teacher. They were just going through the motions, waiting to see what the "real" CIO would tell them to do.

By the third monthly meeting, Stan had talked with IT's internal customers, its middle managers, and the corporation's top executives about their perceptions of his management group. This group was too fragmented to support the corporate change effort effectively. If he had enough time, he felt he could develop them into a collaborative team capable of top-quality decisions. But the rest of the company couldn't wait that long.

Stan stepped back and took a wide-angle look at his management group as a system within a larger system (the IT organization), within a larger system (the corporation), within a yet larger system (its global marketplace). With this perspective, he realized that he needed to revise his approach completely:

> What came to mind was the metaphor of an energy field. I needed to set up a "container" or force field around the group—create conditions that would make it compelling for them to step up, get aligned, and take collective responsibility for acting on what they already knew they needed to do.[13]
>
> One of these conditions was an unflinching dose of the truth. They needed to know how their performance was viewed, and they needed to know that their stakeholders were watching them closely. Was this the right thing to do with a fragmented group with a very limited capacity for collaboration? I figured maybe if I treated them *as if* they were a highly trusting and evolved group of people, they'd rise to the occasion.

Stan began the third monthly meeting by having the CEO come in and talk to the group, coaching him before the meeting to pull no punches:

> He did a great job. He had a lot of IT experience, and he let them know he understood the challenges and the complexities. At the same time, he said in no uncertain terms that IT was the major impediment to improving corporate performance. He was very specific about what a revamped Supply Chain organization could deliver, *if* IT could move rapidly and help it get there—and how much it would cost the company if they didn't.

When the CEO left, Stan laid out the feedback he'd received from the company's senior leadership team and IT's middle managers. Despite viewing them as highly competent professionals, the people above and below them were deeply disappointed in how they functioned as a team. Although the company's individual business units were once content with their performance, now that IT was needed to support the reorganization, these units were holding the function to a new standard.

> I put two glaring examples on the table. Over a year and a half ago, they agreed on a portfolio management process and a reorganization plan. These two changes would have put them just where they needed to be to support the corporate restructuring effort. But they hadn't implemented either one!

Prior to the meeting, Stan had taken a close look at the original portfolio management proposal, and he was ready to make his first real declaration as CIO: The new process had to be implemented by June 1.

> I gave them two and a half months to put their corporate hats on and prioritize projects in a way that would support the new corporate configuration. They expressed a lot of consternation about this deadline, but I knew if they put together the right team, they could do a good job and do it on time.

Stan said he'd also reviewed the stalled reorganization plan and had told his HR manager to get ready to pull together a team of twenty of their best and brightest people from the next two levels. That team would have two months to review the original plan and come back with recommendations: Given the role we now need to play, will this plan get us there and, if not, what modifications are needed? They generated the list of people then and there.

> I took a page from the GE Work-Out process and told them, "In our May meeting, when they come back with recommendations, you need to decide on the spot how you want to move ahead on the reorganization. Implementation needs to start immediately thereafter. I'll be communicating the outcome of that meeting in the monthly net meeting the following week."[14]

Setting decision deadlines for these two projects helped Stan achieve another objective: He got the group's resistance to taking action out on the table.

> To move on portfolio management, they had to have tough conversations with their internal clients, who wanted new forms of support but also

wanted earlier promises kept. Reorganizing meant that their own jobs might change. All very compelling concerns. But when you say them out loud they're a little embarrassing, because you know that the only real alternative to embracing change is to fail because you're living in denial.

During the next two months, Stan made sure the rest of the organization was well-informed that changes were in the works. He frequently reiterated the CEO's message that their purpose wasn't to cut costs or downsize the function but to increase its effectiveness. After talking with his management group about how IT's reorganization process would work, he told those at lower levels that they'd be involved in working out the details.

In the May meeting, when the reorganization team's three representatives came to present their recommendations, Stan said, "A few months from now, I'm not going to be here. You're the ones who'll be leading the reorganization. So I'm going to leave the room, and you're going to act as a collective CIO."

> When I left the room, I felt I'd taken the final step in establishing the force field. They were facing three highly respected people who represented the rest of the organization. They were also very much aware that the whole senior leadership team was tracking their actions. No one dictated to them what IT's new structure had to be, but I felt it'd be hard for them not to step up and make good decisions.

With Stan out of the room, group members occasionally disagreed, but they stepped back and realized they were using different words to mean the same thing. They endorsed the team's recommendations with a few modifications, leaving one piece of the design open, to be determined during implementation. In Stan's view, what made it possible for them to be so productive in this meeting was "the force field, the container, the conditions that had been set up around them." Two weeks later, on June 1, the portfolio management process went live, just meeting Stan's deadline.

In July, Stan and his search committee selected the new CIO. Before she was officially on the payroll, he invited her to attend that month's management group meeting.

> For the first hour Carol sat and listened. During the second hour she asked questions. By the third she was making her views known. By the

end of the meeting, she'd become the new CIO. She made it clear that she supported the direction we'd taken. Any remaining obstacles to change dissolved at that point. Now that she's full time, she's picked up the pace on the reorganization, which will mesh well with the corporate restructuring process that's already under way.

To wrap up, we asked Stan about the sense of purpose that animates the various roles he continues to play in this large corporation:

I've had a remarkable opportunity to shape not only the succession process but also the operating models we've used to remain competitive. As we head into the twenty-first century, I think we have an opportunity to construct something that people can look back at ten years from now and say, "Wow! So that's how you attract, identify, and develop the best leaders. So that's how you organize to be fast, flexible, and responsive amid continuous and often disruptive change."

I'd also like us to become a model for what it looks like for a large corporation to be socially and environmentally responsible. As the senior VP of corporate governance, I work closely with the senior VP of quality to champion social responsibility and environmental health and safety at the top level of the company. Our new CEO is more sensitive to these issues, so that helps.

As a global manufacturing company, we can model ways to excel financially while minimizing our environmental impact. I also want to see us build on current efforts, where we're using our corporate wherewithal to get people who are desperately poor the resources they need to empower themselves by developing their own local economies and by solving their own health, education, and transportation issues. That's why I enjoy going to China and India to advise major firms there on how to govern themselves, so they can attract capital and connect to the more developed parts of the world.

What means more to me than anything else is cross-pollinating with other people who're like little lights all over the planet, doing things that make the world a better place.

LEADING ORGANIZATIONAL CHANGE AT THE SYNERGIST LEVEL

It was hard for Laura to say good-bye to her friends in Boulder, especially those who'd stayed close to her through her husband's battle with cancer and the early months of her grief. As she drove the big U-Haul truck through the wheat fields of Kansas, great feelings of sadness washed over her in waves. For the past year it seemed like everything in her life had been about losing what she'd come to treasure: Eric, whose smile had warmed her heart until the end, and now the wonderful community of friends in Boulder and the mountains she loved so much. She knew now how to let the waves of sadness come and pass away and to face whatever came next.

Only as she barreled toward New England did she feel a spark of excitement about the new life that awaited her. For the past three years, she'd run an innovative health education program at a local university. Although she was only thirty-two, administrators at one of Boston's leading universities had heard about her work and offered her a position in their student health center.

The new job included two roles. She'd spend half her time overseeing an array of initiatives designed to promote student health—programs that dealt with drugs and alcohol, depression and anxiety, eating problems, rape prevention, and sexual health. The other half of the time she'd be renovating and administering a program that gave volunteer pre-med students experience as medical assistants in the university's student health center.

Laura was especially excited about the program for pre-med students. Charles, the student health center director who'd hired her, said the model they'd been using for the program, now over ten years old, no longer worked. He said he wanted her to apply the creativity evident in the Boulder program to the one in Boston. To Laura, this sounded like a dream job. Using innovative forms of education to provide future doctors with a broader vision of health care was very much in line with her sense of life purpose.

When Laura rolled into Boston in early August, she had no preset plan for the medical assistant program. She thought she'd take the first semester to establish herself in her two roles, get to know the students, and think about what an innovative medical assistant program might look like at a top-notch university.

In her first meeting with Charles, he told her to write a letter to all pre-med students, not only to introduce herself but also to tell them the program wouldn't be taking any new volunteers that year. The program, he said, was being downsized. Laura was stunned. She told Charles she was shocked to learn that shrinking the program was one of the changes he had in mind.

Without any hint of apology, Charles explained that this was a costly program and, to remain viable, it had to meet the needs of the health center as well as those of the volunteers. For a long time, the volunteers had filled a real need at the center. But now, with sixty students in the program, they slowed down patient visits and reduced needed contact time with professional clinicians.

Laura wrote the letter. What happened next, she said later, was "absolutely awful":

> What I immediately got back was hate mail. I'm not exaggerating. Some of the students actually came by my office, seething at me and saying "How dare you do this!" I'm a person who's very uncomfortable with conflict, so I found the students' reactions extremely painful.[15]
>
> Then their parents started complaining to the organization on campus that supports pre-med students. I started getting calls saying, "What do you mean, you're cutting people off from the program? This is going to jeopardize their careers!"
>
> When I went to Charles about this, I learned that my letter was the first communication the students had received about any changes in the program. The administration hadn't even told the students that my predecessor was leaving. Charles was totally taken aback by the reaction to the letter. He said he'd talk with the pre-med organization. Beyond that, whenever I asked for help, he pushed it all back on me, saying he knew I was a bright and creative "people person" who could handle this sort of thing.
>
> When I saw that this was the only stance Charles was willing to take, I was tremendously disheartened. For a short time, I got very depressed, feeling like I'd been duped and victimized. I'd left everything dear to me for this supposed dream job, and now I was living a nightmare. I also spent some time kicking myself: Why didn't I insist on more details about the job? Why didn't I ask Charles what had already been communicated to the students?
>
> On top of all this, I was still going through cycles of grief about Eric's death. I'd learned that the best way to deal with grief is not to shut down and wallow in it, but just let the waves of feeling flow through and subside at their own pace. So, while I was making space in my life for these feelings about Eric, I made some space too for the loss I was feeling about my "dream job."
>
> This gave me some inner strength and I stopped feeling so depressed. I knew that in the grand scheme of life this too would pass. And I did feel intuitively that there was some purpose for my being here. I felt that, if I moved ahead, being true to my purpose, things would somehow come together.

At that point I learned that a couple of the students were getting ready to meet, planning to organize the other students and write a letter of protest. My ability to relate to college students has always been my strong suit, so I asked to meet with them.

Meeting with Drew and Benny, two articulate pre-med students, Laura heard firsthand that students viewed the medical assistant program as a very well-organized opportunity that gave them lots of valuable hands-on experience. It also gave them an advantage in applying to top medical schools. After several of these meetings, Laura decided she needed to do something proactive to get the key stakeholders together:

I called a meeting of all the returning medical assistants, and most of them showed up. I also rounded up three of the six other health center administrators to be there with me.[16] Charles said he had a conflict and couldn't be there.

I opened the meeting and said we were here to open the lines of communication about the medical assistant program. I told them about my background and some of the innovative things we did in Boulder. I told them the problems that the health center had with their program. But I said that no decisions had been made about how to solve these problems and that I welcomed their input on that. Then I turned it over to their questions and concerns.

It was a very tense meeting. They somehow thought the program was being shut down, and I had to reiterate several times that it wasn't. Still, the students who spoke up didn't want *any* changes to be made. At the end, I said that I'd continue to meet with students and administrators until we'd worked this through. Then, as everyone left the meeting, a student named Justin came up to me. He was just seething. He told me how betrayed and hurt he felt. He said, "I won't ever forgive you for this!" I was close to tears when I left the meeting.

Over the next two months Laura continued to meet with Drew and Benny, whom the students had asked to speak for their interests. She had one-on-one and group meetings with administrators and health center staff, and she held three more meetings that brought everyone together. It was an extremely difficult, complex process, because everyone had a different agenda, and everyone was upset with everyone else.

Three tiers of nurses worked at the health center. The director of nursing services didn't like the medical assistants program, because the LPNs, the nurses with the least professional training, often sat back and let the volunteers do work the LPNs were supposed to do. Other nurses sometimes became de facto mentors for the volunteers. They loved that role and didn't want the program to change. The physicians, on the other hand, complained that they didn't get the amount of contact time they needed.

The program had always been three semesters. Prior to working at the health center, pre-med students spent a semester receiving sixty to eighty hours of specialized training. The students and their parents felt this initial semester was extremely valuable, but they wanted additional opportunities in the health center to strengthen their med school applications. In contrast, Laura's fellow administrators all wanted to reduce the number of volunteers at the health center, and they each had different visions for the program. A few, she sensed, didn't really care about it. They just wanted everyone to calm down.

From Laura's perspective, the pre-med students were much more unidimensional than the social work and public health students she'd worked with in Colorado. The Boulder students wanted to make a difference in their communities, socially and politically. The Boston pre-med students had a much narrower view of health care and focused only on their own careers. She thought the program would be a lot more fun and more meaningful if the students learned communication and teamwork skills and got some outreach experience. By interacting with people on campus and in the community, they could learn about the larger context of health care.

As far as she could see, Laura was the only person who felt there must be a way to get beyond mere compromise, to revise the program so it was actually better, not only for the students but for all the stakeholders.

> My way of approaching things is to engage with each group in an empathic way and to really feel the situation from their perspective. After meetings, I sometimes called people and asked, "Did I understand your concern correctly? What do you think about this idea?"
>
> Holding all this complexity in mind was kind of crazy-making and bewildering at times. I made lists. I drew diagrams. When I had a clear understanding of all the different perspectives, I came up with several models for a revised program, but I couldn't figure out anything that would meet everyone's needs. Yet I knew there had to be a way.

Pressure was building to find a solution. Laura spent the evening before the fourth large group gathering in the meeting room, filling the walls with flip-chart pages that summarized all the different perspectives. The next morning, as she stood in the shower, water pouring over her, all her ideas rearranged themselves in her mind. Everything suddenly came together. She quickly dressed and wrote it all down.[17]

All at once, I saw how these very disjointed needs and ideas could actually fit together. It was something I could put together quickly enough that I could train people for it the following semester. To tell the truth, it felt like I'd tapped into something beyond my ordinary intelligence.[18]

I got very excited, but I kept asking myself, "What am I forgetting? Will this really work?" I went in and ran the basic idea by a few staff people and asked them if they thought I was missing anything. They said it sounded great. I also talked with Benny and Drew, and they were all for it.

Before the meeting that afternoon, I went into the meeting room and made diagrams of what the program could look like from semester to semester, and I even sketched in a mock curriculum. It all came together in a couple of hours.

In the meeting, I really wasn't sure how they'd react. I thought we might have another big debate. But everybody loved it. They actually stood up and applauded. What a relief!

The new program retained the original three-semester format with its initial semester of training.[19] Although it still included training in basic intake procedures, the students would now experience a much richer learning process:

The new curriculum gets them thinking beyond symptoms. It exposes them to behavior change theory and holistic health models. We bring in social workers and public health people as speakers, so they learn about community health, why people wind up coming to the health center, what the contributing factors are, and why certain groups don't feel as comfortable coming there as others do.

The new program also helps the students develop as leaders by using experiential methods, like ropes courses, to help them learn communication and teamwork skills. Unlike all their regular pre-med courses, to succeed in this training they have to learn to collaborate. In fact, this program, with its emphasis on collaborative group activities, provides the one safe, noncompetitive place on campus where pre-med students can relax and form a circle of friends. It creates a very different kind of learning environment.

Another change: Students spend one semester in the health center and the other in an outreach program on campus and in the community:

> This cuts the number of volunteers in the health center in half. This way, everyone already in the program could complete all three semesters, and we didn't need to stop recruiting new students, although we did have to recruit half as many for each cohort.
>
> The organization on campus that supports pre-med students was OK with these changes, because they felt the increased quality of the program counterbalanced the fact that fewer students could participate.
>
> In the past, mentoring from the nurses was an informal, hit-or-miss thing. Now every student volunteer has a nurse-mentor who stays with them throughout the program. When I talk with the nurses who volunteer as mentors, they always say how much they enjoy sharing something they're passionate about. It gives them a greater sense of pride in the work they do every day.[20]

Each year, Laura has used a variety of different assessment methods to evaluate the program's effectiveness. Everyone is very pleased with it, from the medical assistants and their parents to administrators, health center staff, and the other students on campus. One bright Spring day, two school years after she first arrived on campus, Laura received an unsolicited evaluation in the form of a lovely card. It was from a student who'd been through the program, telling her how much he valued the experience. Later that afternoon, while she was completing some paperwork, he stopped by for a brief visit and thanked her for all she'd done. "It was a brave thing for Justin to do," she said later. "I really appreciated it. It helped bring everything full circle."

THE CAPACITIES OF SYNERGIST LEADERS

As with every previous level of agility, Synergist level competencies develop through a shift in your level of awareness and intent.

Synergist Awareness and Intent

Leaders at every post-heroic agility level have a heightened interest in attending to their ongoing experience. The key difference between the levels of awareness in each of these levels lies in the quality of attention. Catalysts can attend directly but momentarily to their ongoing experience, and they can reflectively recognize assumptions and emotional reactions immediately after they've occurred. Co-Creators can attend a bit longer to the flow of their ongoing experience, giving them the ability to access and verbalize experiences that would otherwise remain out of consciousness.

However, at the Co-Creator level, even when you enter intentionally into the flow state, your awareness is completely absorbed in what you're focused on at the moment. The extent to which this absorption in focal awareness limits your experience of life isn't readily apparent until you experience the level of awareness that emerges at the Synergist level. One person described this discovery in the following way:

> I suddenly realized I'd been asleep all these years, because I wasn't in the moment. I thought I was awake, but I was lost in a dream world. I couldn't actually see the present—and I didn't even know.[21]

At the Synergist level you begin to experience an alert and relaxed present-centered awareness that flows from one moment into the next. There is no mental description or evaluation of what's experienced, just bare awareness. Though a flower is immediately recognizable, it is no longer "a flower," just a vivid sensory experience without a label.[22] These simple moments of presence often give rise to subtle feelings of wonder or wonder. Ted, a Synergist who provides leadership development programs for large corporations, describes it this way:

> The most striking experiences I have when I enter the present moment are experiences of beauty. This happens many times every day with very ordinary things. For example, I'm on an airplane, tapping away on my laptop and, suddenly, I look over and see this Coca-Cola can, or I look ahead and see the light shining through someone's hair. When I really stop and look at things, it just knocks me out how beautiful the details are. I just slow down and take it in, and I get this feeling in my heart. I guess you could call it a sense of appreciation or gratitude.

What distinguishes this level of awareness from Co-Creator awareness is its unforced intentionality, its vividness, and the way your immediate awareness expands beyond the focus of your attention. The flow of present experience becomes so vibrant that whatever you happen to be focusing on stands out sharply from its background. You don't just see the flower (or the Coke can); you see it in contrast to an expanded, slightly out-of-focus, but nonetheless vivid sensory background. As with every other stage, Synergists don't (by any means) operate at this level of awareness at all times. However, in one way or another, they cultivate this awareness, and, whenever they have a genuine wish to do so, they can access it fairly readily.

At the Synergist level you have persistent interest in experiencing life in all its fullness. You also develop an enlivened sense of goodwill, a genuine intention to be of real benefit to others and to yourself. You often experience a sense of purpose that's even more present, palpable, and intangible than the sense of life purpose that emerged at the Co-Creator stage. Like Co-Creators, Synergists are often engaged in projects or organizations that are aligned with their sense of purpose, but they more frequently have specific experiences that feel deeply purposeful.

Like many Synergists, Don and Ted find that their awareness of the world around them often touches their hearts, evoking deeper emotions like joy, appreciation, gratitude, and empathy. While it's quite possible to touch this level of depth at previous levels of agility, at the Synergist level, one begins to experience heartfelt goodwill with increasing frequency even amid difficult everyday life situations.[23]

As you read through the capacities that support the Synergist level of leadership agility, keep two points in mind: First, the eight capacities are more integrated at this level than at any of the previous levels, so their descriptions overlap more than at any other level. Second, Synergists retain the capacities developed at earlier levels, including the capacity for reflection and analysis. In fact, the more you grow into the Synergist level, the more these previously developed capacities are enhanced.

Synergist Context-Setting Agility

When you grow through the post-heroic levels, your *situational awareness* and your *sense of purpose* expand in scope and time frame, but the primary way that they evolve is qualitative: Both capacities deepen.

SITUATIONAL AWARENESS. Virtually all the Synergists in our sample had a well-developed awareness of and concern about global issues. However, most of the Co-Creators in our sample displayed a similar capacity. The primary difference between Co-Creator and Synergist situational awareness is the latter's depth of insight into the human dimension of their larger environment. For this reason, there's a good deal of overlap between Synergists' situational awareness and their stakeholder understanding.

When Stan realized that the IT management team was avoiding a stance of collective accountability, he sensed that the fastest and most effective way to generate that stance was to align the "energy field" around the team in a manner that made this a compelling stance to take. Similarly, when Christine takes leadership initiatives, she detects the "vectors of energy" in the organization that are already moving in the desired direction, and she takes action that intentionally amplifies this positive energy.[24] At one point in Jeff's conversation with Tom, he "held the space" that opened up between them. Although the terminology varies, in each case, these leaders were able to perceive and work with something subtle and significant in the context surrounding their initiative.[25]

SENSE OF PURPOSE. The evolving sense of purpose experienced at the Co-Creator level motivates leaders to undertake initiatives that are personally fulfilling and, at the same time, empowering for others. At the Synergist stage, this sense of living "on purpose" comes alive in the moment with much greater frequency. For example, Ted, the leadership development consultant introduced earlier, spoke not only about moments of beauty but also about moments of purposefulness:

> Many of my leadership development programs involve team meetings where we customize various aspects of the program. It's usually a couple of my consultants and myself working with a similar number of people from the client company. Sometimes in these meetings I have this beautiful feeling of the rightness of the moment—the sense not only of doing something really worthwhile but also of being well used, as if I were made for that particular moment with that particular group or company. Part of what makes these experiences so enjoyable is that they feel so creative. For instance, we might be at a place where the team is stuck, and then a new energy comes in that allows the group to shift and reformulate the issue at hand in a more holistic way.

Synergists often tune in to what might be called "next step intuitions"—inner promptings that help them align with their purpose.

For example, Jeff prepared for his dinner meeting by "going into a sort of meditation on Tom." He experienced a kaleidoscope of images and emotions that lead to an intuitive sense of how to approach their dinner together. In a similar way, when Don follows his intuitions, he often has synchronistic encounters that generate creative possibilities and unexpected next steps.

However, as Ted stressed in our interview, these next-step intuitions aren't always entirely pleasant. As we noted earlier, many of Christine's leadership initiatives are prompted by "a still small voice within, a deep knowing that's a part of myself and yet apart from myself and guiding me." At the same time, one of her strengths is her willingness to acknowledge the feelings of fear and dread that these promptings can generate. To cite another example: Laura had a deep feeling that the new job in Boston somehow represented the next step in her development, yet she found it very difficult to leave Boulder, and even more difficult to navigate the early months in Boston.

Leadership expert John Schuster notes that such feelings of trepidation can arise because, at these "moments of truth," a leader is often challenged to take a big step in personal development. He continues:

> One sign that the real voice, the substantive call, is at work is feeling a kind of fear. If the voice makes you quake a bit, or even a lot, on the big issues you face, then you may well be in the right path. . . .
>
> [This particular fear is about] a need to do something that is not easy, that you may or may not love or be totally equipped for, and which you know will both put something into you and take something out of you. . . .
>
> Another indication that the real voice and not your ego is at work is when the cause or the problem you address is beyond what you could possibly finish in your lifetime with even your most Herculean efforts.[26]

Perhaps one reason Synergists experience these inner promptings is that they frequently return to questions like Why do I work in the first place? or, as Christine says, "When we remember Who we work for, whether you see this as God or nature or the Great Spirit or a vision of what our world could be like, we go to the largest context. If we work for anything smaller, we get lost in personality conflicts, politics, and our own pettiness."

Synergist Stakeholder Agility

Synergists' level of stakeholder agility is made possible by their level of *stakeholder understanding* and their *power style.*

STAKEHOLDER UNDERSTANDING. Different Synergists tune in to others in different ways. However, if we recall Jeff sitting across the dinner table from Tom, Don sitting across from his grantee, and Stan sitting across the desk from Frank, we see that they all have something in common: an ability to attend deeply to other people while maintaining a background awareness of their own bodily presence.

Synergists also have the capacity to hold in mind, in an accurate and empathetic way, the views and interests of multiple and conflicting stakeholders, even under highly stressful circumstances. For example, Laura was able to maintain this level of awareness and remain focused on the common good, even when she was under attack from the stakeholders she most wanted to serve. We also see this capacity at work in Christine's remarkable and persistent ability to convert potential enemies into friends and allies.

POWER STYLE. At the Co-Creator level, you have the ability to use many kinds of power: expertise and positional power, personal and political power, the power of vision and participation, and the power of life purpose and deep collaboration. At the Synergist level, you add to these capacities the power of presence. By *presence* we don't necessarily mean charisma. Some leaders become more charismatic as they grow through the post-heroic levels, while others don't seem to change on this dimension. Still others let their charismatic tendencies mellow, because they detract from authentic presence and connection with others.

By "the power of presence" we simply mean the subtle power and agility that comes from being centered in the present moment. This capacity allows Synergist leaders to take a more playful approach to power than we find at any previous level. Take, for example, Stan's ability to shift gears from a directive power orientation (when he took over HR) to a facilitative orientation (when he first became interim CIO) to a power orientation that was both directive and facilitative. He played with the various sources of power available to him in much the same way that an accomplished artist might play with variations of light and shadow in an oil painting.

The power of presence also contributes to an integrated power style that allows Synergists to embrace their assertive side and their receptive side at the same time. By taking this highly balanced stance, Synergists can remain fully centered in their own sense of what is needed and, at the same time, be highly responsive to the felt needs of stakeholders, even when those needs seem to conflict with their own. For example, Laura took the views and interests of all her stakeholders very seriously, holding them all in mind (along with her own), even when it seemed impossible that important aspects of her own vision would ever be realized. Ultimately, by staying with this ongoing power tension, a solution emerged that worked not only for all her stakeholders but also for herself.[27]

Synergist Creative Agility

Synergist leaders are masters at transforming ill-structured problems into desired results. Their creative agility is supported by their well-developed capacities for *connective awareness* and *reflective judgment.*

CONNECTIVE AWARENESS. At the Synergist level, connective awareness becomes even more wide-ranging and creative than it was at the Co-Creator level. Many Synergist leaders have an ability to work simultaneously with the local and the global. For example, recall Stan's ability to see his IT management group as a system within a larger system (the IT organization), within a larger system (the corporation), within a yet larger system (its global marketplace). Christine has a similar capacity. She can examine an issue like inner-city violence and connect it with projects and people in systems ranging from her own company to the continent of Africa.

Another aspect of connective awareness is the ability to hold in mind multiple and conflicting ideas, emotions, and possibilities. Leaders at the Co-Creator level have the ability to understand differing interests and viewpoints, note key points of commonality and difference, identify shared solution criteria, and then think creatively about solutions that meet everyone's criteria. At the Synergist level, the emergence of present-centered awareness makes it possible to take this capacity for thinking to another level.

Leaders at the Synergist stage often have the novel ability to access "synergistic intuitions" that resolve apparently irreconcilable conflicts in ways that are beneficial for all parties involved. For example, Don's inner question, "How can I help you?" takes him to a deep place where he empathizes so fully with another person's problem that he can accurately feel their pain. When he remains present to the problem and the pain, this triggers a rapid intuitive process that leads to ideas that will benefit a wide range of people. Laura's epiphany in the shower provides another example, as does Jeff's conversation with Tom.

What differentiates this process from thinking at the Co-Creator level is its emphasis on surrendering to a direct experience of the impasse, the "not-knowing," where feelings oppose each other and nothing seems possible. Attending to this experience in a conscious, patient, and caring way liberates energy and opens the way for new, synergistic possibilities. Synergistic intuitions are similar to the intuitive breakthroughs that lie behind many scientific discoveries.[28] The main difference is that Synergist leaders access this level of creativity to address conflicts that arise within and between human beings.

REFLECTIVE JUDGMENT. At the Achiever level, your budding awareness of human subjectivity leads to an emphasis on data-based problem solving. At the Catalyst level, you become attuned to the influence that differing frames of reference have on problem definitions and solution ideas. At the Co-Creator level, you develop an ability to enter unfamiliar interpretive frameworks and imaginatively experience them from the inside out. When you grow into the Synergist level, your present-centered awareness allows you to enter even more deeply into multiple and conflicting ways of framing reality.

At the Synergist level, the more alertly present you are to your everyday life perceptions, the more deeply you understand the subjectivity of all human perception. At the same time, you find that present-centered awareness has a remarkably objective quality, not in the conventional sense of "rational conclusion based on verifiable empirical data" but as a direct, wordless awareness of bodily postures, trains of thought, and emotional reactions.[29]

In a similar way, a Synergist's sense of purposefulness in the moment can have a "feeling of rightness" about it, as Ted put it earlier. So can a breakthrough intuition that seems to work for all key stakeholders. Consequently, at the Synergist level you can sometimes find yourself in the paradoxical position of feeling you really know something, all the time being keenly aware that you are a thoroughly subjective human being.

To resolve this paradox, the leaders featured in this chapter do what scientists do when they have breakthrough intuitions: They find ways to test the validity of their insights. When everything shifted in Laura's mind and what seemed like a multiple-win solution fell into place, she did not walk into the office and announce, "I've just received the answer to all our problems from a source of intelligence beyond my ordinary consciousness." Instead, she first asked herself and a few key stakeholders if the idea would really work for everyone. Then she laid it out in detail at a meeting attended by all the stakeholders and asked for their feedback. Only at the end of that process did she decide that it was really going to work.

The other Synergists in this chapter tested their intuitive breakthroughs by putting them into action, observing the results, and finding that they had real practical value. In most cases, the results not only were beneficial for others, they also contributed to the leader's personal and professional development.

Synergist Self-Leadership Agility

Finally, the capacities of *self-awareness* and *developmental motivation* affect the Synergist's self-leadership agility.

SELF-AWARENESS. Catalysts can reflectively recognize underlying assumptions and emotional reactions immediately after they've occurred. Co-Creators can access and verbalize thoughts and feelings that would otherwise remain just below the surface of conscious awareness. At the Synergist level, you develop an interest in cultivating a direct, present-centered awareness of your five senses, your inner physical sensations, your thought processes, and your emotional responses.[30]

On a physical level, you discover that full attention to muscular tensions helps these tensions relax. When you attend to your breathing, without trying to alter it in any way, it becomes smoother and more relaxed. Simple acts like walking down the hall and driving your car become gateways to a more vivid experience of life. By cultivating this awareness in a wide variety of everyday activities, you receive nonjudgmental glimpses of your habits of physical expression: postures, gestures, facial expressions, and tones of voice.

You also become more familiar with what begins to feel like relentless mental chatter. As one Synergist put it:

> I take a thought and keep it alive by worrying it like a loose tooth. They keep spinning around, and they keep my mind going all the time—thoughts about the past and thoughts about the future, so very little of my being is actually in the present.

Repeatedly, you see your mind take an experience like a walk on the seashore and obscure its freshness with past associations and mental commentary. You see how language, in fact thought itself, biases perception and expression. Through these experiences, you begin to realize that your mental associations and emotional reactions are actually more automatic and habitual that you'd formerly realized.

As you learn to relax obsessive thinking and inhabit your own body, you begin to experience your emotional reactions more directly. At the Co-Creator level, your experience of your feelings is tied to a "story line" about what happened and why, and what might happen in the future. As you grow into the Synergist level, you develop an increasing capacity to drop the story line and experience emotions as energies coursing through your body.[31] For example, you might experience excitement as energy moving up through your torso, wanting to leap into expression. You might experience fear as an energetic tightening in various parts of your body, leaving you with cool hands and a dry tongue.

Here are two distinct examples of Synergist-level emotional awareness, recorded in the journal of a woman in her mid-sixties while taking a three-month sabbatical in the Pacific northwest:

> I notice pain in my chest, light and tender and pain-full. What shall I do with it? Let what happens happen. My breathing becomes deeper, stronger. Then lighter, again. There is water in my eyes. Not trying to understand it, just noticing what happens, I begin to understand in a way that is not transmissible to others. It is my own knowing.[32]
>
> Walking back to my cabin, I knew that I was angry with/at him. I knew that I didn't have to belt him with my anger to [resolve this feeling], though I had no idea how to go about it otherwise. In my cabin, I let me *feel* my anger, feel it totally. I *became* anger. Nothing else existed but anger. When I tried, then, to latch onto who or what I was angry with, I couldn't. . . . "At" or "with" seemed irrelevant. . . . That passed. I wasn't angry any more. All washed away.[33]

This ability to experience emotions in the present provides a more enlivening way to deal with conflicting emotions. Hal, a West Point graduate whose journey into personal growth eventually led him into roles as an academic administrator and a government official, provides an illuminating description of the Synergist's approach to conflicting feelings:

> I am finding that I have many polarities, many contradictory feelings or dichotomies that often leave me confused. To the degree that I force myself to clear it up or deny it, I find that I avoid my real feelings, deceive myself, and end up more confused than ever. My life is a contradiction: tough and weak, love and hate, joy and sorrow, pain and pleasure, feelings and intellect. I am only beginning to accept—to surrender to—the experience of being all of these things. The inner place where my polarities meet is the place where I am stuck, and where my pain exists, and where, after I surrender to myself, my joy overflows and my aliveness grows.[34]

DEVELOPMENTAL MOTIVATION. What Christine calls "the search for a story that's worth your life" is not a search for fame or fortune but a search for life purpose, motivated by the wish to experience life in all its fullness and to be of benefit to others and to yourself. As Denise described it in Chapter Seven, this sense of purpose is "something that keeps evolving as you keep discovering it." At the Synergist level, this process of discovery often unfolds in moments of purposefulness, sometimes feeling prompted to take another step on your path, sometimes simply feeling, as Ted put it, "well-used."

Particularly at the Synergist level, the leadership initiatives that feel most purposeful often challenge you to develop further, both personally and professionally. Quite frequently, these initiatives call on your greatest strengths and, at the same time, evoke your greatest fears and limitations. The opportunity they provide, as Christine has noted, is to use your strengths to stretch beyond your limitations.

Yet Synergists don't need special challenges to motivate them toward continued growth. As we've seen, they feel motivated to bring a present-centered awareness and a sense of goodwill into as much of their lives as possible. In so doing, they gradually and inevitably become more vividly aware of the power and pervasiveness of the habitual reactions that pull them away from their aspirations.

For example, consider the following journal entry by Matt, a young organization development professional. At the time of this entry, he'd been meditating for about three years and had a strong interest in bringing present-centered awareness into his everyday life:

This past week I was able to open my awareness to the present fairly often—a soft, clear awareness that doesn't interfere with what I'm doing at the time.

I'm starting to see how reactive and habitual I am. I began, almost for the first time, to be aware of judgments and daydreams without interfering with them—just seeing them for what they are. When I'm aware of the movement of my attention, I see that it's pulled here and there, as if it has no life of its own.

On Saturday morning, I had a very uncomfortable conversation with my mother. The rest of the day I was constantly getting sucked into negative feelings, resentments, arguments that went around and around in my head. It was very hard to get back to the present moment. Finally, when I was hitting balls against the backboard at the tennis court, I came back into my body, standing, swinging the racket. It was a very powerful experience, like being in another world.

Repeated experiences like these generate the motivation to increase the frequency and depth of these periods of presence. This motivation isn't something you can force. It's an energy that grows naturally when it's fed with attention.

PART THREE

Becoming a More Agile Leader

CHAPTER NINE

Assessing Leadership Agility

The final two chapters of this book are designed to help you use what you've learned in Parts One and Two to increase your leadership agility. This chapter guides you through a more individualized assessment of your leadership agility, noting where it's already strong and where it needs improvement. You can also use this chapter to assess the agility of managers who work for you. If you're a leadership development professional, you can use it to assess yourself and the managers you support. Chapter Ten outlines steps you can take to become a more agile leader.

FREQUENTLY ASKED QUESTIONS

When managers make a thoughtful assessment of their leadership agility, they frequently ask a few key questions. We'll answer these questions, then guide you through your own self-assessment. Feel free to skip any questions that aren't yours.

Leadership Agility and Levels
of Organizational Responsibility

Some people wonder how the leadership agility levels are related to levels of organizational responsibility. Are the earlier agility levels better suited to lower levels of responsibility? Are the more advanced agility levels needed for higher levels of responsibility? Managers often ask these questions because they want to know if higher levels of agility will help them assume higher levels of responsibility. Leadership development professionals also ask these questions as they consider how to use this framework with the leaders they support.

Can you use a manager's level of organizational responsibility to predict level of leadership agility, or vice versa? The stories in Part Two (and perhaps your own experience) show that level of responsibility isn't a reliable predictor of a manager's agility level. For example, you've read about five CEOs who operated at five different agility levels.[1] Similarly, agility level doesn't predict level of responsibility. If it did, one of our Synergist exemplars (Laura) wouldn't be a junior administrator.

Yet, statistically speaking, there is *some* relationship between agility level and organizational responsibility. Table 9.1 summarizes findings from a series of studies that assessed the agility levels of managers at four different levels of organizational responsibility.[2] The table shows that there's no one-to-one correspondence between the two kinds of levels. Yet, on the whole, we see that managers at higher organizational

		Level of Responsibility			
	First-Line Supervisors $n = 37$	Junior and Middle Managers $n = 177$	Senior Managers $n = 66$	Executives $n = 104$	Total $n = 384$
Agility Level	(%)	(%)	(%)	(%)	Rounded Averages (%)[3]
Pre-Expert	24	14	6	3	11
Expert	68	43.5	47	43.5	46
Achiever	8	40	33	39.5	36
Post-Heroic	0	2.5	14	14	7

Table 9.1. Correlations Between Agility and Responsibility Levels.

levels tend to be somewhat more agile than those with lower levels of responsibility.

A more relevant way to ask the question would be, Are higher levels of agility *needed to be effective* at higher levels of organizational responsibility? Studies that have addressed this topic haven't identified threshold levels of agility required for effective leadership at specific levels of responsibility.[4] However, they have found that managers at all responsibility levels, from frontline supervisor to CEO, become more effective as their level of agility rises.[5]

This brings us back to a finding we highlighted in Chapter One: The best criterion for determining the level of agility needed to be effective in your role is the degree of change and complexity you face on a daily basis. In the past, top executives have been more directly exposed to environmental turbulence than those at lower levels of responsibility. However, in recent decades, change and complexity have penetrated organizations to such an extent that higher levels of agility are now required for effective leadership at all levels of responsibility.

Leadership Agility and Leadership Effectiveness

We've said that leadership agility is a master competency needed for sustained success in today's turbulent economy. Does this mean that the four leadership agility competencies are all you need to be an effective leader in today's complex, rapidly changing environment? It does not.

For example, think of everything Ed had going for him when he became CEO of Overmyer AMT: He was bright and had a solid educational background. He had many years of managerial experience and a ready grasp of business and technological issues. He was known for his initiative and his strong track record. These may be only some of the success factors you personally want and need to cultivate in your quest to become an increasingly effective leader.

As we see it, leadership agility is an essential supplement to the full range of leadership success factors. Think of it as a meta-competency because it enhances all your other competencies. For example, whatever skills, mind-sets, and personal qualities you need to become a more effective leader, self-leadership agility enhances your ability to identify and develop them.

Leadership Agility and Corporate Responsibility

A very small percentage of the Achievers we studied incorporated considerations of social and environmental responsibility into their initiatives. This percentage increased noticeably at the Catalyst level. All the leaders featured in the Co-Creator and Synergist chapters incorporated a strong personal commitment to social and environmental responsibility into their initiatives on a regular basis.[6] Does this mean that such a commitment is a prerequisite for higher levels of leadership agility?

Our research was not explicitly designed to answer this question. However, we believe the findings we've just described are a reflection of the capacities developed at each level: Experts are unlikely to be proactive in taking socially or environmentally responsible initiatives, because they give limited attention to the larger context of their initiatives. Some Achievers may undertake socially or environmentally responsible initiatives because they're consistent with their value and belief systems. Others may do so simply because they see them as a way to achieve other highly valued outcomes, like enhanced corporate reputation.[7]

Why are post-heroic leaders increasingly likely to have a strong personal commitment to corporate responsibility? Because their situational awareness, sense of purpose, stakeholder understanding, and power style all develop to levels that motivate them to do so. The primary difference between Co-Creators and Synergists in our sample is that Synergists, on the whole, were prepared to take even greater risks on behalf of these principles. Our overall conclusion: Commitment to social and environmental responsibility isn't a necessary condition for more advanced levels of leadership agility, but in most cases it seems to be a natural outgrowth of developing to these levels.

FINE-TUNING YOUR SELF-ASSESSMENT

In our experience, the best support for increasing your agility is a workshop, coaching relationship, or action learning program that focuses specifically on leadership agility.[8] Beyond this, the primary engine for developing increased agility is self-leadership: Being proactive in assessing your current strengths and limitations, clarifying your development goals, and using your everyday initiatives to experiment with more agile attitudes and behaviors.[9]

Identifying Your Current Level of Leadership Agility

Although no one's leadership agility level is the same at all times, everyone has a home base—a level of agility they return to repeatedly throughout the day.[10] At this point, you may feel you already know your current level of leadership agility. If not, we recommend that you review the chart in Chapter One, Ed's scenarios in Chapter Two, or the chapters from Part Two with which you most strongly identify.

When you assess your level of agility, it's a good idea to compare your own perceptions with feedback from other people. By talking with three or four people, you can conduct an informal, small-scale 360-degree feedback process.[11] Show them the chart in Chapter One. Ask what level best describes the way you operate most of the time in each of the three action arenas. The best people to select will meet two criteria: First, between them, they're familiar with your behavior in a variety of different settings. Second, you can trust them to give you open and honest feedback.

When you get their feedback, it's helpful to ask them to illustrate general comments with brief stories or concrete examples. In the end, you have to make your own assessment. For example, if some people think you lead your team like an Achiever and others think you lead it like an Expert, consider these opinions in light of your own experience and the examples they've provided.

Downshifting

Some managers are so aware that they operate at multiple agility levels, they find it difficult to identify their home base. For example, you may feel that you split your time between the Catalyst, Achiever, and Expert levels. If you identify with a broad set of Catalyst characteristics, this means that the Catalyst level is your home base, but you downshift to other levels of agility when the situation calls for it. For example, if the situation allows, Catalysts often develop a long-range vision. Yet they also have to think about medium-term strategy and short-term tactics. The fact that you downshift doesn't mean you have multiple home bases.[12]

Growing into a New Agility Level

In the preceding example, the idea that your behavior reflects intentional downshifting makes sense if you feel you're fully established at the Catalyst level. Alternatively, you may feel that you're moving frequently back and forth between two levels, like Achiever and Catalyst. If so, you may be in the process of growing from one level to another. Being in transition between levels is quite different from downshifting. The more advanced level feels like a newly preferred way to take leadership, while the previous level feels older and more familiar. It's a developmental process that involves shifting up to a new level of agility, unconsciously falling back into old ways, and repeatedly shifting back to the new level until it gradually becomes home base.

As an example, recall Guy, the call center manager in Chapters Four and Five who was promoted into a new knowledge management position. He'd fully mastered the Expert level, but to be effective in his new job, he needed to move from the Expert level to the Achiever level. We say more about the process of moving from one level to another in the next chapter. Meanwhile, if you feel you're in the midst of a similar transition, we recommend that you make yourself familiar with both levels of agility.

Straddling Two Levels

Here's another possibility: You strongly identify with certain elements in each of two successive levels of agility, but you don't feel you're actively growing into the more advanced level. Many managers find themselves in this situation. For some, it's because they consistently use different agility levels in different action arenas. An example would be someone who operates primarily at the Catalyst level when leading organizational change, but at the Achiever level when leading teams and engaging in pivotal conversations. Other managers straddle two agility levels because they've developed some leadership agility competencies more than others. For instance, a leader might operate at the Catalyst level of creative agility but otherwise operate at the Achiever level. If you've plateaued in a way that leaves you straddling two agility levels, your opportunity is to transform this static split into an active process of growth that will bring you fully into the more advanced level.

For example, in Chapter Four, when we met Carlos, the accounting department manager, he'd mastered the Expert level of agility and had developed a certain degree of Achiever-level stakeholder agility, mainly because he had a strong capacity for stakeholder understanding. However, he had plateaued at this point. To complete his development of Achiever-level stakeholder agility, Carlos needed to forge a more balanced power style. By doing this and also developing his context-setting, creative, and self-leadership agility, he became a highly competent Achiever-level manager.

Unintentional Downshifting and Emotional Hijacking

Some leaders (usually post-heroic) are so aware that they unintentionally shift into lower agility levels that they have trouble identifying with one home base. For example, a Co-Creator leader might say, "I usually try to develop collaborative relationships with my stakeholders, but sometimes, without intending to, I act like an Expert or an Achiever. I either assume I'm right and don't even ask for their input, or I ask for input, but it's really just to get them to buy in to my own ideas."[13] We call this *unintentional downshifting.*

Other leaders hesitate to identify a single home base because of what Daniel Goleman, author of *Emotional Intelligence,* calls "emotional hijacking."[14] This usually happens when a stressful situation triggers a strong reactive emotion such as anger, fear, depression, or professional jealousy. When the emotion takes over, your usual level of awareness and intent collapses down to a narrower level. For example, Larry, the Co-Creator leader, suddenly found himself yelling at his colleague, and Laura, the Synergist, went into a temporary depression when she came under attack from the students she hoped to serve.

Unintentional downshifting is a less extreme version of emotional hijacking. In both cases, emotional reactions arise that take you down a path you never intended. With unintentional downshifting, these reactions redirect your behavior because you're unaware of them. With emotional hijacking, it's because the emotions are so powerful.

People at all five agility levels experience both kinds of reactions. However, at higher levels you're more likely to be aware of the reactions as they're happening, and you're less likely to feed them and make them worse. To the extent that they do take over, you temporarily become much less agile than you are most of the time. In this sense it's quite accurate to say that your agility level fluctuates throughout the day. However, keep in mind that the purpose of the assessment you're doing now is to identify your home base, the leadership agility level you embody most of the time.

ASSESSING AGILITY WITHIN YOUR CURRENT LEVEL

When we say the five levels are stages in the mastery of leadership agility, it's natural to focus on the movement from stage to stage. Viewed in this way, leadership development is like climbing the rungs of a ladder. However, while this metaphor is accurate in some ways, it overlooks an essential part of leadership development: the process of mastery that takes place within each level.

Mastering Leadership Agility Levels

The process of mastering a level of leadership agility is better captured by a metaphor that comes from a particular genre of video games. These games are structured into multiple levels of play. At the outset, you assume the identity of a character who has only a rudimentary set of capabilities. You master each level of play by using the abilities you already have to successfully meet the challenges you encounter. Each successful encounter stretches you, giving you new powers or abilities. By the time you've mastered all the challenges on a particular level, you've also gained a new set of abilities. Once mastered, these abilities provide you with the foundation you need to enter the next level.

While it's possible that you've mastered your current agility level, most managers find they can develop further within their present level. So, if you're like most managers, you'll benefit from informally assessing where you are *within* your current agility level.

THE FOUR LEADERSHIP AGILITY COMPETENCIES. To do this informal assessment, you need to consider the four leadership agility competencies. The Leadership Agility Compass, originally introduced in

Chapter Three and repeated here as Figure 9.1, is a useful tool for this purpose.[15]

Look at the four quadrants. Which leadership agility competencies have you developed the most? Which do you want to master more fully? We recommend that you go back to the chapter that describes your current agility level and find the section toward the end that describes the competencies that emerge at that level. Use these descriptions to assess which competencies you feel you've developed the most and which you'd like to develop further.

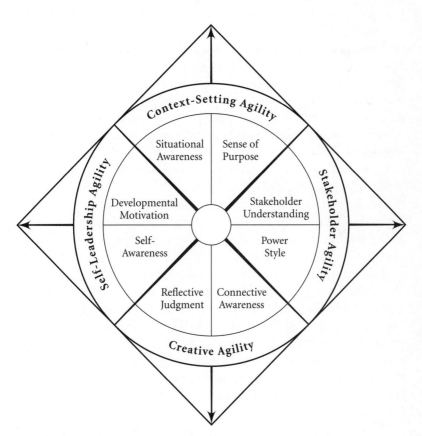

The innermost circle represents the level of awareness and intent that underlies each level of leadership agility.

Figure 9.1. Revisiting the Leadership Agility Compass.

A Real-Life Self-Assessment

Sarah was a bright, competent product development manager in a corporate business unit that made precision equipment for biotech and pharmaceutical labs. Having assessed herself as an Achiever-level leader, she solicited feedback from her colleagues, and discovered that she wasn't very effective in dealing with a particular kind of conversation. The example that caught her attention was a discussion she had with a QA manager who disagreed about a product's readiness to move from R&D to manufacturing. Although Sarah prided herself on being diplomatic, she reacted to the QA manager's opposition by asking loaded questions that made him defensive and even more resistant to her views.

Sarah gained two important insights from this feedback: First, she saw that her own behavior had contributed to the fact that this had been an unproductive conversation. Second, she realized that this wasn't an isolated example. She often reacted to these types of interactions in just this way, with similar results.[16] Third, her reactions in these situations were an example of unintentional downshifting. She decided she wanted to get to the point where she could respond to these situations in a manner that was consistent with her best Achiever-level capacities.

Sarah then used the Leadership Agility Compass to assess her strengths and limitations in responding to forceful opposition. One of her greatest strengths was her creative agility. However, in this type of situation, she had a low level of stakeholder agility, which significantly compromised her ability to find creative solutions. In addition, she wasn't making use of her context-setting agility. Although she knew that disagreements between R&D and QA are to be expected, she rarely took the initiative to frame the conversation in a way that invited cooperative problem solving. At the same time, self-leadership was one of Sarah's strengths: She was willing to take an honest look at herself, and she was willing to use her everyday initiatives to experiment toward greater effectiveness. In the next chapter you'll find out how she fared.

CHAPTER TEN

Developing
Leadership Agility

—ᴍᴠ— T his final chapter begins by helping you set leadership
development goals. As part of this process, you can decide whether
you want to develop further within your current agility level or
whether you want to develop to a whole new level. Either way, you'll
learn how to use "reflective action" to reach your development goals.
To show how this process works, we complete the story of Sarah, the
product development manager, who used reflective action to become
more effective while remaining at the Achiever level. We also describe
how Adam, a communications company VP, used reflective action to
move to the Catalyst level of agility. Finally, we explain how developing your attention can fuel your growth as a post-heroic leader.

SETTING LEADERSHIP
DEVELOPMENT GOALS

Once you've assessed your current level of leadership agility, the next
step in the self-leadership cycle is to set your leadership development
goals. When setting these goals, you need to decide whether you want

to move to a new level of leadership agility or simply to increase your agility within your current level.

Developing to a New Agility Level

In Chapters Four and Five Guy and Carlos both decided to move to a new level of agility. They each made this choice for the same reasons: First, to be effective in their roles, they had to learn new leadership behaviors. Guy wanted to develop skills that would help him succeed in working with stakeholders over whom he had no formal authority. Carlos wanted to become a true manager of his department. In both cases, the behaviors they needed to learn required them to move to the Achiever level of leadership agility. Second, Guy and Carlos were both fully developed Experts who were ready to move to a new level. Most managers who decide to move to a new level do so for these same two reasons. However, some are so primed to move to the next level that just learning about it triggers a strong motivation to go there.

However, simply deciding that you're ready to grow into a new level of leadership agility is not sufficient. As Guy and Carlos did, you also need to identify specific behavioral changes you want to make. Many managers try to make too many changes at once. Start by choosing two to four behaviors you want to learn that are consistent with your next level of leadership agility. As you begin to master these behaviors, you can add more.

Developing Within Your Current Level

While the idea of moving to a whole new level may be very compelling, it's also important to be pragmatic: Start where you are and take your next step. For many managers this means developing further within their current agility level. The story of Sarah, the manager we met in Chapter Nine, provides a good example of how much you can grow as a leader even within your current level.

As you'll remember, Sarah had trouble with a particular kind of work-related conversation: When coworkers forcefully opposed her position on important issues, she reacted by asking loaded questions that made them defensive and even more resistant. These encounters took place with some frequency, usually at crucial points in the product development process. Sarah found these discussions quite unpleasant.

Even more important, she estimated that an effective conversation at any of these pivotal points had the potential to save at least a month of cycle time.[1]

The feedback Sarah received helped her to see that the root cause of her difficulties lay in the power style she had adopted: When others forcefully opposed her, she responded by failing to adequately assert her own views. Why? She felt that, if she asserted herself too strongly, she'd jeopardize an important working relationship. Without realizing it, she tried to compensate for this accommodative style by asserting herself in an indirect and counterproductive manner: She asked loaded questions that felt like biting criticisms. Ironically, this produced the very results she hoped to avoid: She caved in on important issues, and she made the other person angry.

Once Sarah understood her contribution to these negative outcomes, she set her leadership development goals: She wanted to increase her stakeholder agility by balancing her power style and increasing her stakeholder understanding. Building on these insights, she identified three new behaviors she wanted to learn.

To develop a more balanced power style, she would learn to use "advocacy with inquiry" to solve problems in a collaborative manner: Instead of "zinging" the person who opposed her, she would be more forthright in advocating her views. Rather than acquiescing to the other person's views, she would couple her advocacy statements with inquiry: She'd sincerely ask for the other person's views and take them seriously. By inquiring in this way, she could empathize with others, even in the face of forceful opposition.[2]

Sarah chose two other behaviors to work on: She'd take the initiative to frame challenging conversations, letting others know she wanted to resolve the issue at hand in a collaborative way. In addition, if the other person became quite forceful, she would welcome their honesty, match their high energy level, and channel the conversation in a positive direction. Mastering these new behaviors would be challenging enough. If she had tried to do more, she would have overloaded herself.

SELF-LEADERSHIP IN ACTION

Once you've clarified your leadership development goals, the next step in the self-leadership cycle is to use your everyday initiatives to experiment with new behavior.

Sarah's Action Experiments

Sarah decided to try out her new behaviors in any situation where she felt her viewpoint was opposed by another person. Minor conflicts were especially welcome, because they provided low-risk opportunities to practice new behaviors. Sarah found opportunities to experiment with these behaviors on a daily basis. At the end of each day, she used the drive home to reflect and learn from her experiences. Once every week or so, she met with Ron, a senior product development manager who served as her coach and mentor. Ron helped her reflect on her experiments and offered his seasoned perspective on the organizational issues she faced.[3]

A few months into this process, Sarah received a call from a team of scientists who worked for one of her company's customers. The scientists had recently purchased a live cell imager, newest technology available. The new imager used a type of clear bottom plate designed only by Sarah's team and two of her company's competitors. Her customer's problem was that none of the plates on the market actually worked with the new imager.

By meeting with the scientists who used the imager, Sarah learned that the decision about which plate to buy would be made by higher-level managers. They, in turn, insisted on an unqualified endorsement by the imager's inventor, a scientist named Klaus who worked at the company that produced the new device. The scientists with whom Sarah met had already sent Klaus a sleeve of her plates for evaluation. Hoping to get on the inside track, she got permission to contact Klaus directly, and he agreed to send her a copy of his evaluation.

Sarah's Worst Nightmare

When Klaus's report arrived, the data showed that Sarah's plate met all the formally stated specifications except one, an issue she believed was correctable. But it also contained a number of comments implying that other, less clearly stated requirements hadn't been met. Even worse, the whole tone of the report was quite negative. Klaus not only refused to endorse her plate, he seemed to harbor a strong irrational bias against it. One of her fellow managers told her that, while she'd been on maternity leave, he'd clashed with Klaus over an earlier version of the plate, leaving both men angry and frustrated. A few other colleagues reported similar experiences.

Sarah's heart sank. She could see what was coming: She would have to meet with Klaus in person, and it would be exactly the kind of meeting she found most difficult. To get Klaus's endorsement, she knew she'd need to elicit all his criteria for an acceptable plate and gain his trust that her team could meet them. But as she thought about the irrational bias he seemed to hold against her product, she felt stymied. The next day, she talked it over with Ron.

The Reverse Role-Play

Ron knew that the meeting with Klaus posed a real challenge for Sarah. To help her replace her anxiety with a more centered, empathetic orientation, he invited her to try a coaching method we call the *reverse role-play*. This method is especially useful in helping leaders deepen their capacity for stakeholder understanding.[4]

Ron asked Sarah if she'd be willing to spend a few minutes putting herself in Klaus's place. She agreed. Rather than asking Sarah how she thought Klaus might feel, he asked her to imagine that she was Klaus, sitting in a chair and waiting for Sarah to come meet with him about the bottom plate problem. He said, "I know you haven't met Klaus yet, but draw on everything you've heard about him. Sit like you think he might sit, and imagine how he might speak." Because Sarah and Ron had developed a strong bond of trust, she was willing to go for it.

Ron then interviewed Sarah as if she were Klaus: "I understand you recently invented a new state-of-the-art cell imager. How do you feel about that accomplishment?" Sarah (as Klaus) said, "I am very proud of it. It's now the best imager on the market. But I'm very frustrated about these companies that make the bottom plate. No one has done it right! My new imager is worth nothing unless it has a good bottom plate to go with it." Ron asked Sarah to continue to "be" Klaus and to feel his pride and his frustration.

Ron then said, "I understand you're about to meet with Sarah, a manager from one of the companies you just mentioned." As Klaus, Sarah responded, "Yes. I did a report on their bottom plate. I haven't met her, but my last experience with her company was very frustrating." Ron asked, "What could Sarah do in your meeting that would allow you to respond positively to her efforts?" "Klaus" said, "I would want some kind of acknowledgment from Sarah about my previous frustrations in dealing with her company. I'd also need to be reassured, at a technical level and maybe even at a personal level, that I could trust these people with something so crucial to the future of my invention."[5]

When they finished the exercise, Ron asked Sarah what she'd learned. She said, "I feel that giving Klaus a chance to voice his frustrations and feel heard will be an important step in gaining his trust." As a way to do this, she would ask Klaus "what they should have learned" after producing the earlier version of the plate. This would help her understand Klaus's full set of specs within a constructive, "lessons learned" framework. Sarah then surprised herself by saying she owed Klaus a certain measure of gratitude. "Without being asked, he spent many hours testing our plate and producing a valuable analysis our team couldn't have done on its own. I'd like to explicitly recognize the value of what he's done."[6]

The Big Meeting

Sarah also realized that her meeting with Klaus could be a developmental opportunity not only for her but also for Janice and Scott, the two team members who'd be coming to the meeting with her. She decided to coach them on how they could contribute to the meeting in ways that were consistent with the approach she'd developed with Ron. She would take the lead at all the key transition points, but she gave them both important roles to play.

When they met with Klaus, Sarah expressed genuine appreciation for his report and told him she wanted to customize their plate to work perfectly with his new imager. Klaus smiled warmly. But when Sarah asked him what they should have learned after producing the earlier version, his negative feelings came pouring out. He listed problem after problem and expressed a great deal of frustration about all the time he'd wasted. Sarah and her team listened and asked clarifying questions. Then Klaus said, quite forcefully, that he would show them his reports on the earlier version.

Sensing that his past frustrations had now been heard, Sarah responded in a tone and volume that matched his high energy level: She said, "Thank you, Klaus! But we're so close to getting you a plate that meets your specs, I'd rather start from where we are today. How does that sound?" Klaus paused for a moment and responded, "Yes. Let's do that." His tone had shifted dramatically.

Janice and Scott reassured Klaus that they had new manufacturing technologies that would allow them to do what they hadn't been able to do previously. He clarified his full set of specifications, said their plate was already better than their competitors', and said he'd be happy to put in more time to test further iterations. Sarah was so astounded by the shift in Klaus's attitude that she repeated what he'd said, just to make sure she'd heard it correctly. By the time they'd wrapped up this remarkably short meeting, his recommendation of their plate was a virtual certainty. In addition, his help with testing would shorten time to market and ensure sales of his imager (with their plate) to a wide range of companies. Sarah later described it this way:

> We achieved all of our objectives and then some. By using a collaborative approach, we moved from a testy stand-off to a partnership relationship. Within a short period of time, we were first to market with the only plate that works with this brand new technology. My conservative estimate of the financial benefit to the company is at least $750,000 over a five-year period.

By repeatedly practicing self-leadership, Sarah accomplished two objectives at the same time: She succeeded in her initiative, and she became a more agile leader.

THE POWER OF REFLECTIVE ACTION

At its core, leadership agility is a process of stepping back from your current focus in a way that allows you to make wiser decisions and then fully engage in what needs to be done next. We call this core process *reflective action*. Reflective action is both the essence of leadership agility and the best way to develop it.

The Reflective Action Cycle

Reflective action is a four-step cycle that enhances the natural process of learning from experience. In Figure 10.1, each quadrant in the cycle represents one of the four steps.

In practice, you can begin the cycle with any of the four steps. To walk you through it, we begin in the lower-left quadrant with "assess situation and results":

1. *Assess situation and results:* Scan your environment and determine what issues (problems or opportunities) need your attention.

Figure 10.1. The Reflective Action Cycle.

2. *Diagnose:* When you identify an issue that needs attention, before you take action, try to understand what's causing the problem or preventing the opportunity from being realized.[7]

3. *Set intentions:* Clarify the results you want to achieve and determine how you can achieve them.

4. *Take action:* Carry out the steps you've decided to take.

5. *Assess situation and results:* Move on around to Step 1 and assess the results of your actions. Then keep the cycle going.

We all move through the reflective action cycle many times every day. However, we usually do so in a rather unconscious way. As a result, we miss much of the power it has to offer. What makes Sarah's story unusual is the proactive way she engaged in the cycle. Even more unusual is the fact that she also used it to practice self-leadership.[8]

When you practice self-leadership, you move through the reflective action cycle in a way that includes yourself. For example, consider how Sarah approached her meeting with Klaus: When she thought about the problems she needed to solve in that meeting, she included more than the technical issues and Klaus's volatility. She also focused on the challenge of remaining centered when she was forcefully opposed on important issues. When she set her intentions for the meeting, she had two kinds of objectives. One was to win Klaus's confidence. The other was to use the meeting to experiment with more effective attitudes and behaviors. These objectives were so complementary that they merged into a single intention.

The Resilient Attitude

Reflective action involves a willingness to experiment with new behaviors and look honestly at yourself, so it takes a certain degree of curiosity, courage, and self-confidence. It also requires a conviction that you're ultimately responsible not only for your own development but also for your response to whatever life brings your way. We call this the *resilient attitude,* because resilience encompasses everything we've just described. Its motivating force is what gives reflective action its juice.

Your level of resilience depends partly on your developmental motivation. As you know from earlier chapters, each time you move to a new level of leadership agility, your developmental motivation evolves to a new level. Generally speaking, at each new level the attitude with which you respond internally to your own successes and failures becomes more resilient.

In addition to your developmental motivation, your level of resilience also depends on a number of other factors.[9] If you want to maintain a resilient attitude, we recommend three brief daily practices: aerobic exercise, a centering practice (using a relaxation or meditation technique), and a simple "creative practice" that you find both satisfying and invigorating.[10] Experience has shown that doing each of these three practices for an average of just fifteen minutes each day builds a palpable feeling of well-being and a reliable reservoir of resilience.[11]

Making Reflective Action a Foundational Practice

To increase your leadership agility, it's very helpful to make reflective action a conscious daily practice. Each day, pick one issue (major or minor) that you want to address in a conscious and intentional manner. That's step one. Before you jump to a solution, make sure you understand the issue. That's step two. The third step has two parts. The first and most commonly overlooked is to clarify your desired *outcomes.* Then clarify what you'll do to achieve these outcomes. Finally, after you take action (step four), make a little time to reflect and learn from what happened.

Reflective action can be very rapid and intuitive, as in the midst of a conversation, or it can be more sustained and systematic, as in developing a new business strategy. What's important is to practice the four steps until they become second nature. You want to pay enough attention to diagnosis, objective-setting, and planning that it increases your effectiveness, but you don't want to get tied up in self-analysis or self-judgment. You want to learn to move through the cycle with a light touch. The more you nurture a resilient, self-empowering attitude toward the challenges you face, the more your commitment to reflective action will grow.

If you make reflective action a foundational practice, it can also increase your effectiveness in coaching the people who report to you. It helps in two ways. First, it will help you see that effective coaching involves activating and enhancing another person's commitment to reflective action. Second, when you make reflective action a daily practice, you model a commitment to lifelong learning that will serve as an inspiration for others.

LEVELS OF AWARENESS AND INTENT

Sarah's story shows how you can use reflective action to become substantially more agile even within your current level of leadership agility. But what if you're ready to move to a whole new level of agility? In this case, reflective action is still the key: You need to use your everyday initiatives to practice new leadership behaviors and develop the capacities that support them. Now, however, you focus on the behaviors and capacities associated with the new agility level. And here's the real secret: You do this using the *level of awareness and intent* that corresponds to your next level of leadership agility.[12]

What exactly does this mean, and how do you do it? As we've noted, the underlying dynamic of leadership agility is reflective action: You step back from your current focus to gain new insight and make wiser decisions, then engage in what needs to be done next. The process of stepping back corresponds to the first two steps in the reflective action cycle: selecting and understanding an issue. The other two steps capture the process of reengaging in action: you set your intention and do what you've decided to do. The depth and breadth of insight you gain from stepping back depends on your level of awareness. The way you set your intention and take action depends on your level of intent.

For example, because Sarah operated at the Achiever level, when she stepped back, she activated a capacity for robust after-the-fact reflection. She learned from her experience by pausing and reflecting after a meeting, in a coaching session, or on her drive home. When she set her intention and took action, she tapped into the Achiever's level of intent: She wanted to achieve her desired outcomes in a manner that was consistent with her values.

In her quest to develop further as an Achiever, this level of awareness and intent served Sarah well. To move to the Catalyst level of leadership agility, she'd need to engage in reflective action using the Catalyst level of awareness and intent. This would require her to develop the capacity to reflect on her thoughts, feelings, and behaviors *on the spot.* She'd also need to shift her underlying intent to focus on creating contexts that would make possible the sustained achievement of desired outcomes.

Before we provide a real-life example of this process, let's review the five levels of awareness and intent. (Note that each level of awareness and intent includes and goes beyond those developed at earlier levels of agility.)[13]

Heroic Levels

Expert   *Awareness:* A modest reflective capacity

            Intent: To improve and accomplish things

Achiever   *Awareness:* A robust reflective capacity

            Intent: To achieve desired outcomes in a way consistent with self-chosen values

Post-Heroic Levels

Catalyst   *Awareness:* The ability to step back "in the moment" and attend directly but very briefly to a current assumption, feeling, or behavior that would otherwise escape your attention

            Intent: To create contexts and facilitate processes that are experienced as meaningful and satisfying and that enable the sustained achievement of desired outcomes

Co-Creator *Awareness:* A slightly more sustained attention to the flow of your ongoing experience, giving you a more robust capacity for processing painful feelings and for understanding whole frames of reference that may differ from your own

Intent: To tap into an evolving sense of life purpose and actualize it in your everyday life through deep collaboration with others

Synergist   *Awareness:* Sustained, expanded present-centered attention to your physical presence, including your five senses, thought processes, intuitions, and emotional responses

Intent: To engage with life in all its fullness and to be of benefit to others as well as yourself

GROWING INTO A NEW AGILITY LEVEL

Adam had recently been promoted to VP of Central Services for a communications company headquartered in Chicago. He had eight direct reports, and his organization numbered several hundred people. At forty years old, he was a bright, competent manager who consistently exuded a natural enthusiasm, even though the company was going through rough times. The business had been restructured repeatedly in recent years, with several waves of layoffs.

As part of its comeback strategy, the company invested in a leadership development program for high-potential managers. As a participant in this program, Adam received 360-degree feedback and had the opportunity to select a leadership coach. He was also fortunate to have a supportive boss who gave him honest, constructive feedback on a regular basis.

A fully developed Achiever, Adam was a classic heroic leader who didn't like to ask for help. He rarely involved his team in the decisions he made. But he also realized that these tendencies held him back from being the leader he wanted to be. As soon as he learned about the Catalyst level of leadership agility, he knew it was the next step in his development. He wanted to build a participative team, take more time to develop his direct reports, and create a compelling vision for his organization.

Adam was also drawn to the Catalyst level because he wanted to experience a deeper sense of meaning in his life and work. He told his coach about a talk he'd attended recently, given by a retired business leader, who, like Adam, was African American:

It got me reflecting about my life. I'd like to be a CEO someday. But it's not about making money or getting to the top. I focus too much on being "professional," and I don't pay enough attention to my real passion. What am I all about? What's the thing I care about that's bigger than me? I want to get really clear about this and start living it more on a daily basis. That's my quest. I do know that I want to do something that changes the world for the better. I have a real passion for helping people, but I don't know what form I want it to take. My wife and I volunteered to help out with this great after-school program that provides kids with tutors, dieticians, and mentors. They deal with all aspects of a child's life. I was able to get our company to donate computers to the program. Do I want to volunteer for more things? Do I want to join a nonprofit board? I don't know yet.

Meanwhile, Adam was concerned about an upcoming presentation he had to make to a group of VPs in another unit. He'd be making the case for a new way to measure customers' satisfaction with the company's products and services. He was convinced that the new index would benefit the business in a number of ways, but he also knew that this group resisted new methodologies. "I have twenty minutes, max, to present this," he said. "My boss told me my presentations sometimes don't exude enough confidence. How can I project my passion for this new index in a way that will convince them of its value?"

It was an Achiever's question. Adam was thinking of the presentation as a performance: He felt he had to use the force of his personality to persuade a key stakeholder group to support his initiative.[14] His coach took him to the threshold between the Achiever and Catalyst levels: "For just a moment, go beyond your bullet points about company benefits and put yourself in the place of the people in this group. Are there ways that they, personally, will benefit from the new index?"

"Absolutely," Adam said, and he described the benefits. His coach then said, "From the way you talk about this, I can tell that your motivation isn't just to get a win for yourself. You actually care about these people and want to help them succeed." Adam nodded, and his coach continued, "I think that's where your real passion lies. Use your bullet points about company benefits. But also tell them how *they* will benefit. And rather than try to amp up your passion to persuade them, just speak from your heart—person to person—from that feeling that you want to help them succeed."

The meeting went extremely well. There were a few skeptics, but the group as a whole responded positively. Afterward, the group's EVP complimented Adam on the quality of his presentation and assured him that his group would adopt the new index. The next week, when Adam's coach asked him what he'd learned from the experience, he said:

> If you really want to communicate with someone, you've got to get into their world. Find out what's important to them and then just be real. Speak from the heart. This past week, I've been doing that a lot. Like with the two guys who just got moved onto my team. In my first one-on-ones with them, they each held back a lot. The conversations were just surface-level. So I decided to put myself more into their worlds, ask better questions, and get more real with them. It made a big difference. It even helps in talking with my wife.

When his coach saw how easily Adam had put this new behavior into action—and how quickly he transferred it to other situations—he felt that Adam was definitely ready for Catalyst-level self-leadership. In their next session, Adam raised an issue that provided an opportunity to get started. Whenever a male direct report had a performance problem, he could address the issue in a straightforward and constructive manner. However, he found it extremely hard to give negative feedback to women. "I wind up being too nice and just avoiding the issue," he said.

As he reflected on the reason for his avoidance, Adam realized he was afraid he might make the woman cry. Asked how he'd feel if a woman did begin to cry, he said he'd feel deep pangs of guilt. He said he had a similar problem with his six-year-old daughter. His wife complained that he allowed his daughter's whining to manipulate him into letting her do things that she really shouldn't.

Adam's coach suggested that he begin by focusing on his relationship with his daughter. For the next week, each time his daughter tried to do something he had any reservation about, he would simply observe his emotional reactions, *in the moment.* He wouldn't try to analyze *why* he felt as he did, and he wouldn't attempt to act differently. He would simply note the feeling and then let it go. This would build his capacity for Catalyst-level self-awareness, and he'd gain a better understanding of the emotional reactions that held him back.

To Adam's surprise, even though he didn't try to change his behavior, after several evenings of doing the exercise—he began to respond more firmly to his daughter's whining. In other words, as he gained more perspective on the feelings underlying his behavior, the feelings shifted and his behavior changed. His wife was amazed.

Adam continued to practice this exercise with his daughter at least once each evening. Two weeks later, he initiated a meeting with a woman whose performance issues he'd been avoiding. They had several candid conversations about her strengths and limitations, which ultimately led to a change in her job description.

As Adam began to practice Catalyst-level awareness in other situations, he observed other counterproductive emotional reactions. For example, he noticed that, whenever he was challenged, he felt he "had to be right."

The feeling is: If I'm not right, there's something wrong with me. For instance, I brought in some consultants to assess one of my units and make recommendations. The director who runs that unit came and complained to me. He felt that everything was under control and that I'd gone around him. That's when I noticed the feeling that I had to be right. I was so busy defending my position that I didn't get into his world and understand where he was coming from.

Adam's coach told him that heroic leaders have these feelings frequently, but they're often not aware of them. Because he knew Adam wanted to become a more participative leader, he asked him to consider his perception that the director's unit needed outside help. He then showed Adam how to act on that perception, and others like it, as a Catalyst would: Discuss it with the director first. Combine advocacy and inquiry. Have a conversation where each person's assessment and the reasoning behind it could be fully heard. Then, if he still believed that consultants were needed, he could use his authority and make that decision.

Adam was more resilient than the average manager. But when a new round of layoffs was planned, he told his coach that his stress level was rising. He already had a regular aerobic practice: He ran every day. So his coach introduced him to the other two resilience practices mentioned earlier in this chapter. Adam wasn't sure he wanted to learn to meditate, but he decided to take fifteen minutes of "alone time" every evening to relax and decompress. When it came to choosing a creative practice, he said he'd always wanted to learn to fly. He couldn't fly fifteen minutes a day, of course, but he took fifteen minutes most evenings to read about flying, and he took a flying lesson every weekend. He found it to be a thrilling experience.

Over the next several months, Adam found frequent opportunities to shift into Catalyst-level awareness, both at work and at home. Although many of his peers were in a constant frenzy, Adam became calmer, less frazzled, and more centered. Previously, his confidence was based on how well he thought he was performing. He now felt a growing sense of confidence in himself as a person. "I feel I can let people see the human side, the real me," he said. "I feel like I'm connecting with people more, person to person." His boss noticed the change as well. "You're speaking with more confidence," he said. "Asking more questions, not shooting from the hip so much. That's great!"

Adam also moved into more of a coaching relationship with his direct reports, particularly those who were more experienced:

> In the past I used to watch what Jason did very closely. I was always in there controlling and dictating. I would justify that on the basis that he was managing really important projects. I'd have him run things by me, and if I felt uneasy about his approach, we'd talk about it until my concern became his concern. But on his last big project I tried something new. This was an employee engagement survey, a huge company-wide project with high visibility. I had virtually no input into the design or management of the project. All I did was to coach him to become a more effective leader. For instance, I helped him identify the project's stakeholders and think about the best ways to work with them.
>
> I was able to do this partly because I realized that my directors are really intrinsically motivated. So my job isn't to make them feel motivated. It's to create conditions where their intrinsic desire to learn and achieve is channeled in the right direction.
>
> The other shift is that I no longer feel I need to get the credit. For me, this project was about Jason and his development. From the perspective of my Achiever self, I didn't really contribute anything. But from a Catalyst perspective, my contribution was the coaching I provided: Asking questions, listening, being a sounding board, and providing encouragement. If he'd headed off in the wrong direction, I would have stepped in to get him back on track. But the fact is, with some regular coaching, he did an outstanding job. As I see it now, part of my job is to train my people to be better leaders, to help them learn how to collaborate in a company that doesn't yet know how to collaborate.

In a similar vein, Adam began to involve his management group in making important decisions. His directors responded very positively to this development, and they began to function more like a real team. For example, because of the company's financial difficulties and a perception that some top executives were just out for themselves, morale had become a real problem in most parts of the company. Adam brought his team together to discuss what they could do in this challenging environment to remain true to their own values and ensure that their organization did the same. Word about his leadership began to spread, and people from other units began to ask if he had a place for them in his organization.

When the company's top executives ordered Adam and his peers to institute another round of layoffs, he called a meeting with his team, and they made the decisions together. "It was gut wrenching," he said later, "but we did a good job, and we did it in three hours—much faster than I could have done on my own." Two weeks later he pulled his team together to create a vision and strategy that they then presented to the rest of the organization. Adam felt this was an important step, not only because it brought his management team together and set a clear direction, but also because of what it modeled for the rest of the organization. "I want our people to see us as a real leadership team," he said. "I want this to set the tone for how people operate down the line."

Adam attributes most of the changes he's made, at work and at home, to his newfound ability to shift into the Catalyst level of awareness and intent:

> I do that a lot now: I ask myself what I'm feeling and then let it go. If you're not on the right path, this little practice helps you get there. If you are on the right path, it makes things more interesting.
>
> My job requires me to travel a lot. Usually not more than two weeks at a time. Recently I was on the road for four weeks. During the third week, I was talking with my wife, and she told me how much my daughter missed me. A special event at her school was coming up in two days called "Daddies and Donuts." You come to school and your child shows you all the things she's been doing there. But I was down in Jackson, Mississippi, and I had a full day of meetings to attend that day.
>
> After the phone call I was in back-to-back meetings, but I kept thinking: What's really important? If I died tomorrow, what would my

life be about? Fortunately, the meetings I had scheduled for the next day were with direct reports, not with customers. I booked a flight back to Chicago that evening and spent the morning at "Daddies and Donuts" with my daughter. I was back in Jackson in time for dinner with my business colleagues. I am *so* glad I did that. It made a huge difference for my daughter.

My wife says she sees a big change happening in my life. There's no way I would have done that even three months ago. I feel like I'm getting closer to living my values, just clearing all the extraneous BS out of my life. When I'm at work, I want to give it my full attention. When I come home, I want to be at home. This past weekend I left all my work stuff at work for the first time ever. When we came home from church on Sunday, I suddenly got this feeling: "Go and give some blankets to the homeless. Just go do it." So I did.

ATTENTIONAL PRACTICE

Reflection is a mental process that allows you to recall and think about previous thoughts, feelings, and behaviors after they've occurred. At any level of leadership development, heroic or post-heroic, reflection can be a powerful ally. The great strength of Achiever-level awareness is its capacity for robust reflection. Its key limitation is that it always takes place after the fact. As an Achiever, you can act or you can reflect, but you can't do both at the same time.

Adam's feeling that he had to be right, his fear of making a woman cry, his desire to get credit for his subordinates' successes, his assumption that he couldn't risk a day away from work to be with his daughter—these are good examples of reactive feelings and assumptions often missed by Achiever-level awareness. To discover how these kinds of reactions operate on the spot, you need the more subtle form of reflective awareness that develops at the Catalyst level.

You can activate Catalyst-level awareness as Adam did, by attending directly to an assumption, feeling, or behavior that would otherwise pass you by. These moments of heightened consciousness produce new insights, giving you greater freedom to adjust your behavior. However, at the Catalyst level, the impulse to move away from direct experience (via action or analysis) kicks in very quickly, limiting the depth and power of your insight. While some behaviors may yield easily to Catalyst-level awareness and intent, more deeply ingrained reactive patterns often do not. To develop an awareness that has greater depth and power, you need to strengthen your ability to attend to the present experience.

The Power of Attention

Attention, as we define it, is the direct, nonconceptual awareness of physical, mental, and emotional experience in the present moment. (Other terms sometimes used for attention are *presence* and *mindfulness*.) For most people, reflection is much more familiar than attention. Everyone has some degree of free attention. But our attention is usually so absorbed in our experiences and reflections that we're not cognizant of it as a distinct mode of awareness. Yet it's by developing this capacity to live "in attention" that you can move into and through the post-heroic levels of leadership agility.[15]

What makes it possible to move to the Co-Creator level of agility is the development of a more sustained attention to thoughts, feelings, and behaviors. For example, you're sitting in your office preparing for a presentation when you notice a tightness in your chest and "butterfly" feelings in the pit of your stomach. Reflecting in the moment, you realize that you're feeling anxious. As you hold the feeling of anxiety in attention, you recognize it as a fear of rejection that pops up in different parts of your life. You notice that your first reaction is to want this feeling to go away. But as you attend to your anxiety in a nonjudgmental way, you begin to relax.

This movement back and forth between direct attention to experience and reflection on the meaning of the experience is a hallmark of the Co-Creator level of awareness. However, because your attention remains absorbed in your experience (the anxiety) and in your reflections about it, you may not be aware of the role that attention plays in making this level of awareness possible.

Meditation as Attentional Practice

For most people, attention as a distinct mode of awareness first becomes clearly evident through direct sensory experiences of the present moment. One of the most reliable ways to cultivate this quality of attention is through a meditation practice that emphasizes present-centered awareness. We found that leaders are much more likely to practice meditation at the Co-Creator and Synergist levels than they were at earlier agility levels. Forty percent of the leaders in our Co-Creator sample meditated regularly, while another 10 percent did so in a more sporadic way. In our Synergist sample, 50 percent had a daily meditation practice, and 35 percent had a "semi-regular" practice.[16] However, we've also found that managers at all levels of agility can learn to meditate.

The particular form of meditation doesn't matter, as long as it helps you develop your attention. For example, four of the leaders featured in this book practice some form of Buddhist meditation.[17] Alison (Chapter Seven) practices Transcendental Meditation, which comes from India's Vedic tradition. Several of Jeff's partners (Chapter Eight) practice chi gung, tai chi, and other Taoist practices.[18] Other Synergists in our sample practice forms of meditation from the Jewish tradition[19] and the Sufi tradition.[20] Ted (Chapter Eight) practices a traditional form of Christian meditation called "the centering prayer."[21] In addition, every morning, before he and his wife get out of bed, they each say a "gratitude prayer":[22]

> She says three things she's grateful for, and I say three things I'm grateful for. I'm sure this has a lot to do with the fact that I keep noticing moments of beauty throughout the day.

Some of the leaders we've just mentioned are members of the religion with which their particular form of mediation is associated, but just as many are not.[23] Other leaders practice forms of meditation that are distinctly areligious.[24] One example is the "relaxation response," a form of meditation developed by Dr. Herbert Benson at the Harvard Medical School.[25] The trick is to find a practice that works for you and to carve out a brief period of "alone time" to do it each day.

Other Ways to Develop Your Attention

Some leaders in our sample found other ways to develop Co-Creator and Synergist-level awareness. For example, Srini and Marilyn (Chapter Seven) developed Co-Creator awareness by participating in forms of psychotherapy that fostered this awareness. For many years, Laura (Chapter Eight) has attended a weekly shamanic drumming circle, a practice that's deepened her awareness and developed her intuition.[26] Although Stan (Chapter Eight) practiced yoga and Transcendental Meditation regularly throughout his twenties, he practices neither today. Yet, for decades, he's actively cultivated an awareness of the present moment in everyday life.

Here's what we've observed about those Synergists who don't have a regular meditation practice: They've each made a commitment, in both their personal and professional lives, to enter repeatedly into the flow of their ongoing experience. We see this in Laura's ability to ride the waves of grief and depression, and in Christine's practice of "feeling the fear and doing it anyway."[27] By doing this so fully and frequently in their everyday lives, they repeatedly break through the absorbed awareness of the Co-Creator into the more vivid presence of the Synergist.

ATTENTION AND LEADERSHIP AGILITY

The psychological and health benefits of meditation have been well-documented.[28] Sitting meditation can become a true oasis from the stresses of everyday life, a way to access the wellspring of peace and joy that we all have at the core of our being. Further, if you practice regularly, the states of mind you experience in meditation will spill over into your everyday life, at least to some extent. Scott, an internal leadership development professional, began a daily sitting practice while making the transition to the Catalyst level of agility. After about six months, he described the effect of this practice on his life:

> I have more energy, I have better focus, and I'm more resilient. I don't necessarily feel an instant benefit each time I meditate. Sometimes when I sit down in the morning and meditate, it seems like I get nothing out of it at the time. But I do it anyway, because so often I find that I'm more resilient later in the day.

If you establish such a practice, you'll probably experience spontaneous moments of presence during the day. In the beginning, these moments usually occur in emotionally neutral situations: doing yard work, climbing a flight of stairs, sitting down in a chair. When you notice these moments of heightened attention, relax into them. Without becoming self-conscious or interfering with anything you're doing, let this awareness extend itself, even if it lasts only a few more moments. You can aid this process by beginning each morning with the intention to use the day to become more present in your life.

If you expect instant, dramatic results, you're likely to be disappointed. However, if you come back to this awareness many times each day, your attention will grow and become stronger. It will gradually extend itself over longer periods of time, and it will become more spacious and panoramic. If you stay with this practice, you will eventually learn how to be present amid more complex circumstances.[29] Recall how Jeff prepared for his dinner meeting with Tom: He was able to remain present even while he reflected on the past and anticipated the future. Ken was able to remain present much of the time during his difficult emotional encounter with his employee. Both had worked for years to bring present-centered awareness into their everyday lives.

Even in the early months of meditation practice, bringing increased attention to challenging circumstances can help you develop the mental and emotional capacities you need for increased leadership agility. For example, like Adam, Scott accelerated his growth into the Catalyst level by bringing increased on-the-spot attention to his feelings and assumptions. As he describes it:

> My meditation practice has given me more perspective on the things that happen in my life. When I say that, it's not like I'm more detached from my experience. I'm actually more aware of my feelings and more connected with them.
>
> Being more aware of my feelings has changed the way I relate to my coworkers. By seeing how reactive my own feelings are, I also see how other people are driven by their own automatic reactions. This just naturally makes me less judgmental and more empathetic, even when my coworkers do things that make life more difficult for me. Just yesterday I was in a meeting where someone implied I'd made a mistake that slowed down a project. Because I was aware of my reactions, instead of going into attack mode, as I would have in the past, I handled it in a much more productive way.

Scott makes several important points. First, his meditation practice has made it easier to bring Catalyst-level awareness into his everyday life. Second, applying this new level of awareness in the workplace has helped him develop his mental and emotional capacities to the Catalyst level. The capacities he specifically mentions are his self-awareness and his stakeholder understanding. In terms of self-awareness, he's more directly aware of reactive feelings that, formerly, he would have overlooked. He is more connected with his feelings and, paradoxically, has more perspective on them. Even when others criticize him, this new level of self-awareness allows him to be less defensive and more empathetic, because he realizes that other people are driven by their own emotional reactions.[30]

At the beginning of this book, we talked about the power of taking an integral approach to leadership agility, one that works both from the outside in and from the inside out. From an outside-in perspective, it's essential that you set leadership development goals that identify specific behaviors you want to change. Scott's example emphasizes the leverage you gain when you also approach leadership development from the inside out: When you repeatedly cultivate a new level of awareness in the midst of action, your mental and emotional capacities develop accordingly. These capacities, in turn, support more agile leadership behavior.

THE CHALLENGE AHEAD

We began this book by highlighting two deep trends that pervade our world: accelerating change and mounting complexity. The leaders we've featured operate in a wide variety of industries and sectors. Yet, in every story the challenge they faced required an effective response to complex, rapidly changing conditions. Whether the initiative involved organizational change, team development, or pivotal conversations, this was always the central challenge.

To develop organizations that are effective in anticipating and responding to change and complexity, we need agile leaders—not just at the top but at all organizational levels. Yet we face a significant leadership agility gap: About 10 percent of today's managers still operate at Pre-Expert levels, 45 percent are Experts, and 35 percent are Achievers. Only about 10 percent have developed into the post-heroic levels. Beth (Chapter Four) and Sarah (Chapters Nine and Ten) have shown us that heroic leaders can become more effective even within their current level of agility. But in this new era, with its increased demand for continuous change, true teamwork, and collaborative problem solving, we need to at least double the percentage of leaders who operate at post-heroic levels. Imagine what would happen if half of today's managers developed to their next level of agility: Five percent would remain at pre-Expert levels, about 28 percent would be Experts, about 45 percent would be Achievers, and about 27 percent would be post-heroic leaders.

To put it more graphically: What would it be like if half of today's Experts (managers like Tony, Beth, Guy, Carlos, and Kevin), became Achievers, as Guy and Carlos did? What would happen if half of the Achievers (people like Rachel and Mark), began to lead like Brenda, the environmental health and safety officer; David, the software EVP;

Joan, the consulting firm COO; and Robert, the oil company president? How might this change your organization? How would it change the world in which we live?

If we want our organizations and our world to change for the better, we can't sit back and hope that others will develop the wisdom and skill to do it for us. Mahatma Gandhi, one of the greatest leaders of the twentieth century, famously said, "You must be the change you want to see in the world." Whatever others may choose to do, we can each make the commitment to become leaders who change things for the better.

Through our work with leaders, we've become convinced that agile leadership and personal development go hand in hand. Most of us spend about half our waking hours on the job. Depending on how you approach it, work can grind you down or polish you like a jewel. By approaching your leadership challenges with greater mindfulness, you can develop your agility, make a difference in the world, and enjoy the person you become in the process. If this rings true for you, we hope this book will serve you as a guide and companion for years to come.

Research Behind
This Book

W e developed the framework presented in this book from two sources:

- A long-range, three-phase research project that began in the early 1970s
- Three decades of direct experience coaching, teaching, training, and consulting to leaders in organizations based in the United States, Canada, and Europe

This Appendix is divided into two parts. The first summarizes our three-phase research effort and cites the primary influences on our thinking about stages of leadership development. The second part describes the research methods we used in the intensive third phase. It also explains the reasoning behind our estimates of the percentage of managers at each level of leadership agility.

THREE PHASES OF RESEARCH
Phase One: Understanding Developmental Stages

Our initial exposure to leadership and to stage development psychology as fields of study came in 1972 when we took a course called "Toward an Action Science," taught by William R. Torbert. Our experience in this course led to a graduate-level paper that synthesized existing developmental stage theories into an original framework that focused on the five adult stages that later became the focus of this book. The final version of this paper, completed in 1976, also incorporated a number of findings from Jane Loevinger's then-new book, *Ego Development*, which was itself a powerful synthesis of previous research and theory on stages of personal development.

This paper also drew on a number of in-depth interviews we conducted with people who'd developed into what we now call the Catalyst, Co-Creator, and Synergist stages. In addition, several people graciously provided us with access to journals they kept during periods of intensive personal growth. At that time our primary focus was on what we now call self-leadership agility. The information we gleaned from these sources contributed a great deal to our understanding in this area.

This constellation of data, along with reflection on our own experience, led to the paper's most original contribution: We described a distinct "level of awareness" underlying each of the five developmental stages described in the paper. We found confirmation for this perspective a year later when philosopher-psychologist Ken Wilber published his first book, *The Spectrum of Consciousness*.

Phase Two: Connecting Stages and Leadership

During the late 1970s, amid our graduate training and early consulting work, we conducted a new research project, using an in-depth interview technique called "modeling" to map the thought patterns that underlie the behavior of high-performing leaders and other professionals. However, it wasn't until the early 1980s that we embarked on a research project that explicitly connected developmental stages and leadership effectiveness. This project was one of a larger set of studies conducted around this time, which established a positive connection between developmental stages and leadership effectiveness.

During the first half of the 1980s, a number of new books on developmental stages were published that deepened our understanding of the subject: Robert Kegan's *The Evolving Self*, James Fowler's *Stages of Faith*, and a number of more conceptual books by Ken Wilber.[1] But the spark for doing a new phase of research on stage development and leadership came in 1982, when we attended a graduate course on adult development taught at Harvard by Harry Lasker, who'd recently conducted the first academic study that looked at differences between managers at different stages of development.[2]

To assess the "ego development" stage of each manager in his study, Lasker used the Washington University Sentence Completion Test (SCT), a research instrument designed and painstakingly validated by Jane Loevinger and her associates.[3] This study established a positive empirical relationship between stage development and effective leadership. Lasker also led training programs designed to help managers move beyond their current stage of development. These experiences gave Lasker a number of deeper insights into the inner psychology of Loevinger's stages, which confirmed and expanded upon our earlier research.[4]

In 1983, inspired by our exposure to Lasker's work, we received the training needed to score the SCT, and we conducted a six-month research project designed to further our understanding of the relationship between developmental stages and leadership effectiveness. Participants in the study were willing clients from the company called FSS in Chapter Six.

For this project, participants completed Loevinger's instrument, then we scored the responses and conducted interviews where we arrived at a mutual assessment of their developmental stage.[5] Because each participant had attended our training program in collaboration skills and was also a coaching client, we were able to identify key differences in the ways that leaders at the Expert, Achiever, and Catalyst stages functioned in the action arena of pivotal conversations.[6]

In 1984, we were asked to conduct a research project at Polaroid Corporation, doing in-depth interviews with managers who'd attended a variety of personal development workshops. This study, which further advanced our understanding of the relationship between personal development and effective leadership, showed that a high percentage of managers exhibited new behaviors that led to measurable—and in some cases dramatic—financial benefits for the company.[7]

During this period Bill Torbert and his associates at Boston College began a program of intensive academic research that built on Lasker's initial inquiry.[8] Taken as a whole, these studies form a critical mass of findings showing that leaders at more advanced stages of development, as measured by Loevinger's instrument, are more effective than their counterparts in carrying out a variety of leadership tasks. In 1987, Torbert reported these findings in *Managing the Corporate Dream,* the first book ever published on stage development and leadership effectiveness.

A Sustained Interlude of Practical Work

By 1980, we were coaching and consulting to leaders full time. During the ensuing decade, what we'd learned from Lasker, Torbert, and Kegan and from our own research found its way into our work with leaders. However, we felt that it wasn't yet the time to use an explicit stage development framework in our work with clients. Instead, we used the framework implicitly, and, as our practices evolved, we continued to learn and invent new ways to work with clients.

For more than twenty years, this is the approach we took to our work. Then, in the late 1990s, we noticed that interest in stage-development frameworks was starting to grow. Bob Kegan published *In Over Our Heads* in 1994. Two years later Don Beck and Chris Cowan published *Spiral Dynamics,* a framework of developmental levels based on the work of the late Claire Graves. By the year 2000, Ken Wilber had written or coedited seventeen books, almost all based on his evolving framework of developmental levels, and his ideas had become popular among a growing global network of leading-edge thinkers.[9]

Phase Three: A Burst of R&D

The idea for this book was conceived one afternoon in February 2001, when we discovered that we'd each been separately outlining the same book. As we continued to talk, an ambitious research project emerged. The project's primary aim was to complete the grid presented in the Introduction, so that leaders would have a practical guide to all five levels of leadership agility in the three arenas of pivotal conversations, leading teams, and leading organizational change. A secondary aim was to answer a number of nagging questions we had about the relationship between stage development and leadership effectiveness.

We decided that this project would draw on three sources of data: a review of eight decades of research on nine developmental stages (the five covered in this book plus the four preceding stages); existing research on the relationship between developmental stages and leadership effectiveness; and data from 220 managers in the form of client experiences, in-depth interviews, and detailed action-learning journals. This study, which took four years to complete, resulted in many insights that advanced our understanding beyond anything previously written on the subject.

Stages and Levels

Our review and synthesis of previous research on stages of personal development benefited from a study of the stages prior to Expert as well as the stages from Expert to Synergist. (For an overview of our own stage descriptions with a chart comparing our stage development framework with those of others, see Appendix B.) Our descriptions of the five levels of leadership agility come primarily from our own research, but we've also drawn on the work of William Torbert (even borrowing his Expert and Achiever names) and on unpublished doctoral dissertations written by Christine Harris, Keith Merron, and Salathiel Smith.[10]

In addition, we've benefited from David Bradford and Allan Cohen's work on team leadership. Although they don't use a stage-development framework, their distinction between heroic and post-heroic leadership mirrors the distinction between conventional and post-conventional stages of development. More specifically, their Technician and Conductor correspond to the Expert and Achiever team leader, and their Developer spans the Catalyst and Co-Creator levels of team leadership agility.[11] In a similar way, we've benefited from the research-based distinction between "segmentalist" (Expert) and "integrative" (post-Expert) managers reported in Rosabeth Moss Kanter's *The Change Masters.*

RESEARCH METHODS

We now turn to the methodology we used during the third and final phase of research for this book.

Sample Size

The total number of subjects we included in our recent four-year research project was 604: 384 managers from four research studies reported in William R. Torbert's *The Power of Balance: Transforming Self, Society and Scientific Inquiry*,[12] and 220 managers who were clients, interviewees, or evening MBA students.

Data Sources

Other than the fictional scenarios presented in Chapter Two, all of the stories presented in the book come either from our work with clients or from in-depth interviews. Shorter examples are also taken from journals kept by interviewees or by practicing managers in evening MBA courses.

Interview Format

In-depth interviews were used in all three phases of our overall research project, each lasting between forty-five minutes to two and a half hours. We used two distinct interview formats—one designed to assess a person's stage of personal development and another to assess level of leadership agility in at least one of three action arenas (pivotal conversations, team leadership, and organizational leadership). In many cases, leaders participated in both kinds of interviews.

To qualify for a particular level of leadership agility within a specific arena, we needed to see solid evidence that a leader had reached the corresponding stage of personal development, and the story provided had to show evidence that the leader consistently employed a wide range of capabilities, consistent with that stage, in taking action.

Assessment of Developmental Stage

We assessed each leader's stage of development by using a well-tested research instrument designed for this purpose, supplemented either by a "clinical assessment," if the leader was a client, or by an interview. Prior to the third phase of our research, the instrument we used was the Washington University Sentence Completion Test (SCT). For the third and most intensive phase of our research, we used a slightly different well-tested research instrument, the Leadership Development Profile (LDP), developed by Susanne Cook-Greuter.[13]

How We Estimated the Percentage of Managers at Each Stage

To make a rough estimate of the number of managers at each stage of adult development, we relied on four research studies reported by Torbert, which assessed the developmental stages of a total of 384 managers at a full range of organizational levels.[14] The percentages of managers at each stage are captured in Table A.1.

| | First-Line Supervisors $n = 37$ | Level of Responsibility | | | |
		Junior and Middle Managers $n = 177$	Senior Managers $n = 66$	Executives $n = 104$	Total $n = 384$
Agility Level	(%)	(%)	(%)	(%)	Rounded Averages (%)
Pre-Expert	24	14	6	3	11
Expert	68	43.5	47	43.5	46
Achiever	8	40	33	39.5	36
Post-Heroic	0	2.5	14	14	7

Table A.1. Correlations Between Agility and Responsibility Levels.

To underscore the tentativeness with which we generalize from 384 U.S. managers to the entire population of managers, we decided to round the total percentage found at each level. In determining how we might most accurately round these numbers, we took into account our experience that, when leaders are interviewed, in a few cases their actual stage turns out to be a stage beyond what the SCT or LDP indicates. Taking this observation into account, we rounded the first three "total" percentages down 1 percent each. This brought the post-Achiever percentage to 10 percent. We calculated estimates for these three stages by assuming the same relative distribution within these stages that Susanne Cook-Greuter found for her sample of 4,510 individuals.[15] The resulting estimates can be summarized as follows:

STAGE	PERCENTAGE
Pre-Expert	10
Expert	45
Achiever	35
Catalyst	5
Co-Creator	4
Synergist	1

Stages of Personal Development

As part of our last four years of research, we reviewed the major stage development frameworks and created our own framework of developmental stages that synthesizes previous stage descriptions and incorporates the empirical research described in Appendix A. In Table B.1, you'll see how our stages align with those articulated by Ken Wilber, Robert Kegan, Bill Torbert, and Susanne Cook-Greuter.[1] Most of this Appendix consists of a condensed version of our stage descriptions. It begins with the pre-Expert stages (not described elsewhere in the book) and goes on to summarize the stages from Expert to Synergist.[2] It ends by answering frequently asked questions about developmental stages and by discussing stages that lie beyond Synergist.

THE THREE PRE-CONVENTIONAL STAGES

Generally speaking, the first three stages cover the period of life from birth to the preteen years. If you have children of middle-school age or younger, these stages may give you new insights into why they do what they do. You may also find it to be an interesting way to reflect on your own childhood.[3]

The Explorer Stage

At birth, an infant's awareness is immersed in a sea of physical sensations. Newborns can't yet organize these sensations into the perception of physical objects, and they aren't yet capable of goal-directed behavior. However, the infant's physical instincts and reflexes serve as the foundation for the first stage of human development, which typically lasts eighteen to twenty-four months.

Picture an infant reaching out, grasping a rattle, shaking it, then mouthing it, an action repeated frequently during the early months of life. With each repetition, the infant moves through a cycle of awareness, intention, and action. The awareness part of the cycle leaves visual, auditory, and tactile memory traces. The action part of the cycle leaves memory traces that link the initiating impulse to certain muscular movements. Over time, as these impulses and muscular memory traces develop well-established connections, the infant learns to perform this action with dexterity.

This is the infant version of reflective action. Jean Piaget, the French psychologist who began research on developmental stages in the 1920s, found that it's only through countless such cycles of movement and awareness that the Explorer-stage child develops "object permanence," the ability to organize disparate sensations into recognizable physical objects.[4] At the same time, the infant develops an ongoing desire to pursue interesting, pleasant experiences and avoid unpleasant ones. By the second birthday, the once helpless newborn has become a toddler. Capable of simple goal-directed behavior, toddlers now experience themselves as robust physical beings distinct from the rest of the physical world.

The Enthusiast Stage

The second pre-conventional stage of development begins around the second birthday (the onset of "the terrible two's") and lasts until sometime between the sixth and seventh birthdays. The Enthusiast is constantly on the move, a creature of rapidly shifting moods—alternately exuberant, serene, fearful, and defiant. During this stage, children grow beyond their primarily physical sense of identity and begin to experience themselves as emotionally distinct from others. *I, me,* and *mine* are words said with real conviction. Enthusiasts find they can exert their own will, though they can't always get what they want.

Through symbolic play and the acquisition of language, preschoolers develop what Piaget called "representational thinking," the ability to think about the world using emotionally charged words and images.[5] Just as object permanence enabled the Explorer to integrate multiple sensory impressions (sight, sound, and so on) into the perception of a unified physical object, representational thinking allows the Enthusiast to integrate multiple perceptions of the same types of objects into words and images (for example, *dogs* and *cats*) that represent what all such objects have in common.[6]

Enthusiasts also develop the most basic understanding of time.[7] At around three years, children begin to talk about things they want to do the next day: "Tomorrow Sally will be here, and she'll bring her new doll." At about four years, children begin to anticipate concrete events farther in the future: "Mommy and Daddy promised me a bicycle on my next birthday!" By the time children have fully developed into the Enthusiast stage, they have a consistent understanding of the difference between past, present, and future.

Enthusiasts aren't aware that other people might perceive situations differently than they do. For example, while a young preschooler talks on the phone with her grandfather, he asks, "Is your mother there?" She says, "Yes, Mommy's right there." She points to her mother, expecting that he can see her as easily as she can. Similarly, a five-year-old looking out the car window on a moonlit night sees a moon that moves alongside the car. Children of this age can't yet conceive of a moon that exists independently of their own perception. At this stage, children are so enmeshed in imagery that they don't distinguish between imagination and reality. Animated conversations with dolls and stuffed animals are part of the charm of the Enthusiast's world.

While the Enthusiast stage brings a level of autonomy and initiative that simply isn't possible at the Explorer stage, Enthusiasts remain slaves to their impulses, unable to clearly distinguish between imagination and reality. The capacities to regulate impulses and to see beyond immediate perceptions come only with the new stage of development that emerges during the grade school years.

The Operator Stage

Children develop through the Operator stage during their grade school years. Piaget called the level of awareness that emerges at this stage "concrete operations," the ability to think about the properties of specific objects (their color, shape, volume, and so on) and organize them accordingly. Concrete operational thinking also allows grade-schoolers to step back from the imagery that permeated their world during the Enthusiast stage and distinguish between imagination and physical reality.

At the same time, Operators develop the ability to regulate their impulses by anticipating the short-term consequences of their action. Together with operational thinking, which allows grade-schoolers to grasp the logic of rules and roles, this capacity enables them to conceive and carry out all kinds of little plans and schemes, allowing them to become the real (though small-time) Operators we see as the lemonade stand entrepreneur, puppet show producer, and collector and trader of favorite objects.

THE THREE CONVENTIONAL STAGES

The stages of conventional development begin with the Conformer stage, which is the stage immediately prior to Expert. Most girls grow into the Conformer stage around age eleven or twelve, while boys usually enter it about a year later. By age fourteen or fifteen the vast majority of high school kids are well-established Conformers. Most people grow into the Expert stage during their late teens. A few who grow into the Achiever stage begin to do so as early as the last year of high school. Most make this transition in college or in their mid-twenties, but some develop into this stage later in life, usually in their thirties or forties.[8]

The Conformer Stage

The level of awareness that emerges at this stage is the most basic level of abstract thought, which allows the young adolescent to think in hypothetical terms, to see what *is* in light of what *could be* and *should be*. This development has a profound effect on adolescents' perceptions of interpersonal relationships. Grade-schoolers know that other people can see things differently than they do, but it doesn't occur to them that others might see *them* differently than they see themselves. However, with adolescents' new ability to imagine hypothetical possibilities, they are quite aware of the fact that other people have feelings and opinions about them. What they imagine often has more to do with their own hopes and fears than with what others actually think, although at this stage this is usually a difficult distinction for them to make.

Conformers very much want to gain the approval and avoid the disapproval of those people and groups they regard as significant. This preoccupation, along with increased impulse control and the ability to think abstractly, gives them the motivation and ability to present themselves in ways they feel will establish the connection they want with the people who matter most.

Yet Conformers are rarely aware that this is their underlying intention. One manager who remained in this stage until her early thirties later described it this way:[9]

> I grew up in a small town in Tennessee. I started college but dropped out my freshman year to get married. My husband and I moved to Atlanta, had two children, and made our home in one of its affluent suburbs. I wanted very much to be a part of the social group in that community, so I threw myself into everything from volunteer work to social clubs and the PTA. I didn't realize it at the time, but what I was really doing was trying to create the image I wanted others to see. I did this for years without being conscious that none of this was of any real interest to me.

The Expert Stage

The vast majority of managers grow into the Expert stage during late adolescence or shortly thereafter. As they do so, they develop a strong problem-solving orientation and an ability to think more independently and analytically. However, at this stage, the focus is more on completing tasks and projects than on achieving long-term goals. When facing multiple tasks, each important for different reasons, it's often hard to step back and prioritize them in the midst of action.

Whereas Conformers have a strong interest in fitting into desired social groups, Experts develop an interest in standing out. They expect themselves and others to live up to rather rigid standards, and their ability to empathize with others and to understand those who hold views that conflict with their own is fairly limited. When their priorities conflict with those of others, they're likely either to assert themselves without taking others' needs into account or to accommodate themselves to others' priorities. Balancing assertion and accommodation is difficult.

At the Expert stage, people have a strong interest in improving and accomplishing things. Rather than trying to do things the "one right way," as they did during the Conformer stage, they now see that problems have many possible solutions. However, they tend to tackle one problem at a time, each as an isolated task, and they find it difficult to step back to see how various problems might be related. Without realizing it, they allow limiting personal opinions and biases to influence their approach. Yet because they tend to assume that their judgments are correct, they're not likely to test their views against objective data or differing viewpoints.

Experts develop an introspective awareness that makes it possible to recognize recurring inner moods and develop a more independent self-image. Their self-esteem now comes from developing their own beliefs, being respected for their knowledge and skills, and being able to persuade and convince others. When they feel they're not improving in these areas, they can be quite self-critical. This self-critical tendency and the need to be right combine to make it unlikely that they'll seek feedback from others.

The Achiever Stage

At the Achiever stage people develop a robust reflective capacity and a greater awareness of the societal and institutional context within which they live and work. Using these capacities, they create their own internally coherent view of the world and an explicit, consciously examined set of principles and ideals to live by. They can think strategically, and their ability to envision future outcomes can make it highly compelling to pursue objectives that may take as long as two to five years to achieve.

Achievers' ability to imagine themselves in another's situation gives them a greater capacity for empathy than they had at the Expert stage. They're receptive to differing viewpoints when they think these views might help them achieve their desired outcomes. In dealing with differences they may be assertive (focused on persuading others) or accommodative (focused on understanding and including others). Either way, there's a good chance that they'll try to balance their predominant style, to a certain extent, with its opposite.

When they're solving important problems, they want these problems to be diagnosed and solved using verifiable data. Because they have a more robust reflective capacity than they had at the Expert stage, they can see how individual problems are related. They can use various frameworks to conceptualize or reconceptualize issues, and they can develop innovative solutions by taking what was successful in one context and applying it in another.

Achievers develop a level of self-awareness that allows them to reflect on recent events and remember why they acted as they did. Through these reflections and a newfound ability to recall what they were like at many different periods of their life, they develop a solid sense of their own identity. Because they can vividly imagine the future effects of their actions, they have a strong sense that they control their own destiny, and their professional self-esteem comes primarily from believing they've contributed to the achievement of significant outcomes.

THREE POST-CONVENTIONAL STAGES

Research studies focusing on adults who have at least a college education indicate that approximately 12 percent have grown into one or more of three post-conventional stages: Catalyst, Co-Creator, and Synergist.[10]

The Catalyst Stage

In the Catalyst stage, people begin to feel more at ease with change and uncertainty, and they develop a broader, longer-term view of the environment within which they live and work. As a result, their aspirations tend to be more visionary than they were in the Achiever stage. They also develop a strong interest in the quality of life and the process of human experience. Because they recognize that sustained achievement of desired outcomes takes place within a larger context of human relationships, enhancing these relationships becomes an important priority.

Catalysts have a deeper capacity for empathizing with others, because they can now imagine fairly accurately what it's like to be another person, facing whatever situation they're facing. They develop a real curiosity about frames of reference that differ from their own, and they listen to other views because they genuinely want to consider new possibilities. In responding to people whose views differ from their own, they move more fluidly between assertiveness and accommodation.

Their enhanced ability to "try on" differing frames of reference makes their thinking more creative than it was at previous stages. Their enhanced awareness of the power of frames of reference often leads them to question their assumptions and those of others when framing problems and developing solutions. They're more likely to see that specific problems are part of a larger pattern of issues caused by deeper, unresolved organizational issues, and they're more aware that solutions can have unintended consequences.

At the Catalyst stage, people develop a new capacity for self-observation that allows them to recognize feelings, assumptions, and priorities that would otherwise escape their conscious awareness. They begin to realize how much their need to achieve comes from a desire for approval and recognition. They also discover that the primary determinant of their self-esteem is their own attitude toward their successes and failures. They become more proactive in seeking and applying feedback, more willing to accept and deal with inner conflict, and more adept in responding to new and uncertain situations.

The Co-Creator Stage

Co-Creators add to the Catalyst orientation a more fully experiential awareness that develops the intellectual and emotional capacities needed to create deeply interdependent relationships. Co-Creators become interested in committing themselves to relationships and enterprises that reflect an intangible and evolving sense of life purpose, a direction that increases inner fulfillment while enhancing the lives of other human beings.

Co-Creators develop the capacity to enter more fully into differing frames of reference, and this development deepens their capacity for empathy. They prefer relationships characterized by shared purpose and collaboration, where mutual commitment and respect for individual autonomy are experienced as complementary opposites. Their capacity for developing these kinds of relationships is supported by their ability to balance self-assertion with appropriate receptivity to others' needs.

At this stage people can step back from multiple frames of reference (including their own), and identify where these frames conflict and where they have common elements. When they're faced with opposing viewpoints, they're quite capable of making tough choices. However, on important issues, they generally prefer not to take sides immediately but to explore what is possible by bringing those with differing perspectives into relationship with one another. Their capacity for integrative thinking gives them the ability to engage in creative problem-solving dialogues that can lead to true win-win solutions.

Co-Creators develop a level of self-awareness that allows them to stay with difficult and unfamiliar feelings longer than they would have at the Catalyst stage. As they become aware of a wider range of feelings and assumptions, they discover inner conflicts. By experiencing and working through these conflicts, they begin to integrate into their conscious personality various parts of themselves that they'd formerly walled off or ignored. As they become more attuned to their real thoughts, feelings, and behaviors, they increase their capacity for authentic self-expression and for experimenting with new perspectives and behaviors.

The Synergist Stage

At this stage people develop a strong wish to engage with life in all its fullness, a deep concern about human issues, and an evolving sense of life purpose that's in some way linked to that concern. Even when they live and work in contexts where their commitments are not shared, they continue to take initiatives that are aligned with their sense of purpose. Many Synergists have compelling feelings about being at the right place at the right time and intuitions about next steps that keep them "on purpose."

Although they can now make use of many forms of power, Synergists cultivate the "power of presence," a subtle form of power and agility that comes from being centered in the present moment. As this capacity develops, they may sense subtle energetic dynamics within people, groups, and organizations that would have escaped their awareness at previous stages. They're also able to remain focused on the common good while holding in mind, in an accurate and empathetic way, conflicting stakeholder views and interests, including their own.

When they're working with others to solve ill-structured problems, Synergists' well-developed capacity for holding mental and emotional complexity often gives rise to "synergistic intuitions" that resolve apparently irreconcilable conflicts in ways that are beneficial for all parties involved. However, even when their intuitive breakthroughs seem to do just that, they usually test the practical validity of these insights by getting feedback from others and by testing their ideas in action.

The wish that Synergists have to engage with life in all its fullness leads them to cultivate a direct, present-centered awareness of their five senses, their physical presence, their thought processes, and their emotional responses. As a result, they develop an enhanced, nonjudgmental awareness of their habitual patterns of thinking and emotional reactions. This awareness motivates them to further develop their attention, so they can gradually free themselves from the domination of reactive mental and emotional patterns. It also opens them to the joy and wonder of being alive.

FAQS ABOUT DEVELOPMENTAL STAGES

When people are introduced to the idea of developmental stages, they often have a number of questions. Here, we answer some of the most basic and frequently asked questions. Feel free to skip any of these questions that aren't your own.

Does everyone always develop through these stages in the same order?

Yes. Maybe it's the words *everyone* and *always*, so overused at the Conformer stage, that make some people pause when they hear this answer. After all, how many things in life are *always* true for *everyone*? Yet multiple cross-cultural, longitudinal studies have repeatedly confirmed that this developmental sequence is universal. In these studies, researchers have found no examples of people who've skipped a stage or moved through the stages in a different sequence.[11]

Perhaps the easiest way to confirm this conclusion for yourself is to reflect on some of the earlier stages. After the Explorer (infant-toddler) stage, children spend the rest of their preschool years developing through the Enthusiast stage, where they acquire language and learn to think in words and images. It's difficult to imagine how a toddler could skip this stage and, still unable to speak and think in words, go directly to the Operator (grade school) stage, and begin to make conceptual distinctions like this one: When you pour water from a tall, skinny beaker into a short, fat beaker, the volume of water remains the same, even though it's taken on a different shape.

Similarly, it's hard to imagine a five-year-old child in the Enthusiast stage skipping the Operator stage and suddenly developing the capacity for abstract thought, which emerges at the Conformer stage. Because each stage emerges from and builds on the one before it, it's even harder to imagine a child who could develop through the first four stages, but in a different order. The same is true for the adult stages. You can't reach the Achiever stage without first developing to the Expert stage. As an Achiever, you don't suddenly develop into the Synergist stage, then later go back and develop through the Catalyst and Co-Creator stages.

Even if the sequence of these stages doesn't vary, isn't it possible for a person to reach a particular stage of development and then regress to an earlier stage?

The type of regression that can and does happen is almost always temporary. For more than two decades, Robert Selman and his colleagues at Harvard University have studied children at play from a stage development perspective, using their insights to devise ways to help kids create healthy, age-appropriate friendships. Their research, based on endless hours of direct observation, has shown that playtime conflict can deteriorate to a point where children behave as if they were at earlier stages of development. Most parents need no convincing on this point.[12]

The same thing can happen to any adult. You can probably think of examples from your own experience. To investigate this question, developmental psychologist Harry Lasker conducted research with graduate students at Harvard. When these students participated in highly concrete, competitive games with strict win-lose structures, they often behaved as if they were at earlier stages of development. Once the experiments were over, they returned to their previous level of functioning.[13]

In a note to the Introduction, you said that these stages do not refer to age-based life eras or to the "passages" between them, such as the midlife crisis. But for many of the stages you describe, especially the earlier ones, you refer to the ages when people are most likely to be in each stage. Are these stages age-related or not?

During the early stages of life, it's relatively easy to predict developmental stage by knowing a person's age. However, the research shows that, with each new stage, the link between stage and age becomes increasingly approximate. By the early twenties, any close connection between age and stage disappears.[14] This statistical disconnect between adult age and stage reflects the fact that adult stage development is not automatic. Consequently, although the early stages are closely correlated with age, it's really impossible to predict an adult stage from someone's age. We've provided information about what is known about stage and age to make it a bit easier to relate the stages to your own life.

If an adult has a high IQ, does this indicate
a more advanced stage of personal development
than other people?

An adult with a high IQ, as measured by standard intelligence tests, could be at the Expert stage, the Synergist stage, or anywhere in between.[15] Stage development, as we're defining it here, refers to the growth of the whole person. As people grow from stage to stage, they develop capacities that allow them to deal more effectively with change and complexity.

When you say that people at the more advanced
stages are more developed than other people,
aren't you promoting a hierarchical or elitist way
of thinking about human beings?

The framework we've presented in this book outlines stages of human development, not a status hierarchy. We're not saying that those people who currently occupy the top levels of today's business, political, or social hierarchies are necessarily well-developed human beings. (It's easy to think of a number of people in these positions who are not very highly developed.) What we're saying is that, as you develop, your ability to deal effectively with change and complexity increases. Put differently, growth through the stages is not about moving toward perfection. It's about moving toward *wholeness*.[16]

Developing in this way doesn't make you better than others, but it can make you a more effective leader in today's turbulent world. In fact, as you develop beyond the Achiever stage, you become less egotistical and less judgmental and hierarchical in your attitudes toward yourself and other people. You honor and respect others, simply because they are fellow human beings.

STAGES BEYOND SYNERGIST

In the 1950s, most stage developmental psychologists believed that the Achiever stage represented full adult development.[17] Today, many believe that the Co-Creator or Synergist stage represents the apex of human development. Our view of the Synergist stage aligns with that of Ken Wilber and Bill Torbert, who see it as a potential gateway to further, even more rarely accessed stages of human development. (See Table B.1 at the end of this Appendix.)

In Wilber's early work, he called his equivalent of the Synergist stage "the centaur," a term intended to convey a more conscious connection between body and mind.[18] While the Synergist stage marks the culmination of post-conventional development, it can also serve as the first stage of what Wilber calls "transpersonal" development.[19] By using this terminology, Wilber points to a process of transformation that goes beyond development of the individual personality. Though it may affect the personality, transpersonal development refers primarily to the cultivation of more selfless inner potentials—for example, deep equanimity, wisdom, and compassion.

In Wilber's framework, which is based on extensive examination of both ancient and modern forms of personal transformation, transpersonal development potentially includes nine distinct stages. In *Integral Psychology* and in other works, he organizes these nine stages into four levels of development, which he calls psychic, subtle, causal (or formless), and non-dual. In *Action Inquiry, The Power of Balance,* and earlier books, Bill Torbert describes three stages beyond what we call the Co-Creator: the Alchemist stage, the Ironist stage, and a further stage he simply designates with a question mark. His Alchemist stage corresponds to Wilber's psychic and subtle levels, his Ironist stage corresponds to Wilber's causal (or formless) level, and his question mark refers to Wilber's non-dual level.[20]

Because Torbert's three most advanced stages and Wilber's four transpersonal levels each includes multiple stages, they can be described as "zones" of development, similar to the Pre-Conventional, Conventional, and Post-Conventional "zones," each of which includes several stages.

We should note that the Synergist stage, as presented in this book, represents only the beginning of what Torbert calls the "Alchemist" stage. Rather than attempt to clearly define where the Synergist stage ends and the next stage begins, we prefer to leave this question, particularly as it applies to leadership, for further research.

Table B.1. Comparison of Developmental Stages.

Wilber	Kegan	Loevinger	Cook-Greuter	Torbert	Joiner and Josephs
Pre-personal					
Sensorimotor	Incorporative	Pre-social	Pre-social		Explorer
Phantasmic-emotional		Symbiotic	Symbiotic		
Rep-mind	Impulsive	Impulsive	Impulsive	Impulsive	Enthusiast
Concrete operations	Imperial	Self-protective	Self-protective	Opportunist	Operator
Personal				**Conventional**	**Heroic**
Formal operations	Interpersonal	Conformist	**Conventional** Conformist	Diplomat	Conformer
		Conscientious/conformist	Conscientious/conformist	Expert	Expert
	Institutional	Conscientious	Conscientious	Achiever	Achiever
Post-formal/vision-logic	Inter-individual	Individualistic	**Post-conventional** Individualistic	**Post-conventional** Individualist	**Post-heroic** Catalyst
		Autonomous	Autonomous	Strategist	Co-Creator
		Integrated	Construct-Aware	Alchemist	Synergist
Transpersonal					
Psychic			Unitive	Ironist	
Subtle				?	
Causal (formless)					
Non-dual					

Notes for Inquiring Readers

INTRODUCTION: THE MASTER COMPETENCY

1. These five levels of leadership agility are not to be confused with the "Level 5 Hierarchy" Jim Collins presents in *Good to Great.* According to our analysis, Collins's "Level 5 Leader" corresponds to the fully developed Achiever, our second level of leadership agility.

2. This Introduction includes a brief overview of the experience and research that forms the basis for this book. Additional detail can be found in Appendix A.

An Integral Approach

3. An example of this approach can be found in the relatively recent emphasis on "emotionally intelligent" leadership. See *Working with Emotional Intelligence,* Goleman; *Primal Leadership,* Goleman, Boyatzis, and McKee; and *Resonant Leadership,* Boyatzis and McKee.

4. We use the term *integral* partly because the perspective upon which our book is based is consistent with the "integral" approach advanced by Ken Wilber in a series of books that include *Integral Psychology* and *A Brief History of Everything.* We would be the first to acknowledge that the material in our book would be "more integral" if it described how organizations and societies might evolve through a parallel series of levels. However, such an undertaking is quite beyond the scope of this particular book.

Stages of Personal Development

5. The overview of stages we present here (and in more detail in Appendix B) is a synthesis, based on an extensive study of existing developmental stage frameworks, all created by Western research psychologists. Although we believe that further stages exist (as identified, for example, by William R.

Torbert and by Ken Wilber and his associates), we haven't attempted to describe these additional stages in this book. See *Action Inquiry*, Torbert and associates; *Transformations of Consciousness*, Wilber, Engler, and Brown; and *Integral Psychology*, Wilber.

6. Age-related references are for children in advanced industrial societies. While the timing of development through the pre-conventional stages is closely related to a child's age, as people grow older, it becomes increasingly difficult to predict their stage from their age. Consequently, in this field the adult stages don't refer to age-specific life eras or to the "passages" between them, such as the midlife crisis. Instead, they refer to qualitatively more advanced levels of intellectual and emotional maturity.

The idea of age-related stages of adult development comes from a companion field called *lifespan* developmental psychology, which focuses on the age-specific "psychosocial tasks" that need to be resolved over the course of a person's lifespan. During the 1970s, Daniel Levinson and his colleagues published *The Seasons of a Man's Life*, which described age-related issues faced by a sample of American males aged eighteen to forty-seven and what it took to resolve these issues successfully. In *Passages*, Gail Sheehy used a similar perspective to outline age-related stages of life (which we call "life phases") as experienced by both men and women. In that book, "passages" refer to the transitional periods between life phases, including a midlife passage that takes place during a person's late thirties and early forties. In 1978, Edgar Schein published a book called *Career Dynamics*, which showed how these insights could be used to better understand and foster the career development of corporate employees.

7. We're using the terms *pre-conventional, conventional,* and *post-conventional* as they're currently used by William R. Torbert and Susanne Cook-Greuter. (See Cook-Greuter's "A Detailed Description of the Development of Nine Action-Logics in the Leadership Development Framework.") These terms originally come from the work of Lawrence Kohlberg, a research psychologist who did pioneering work on stages of moral development. Some researchers have critiqued Kohlberg's description of his two post-conventional stages as being philosophically or gender biased, or both. (See "Moral Development in Late Adolescence and Adulthood: A Critique and Reconstruction of Kohlberg's Theory," Murphy and Gilligan, and "Critical Political Theory and Moral Development: On Kohlberg, Hampden-Turner, and Habermas," Reid and Yanarella.) Although we believe that these are valid critiques, they don't overturn the claim that thinking about moral issues evolves through a sequence of stages. Still, in our conventional and post-conventional stage

descriptions we've drawn on Kohlberg's work only to the extent that his findings have been confirmed by other researchers, including ourselves.

8. The particular social conventions to which a person feels compelled to conform at this stage vary enormously, depending on the specific groups to which a person wants to belong. Church groups and motorcycle gangs have very different conventions. However, for group members at the Conformer stage, the underlying desire to gain acceptance through conformity to group norms is the same.

9. In addition, growth into this stage is often stimulated by the experience of attending junior college or entering military service.

10. These stages, which we call Catalyst, Co-Creator, and Synergist, are described in Appendix B. The corresponding three leadership agility levels are described in Chapters Six through Eight. Research has shown that only about 10 percent of those adults who graduate from college have developed beyond the Achiever stage of development. This estimate is based on four "highly educated" samples reported in Robert Kegan's *In Over Our Heads* (p. 195) and a larger highly educated sample reported in the Cook-Greuter paper cited in Note 7.

11. For a comparison of our stages with those of Kegan, Wilber, and others, see the chart in Appendix B. Appendix B and its notes also provide a complete list of researchers and theorists we've drawn upon in creating our own synthesis. For reasons discussed there, we have not used *Spiral Dynamics* as one of these sources.

12. Wilber's developmental framework is unique in that he draws on both ancient and modern sources to map the full range of human development, which ultimately extends beyond the post-conventional stages. His books have been translated into twenty languages. As an introduction to his thinking, we recommend his *Integral Psychology* and *A Brief History of Everything*. For an overview of his work, see *Ken Wilber: Thought as Passion,* Visser.

Levels of Leadership Agility

13. Most of these studies were overseen by William R. Torbert of the Carroll School of Management at Boston College. These studies showed that "stage of ego development" is a statistically significant measure of what we call level of leadership agility. (For more on stages of ego development, see *Ego Development,* Loevinger.) These studies used a well-validated psychometric instrument called the Washington University Sentence Completion Test (SCT) to assess managers' stages of ego development. (See *Measuring Ego Development,* Hy and Loevinger.) The most current summary of Torbert's work in this area can be found in Part II of *Action Inquiry,* Torbert and

associates and in the *Harvard Business Review* article "Seven Transformations of Leadership" by Rooke and Torbert.

14. For more information on this project and the research methods we used, see Appendix A.

A Few Words About Wording

15. The distinction between management and leadership was first publicly articulated in a speech by Warren Bennis at the Federal Executive Institute in 1975. Now considered one of the world's foremost authorities on leadership, Bennis is an unusual leadership theorist in that, earlier in his career, he spent a number of years in high-level leadership roles. His distinction between leadership and management originally grew out of his personal experience as president of the University of Cincinnati during the early 1970s. He accepted this position because he wanted to transform the second-largest "multiversity" in the country into an innovative learning community that would bring theory and practice together and help solve the problems of the larger society. Ten months into the job, sitting in his office at four in the morning "bone weary and soul weary," a huge mass of papers stacked on his desk, he had an epiphany: He'd become so enmeshed in managing stakeholder relationships and attending to administrative tasks that he wasn't communicating his vision, and he wasn't mobilizing the initiatives needed to make that vision a reality. This experience led to his basic insight: As he saw it, he was *managing* the university, but he wasn't *leading* it. See *The Unconscious Conspiracy: Why Leaders Can't Lead,* Bennis.

Bennis was distinguishing between two types of activities: leading and managing. In our terminology, it was, essentially, a distinction between two levels of leadership agility: Achiever and Catalyst. Where, then, is the source of the idea that leaders and managers are two fundamentally different kinds of people? A year after Bennis articulated his distinction between leading and managing in *The Unconscious Conspiracy,* Abraham Zaleznik published an influential article in the *Harvard Business Review* called "Managers and Leaders: Are They Different?" Zaleznik said that managers and leaders are two "completely different" personality types, the result of very different childhood experiences. The implication was that only those who fit a particular personality type can be effective leaders. Zaleznik's manager versus leader theory was later taken up, with some qualifications, by Harvard leadership guru John Kotter, whose published work indicates that he thought Zaleznik, not Bennis, was the originator of the distinction between leadership and management (*A Force for Change: How Leadership Differs from Management,* Kotter, p. 166, endnote 10).

Zaleznik's theory, based solely on anecdotal data, has been directly disconfirmed by at least two important empirical studies. During the late 1970s, Bennis interviewed ninety exceptional leaders. He found that the differences in these leaders' personalities were far more striking than their similarities. Some were intuitive and imaginative, others highly analytical. Some were extraverted, others introverted. Some were highly articulate; others were not. This study also led Bennis to conclude that the idea that exceptional leaders are charismatic is a myth. Most, he said, are not (*Leaders*, Bennis and Nanus).

During the late 1980s, John Kotter conducted several research projects that looked at the behavior of executives from a diverse group of corporations. A key conclusion: The most effective executives both lead and manage, often weaving these two types of activity together in the same interaction. This finding further disconfirms Zaleznik's theory (described in Note 15) that managers and leaders are two completely different kinds of people. It also shows that, while the distinction between the two activities is a useful one, it's best to be good at both (*A Force for Change*, Kotter, p. 104).

16. You may be thinking, "Leadership isn't just about intent—it's about getting results." That's our definition of *effective* leadership. But leadership isn't always effective.

17. One variable we have not changed is company size. In a very few cases, in order to fully illustrate a particular level of leadership agility in a particular action arena, we grafted onto a leader's story a brief example from an interview with another leader who operated at the same agility level. Technically, we could say that these few stories are composites, but that would be an overstatement, because the grafted elements are, at most, a few paragraphs in length.

18. A number of the stories in this book come from our experiences with clients. Some are Stephen's clients, some are Bill's, and some are joint clients. Similarly, some research for this book was conducted by Bill, some by Stephen, and some by both of us. Because this book is a thoroughly collaborative effort, and because continual references to one or the other of us seems awkward and unnecessary, we've used "we" throughout to refer to Bill, Stephen, or both of us together.

CHAPTER 1: AGILITY IN A WORLD OF CHANGE AND COMPLEXITY

1. "Robert" is one of our clients. We tell this story in more detail in Chapter Six. Among other things, we designed and facilitated the creative thinking sessions that Robert and his management team used to develop their

breakthrough strategies. The lead consultant on this project was Sheila Shuman, who subsequently changed careers and became a Jungian therapist. For more information on our customized Breakthrough Strategy Process, go to www.changewise.biz/os-bsp-overview.html.

The Agility Imperative

2. "Connective technologies" include telecommunications technologies; the Internet, e-mail, and other computer-mediated communication technologies; and personal communications technologies.

3. Organization design experts first used the term *agile* in the early 1990s to describe manufacturing firms that could quickly adapt to meet changing customer needs (*Agile Manufacturing,* Kidd; *Pathways to Agility: Mass Customization in Action,* Oleson; *Response Ability: The Language, Structure and Culture of the Agile Enterprise,* Dove; and *Transitioning to Agility: Creating the 21st Century Enterprise,* Gunneson). By the end of the millennium, the concept of agility had broadened to mean "the ability to anticipate and respond rapidly to changing conditions" ("Building Agility and Resiliency During Turbulent Change," McCann). It was also being applied in the service sector to IT projects, and to the IT systems needed to support agile organizations (*Agility in Health Care,* Goldman and Graham; and *Cooperate to Compete: Building Agile Business Relationships,* Preiss, Goldman, and Nagel. Books and articles on agile IT are legion). In 2003, a study of fifty government agencies in eight countries, conducted with the London School of Economics, concluded that agile agencies not only exist, they significantly outperform other agencies on virtually every important metric—from productivity to employee and customer satisfaction ("Agile Government: It's Not an Oxymoron," Baker, Durante, and Sanin-Gómez). Also see *Built to Change: How to Achieve Sustained Organizational Effectiveness,* Lawler and Worley.

4. As organizational theorists have pointed out, to enjoy sustained success, companies need to develop a level of organizational agility that matches the increasing level of change and complexity in their business environment. Some organizational theorists prescribe "organizational agility" for environments where change is continuous and "organizational resilience" for even more turbulent environments where disruptive change has become the norm ("The Quest for Resilience," Hamel and Valikangas, and "Organizational Effectiveness: Changing Concepts for Changing Environments," McCann). Because of the way we define agility, we say that extremely turbulent environments require organizations, teams, and individual leaders

to have higher levels of agility, and we define resilience as a necessary but not sufficient condition for agility. For a discussion of the relationship between resilience and agility at the individual level, see Chapter Ten.

5. "The Present State of Leadership and Strategies for Preparing Future Leaders," Taylor.

6. This survey was conducted by the global career-management services firm, Lee Hecht Harrison, in 2004. Researchers gave a list of leadership competencies to 130 senior executives and human resource professionals in Fortune 500 companies, universities, and professional service organizations and asked them which competencies were most critical for their organizations. When the responses were in, three competencies clustered together at the top: "delivering measurable business results," "influencing others to assume leadership in their roles," and "agility."

Five Levels of Leadership Agility

7. The names for our Expert and Achiever levels are borrowed from the pioneering work of William R. Torbert. See *Action Inquiry: The Secret of Timely and Transforming Leadership*, Torbert and associates.

8. In *Power Up*, Bradford and Cohen identify two forms of heroic leadership, the Technician and the Conductor. Although they don't use the terminology of levels of agility, their Technician corresponds to our Expert, and their Conductor corresponds to our Achiever. Also see their earlier book, *Managing for Excellence*.

9. In this chart, the percentage of managers at each level is an approximation, extrapolated from four research studies involving a total of 384 managers. For more information about how we arrived at these estimates, see the last part of Appendix A.

10. Conceptually, Bradford and Cohen's post-heroic leader, which they call the Developer, spans our Catalyst and Co-Creator levels. However, the primary story upon which *Power Up* is based appears to capture a leader's transition from the Achiever to the Catalyst level.

Agility Levels and Personality Types

11. Tools such as these are often used to help people appreciate the contributions that diverse personality types can bring to a team effort. The Myers-Briggs Type Inventory identifies four "basic temperaments," sometimes called Idealist, Rational, Guardian, and Artisan, which are then subdivided into a total of sixteen personality types. See *Type Talk*, Kroeger and Thusen,

and *Please Understand Me II*, Keirsey. The names we've just given for the four temperaments come from a very useful pamphlet called *The 16 Personality Types*, Berens and Nardi. The DISC Personal Profile System posits four basic personality types: Decisive, Influential, Steady, and Compliant. (See www.discprofile.com.)

12. *The Essential Piaget*, Piaget; *Essays on Moral Development*, Volume 1: *The Philosophy of Moral Development*, Kohlberg; *Ego Development*, Loevinger; *The Evolving Self*, Kegan.

13. For example, the classic study of high-performing leaders, reported by Bennis and Nanus in *Leaders* two decades ago, found no correlation between personality type (including charismatic personality) and effective leadership. More recently, we conducted an in-depth study of twelve managers representing seven Myers-Briggs personality types and found no correlation between any dimension of MBTI personality type (introvert-extravert, intuitive-sensing, thinking-feeling, or judging-perceiving) and level of leadership agility.

CHAPTER 2: THE FIVE EDS
A Leadership Challenge

1. This would mean that you have developed the mental and emotional capacities needed to operate at the Achiever level (that is, developed to the Achiever stage), but haven't yet translated these capacities into Achiever-level behavior into two of three basic leadership arenas. We discuss this further in Chapter Nine.

Initial Self-Assessment

2. For more information about the research behind this book, see Appendix A.

3. If you feel you need more information about leadership agility levels before you can answer these questions, don't worry. You'll have an opportunity to come back to this question in Chapter Nine, after you've learned a good deal more about each agility level.

4. For example, your overall level of agility can sometimes drop for a time when you move from one organization to another, especially if you need to adjust to a different kind of organization or learn a new industry. Your agility level can also dip temporarily when you're under high stress. At the same time, increasing your agility level can increase your capacity for dealing with stress.

CHAPTER 3: FOUR COMPETENCIES FOR AGILE LEADERSHIP

1. One symptom that a behavior at a new level of agility is not sticking is the occurrence of frequent lapses into old behavior with little awareness or concern about them. Another indication is when leaders repeatedly enact "new" behaviors in ways that are consistent with their current agility level. Example: An Achiever asks for input from stakeholders simply to gain buy-in, without being genuinely open to their influence.

2. As you'll see in Chapter Ten, these methods are also highly efficient, because they help you use your everyday initiatives to accelerate your development as a leader.

The Leadership Agility Compass

3. We've borrowed the term *self-leadership* from *Mastering Self-Leadership*, 3rd edition, Charles Manz and Christopher Neck.

4. When your team or organization as a whole becomes the issue you need to address, context-setting includes the same basic steps, only instead of clarifying intended outcomes for a single initiative, you set the strategic direction for the team or organization, a process that may include defining mission, vision, values, and strategic objectives.

5. Peter Senge often emphasizes the power and efficacy of a deep sense of purpose. For example, he says, "Without a deep sense of purpose, it's difficult to harness the energy, passion, commitment, and perseverance needed to thrive in challenging times." ("Creating Desired Futures in a Global Economy," Senge, p. 4). Our research indicates that leaders who operate at post-heroic levels of agility are often what Robert Greenleaf has called servant leaders: "[Servant leadership] begins with the natural feeling that one wants to serve, to serve *first*. Then conscious choice brings one to aspire to lead. That person is sharply different from one who is leader first, perhaps because of the need to assuage an unusual power drive or to acquire material possessions. . . . The difference manifests itself in the care taken by the servant—first to make sure that other people's highest priority needs are being served. The best test, and difficult to administer, is: Do those served grow as persons? Do they, *while being served,* become healthier, wiser, freer, more autonomous, more likely themselves to become servants? And, what is the effect on the least privileged in society; will they benefit, or, at least, not be further deprived?" *Servant Leadership,* Robert Greenleaf, pp. 13–14.

6. Much has been said in recent years about the counterproductive effects of the intense pressure placed on top executives in public companies to make quarterly numbers. This systemic pressure is enormous, so we don't minimize it in any way. However, we find that executives at more advanced agility levels are more likely to respond to these pressures in ways that take into account both long-term needs and short-term demands. For example, when Robert, the oil company president, set the context for his strategic thinking initiative, the firm badly needed a short-term increase in its stock price, and Robert established this as one criterion for new strategy ideas. However, as a Catalyst leader, he was also very clear that the new strategies also had to fulfill a long-term vision of creating a company whose business performance and operating culture were benchmarked by other companies. (See "Temptation Is All Around Us: Daniel Vasella of Novartis Talks About Making the Numbers, Self-Deception, and the Danger of Craving Success," Leaf, and "How to Escape the Short-Term Trap," Davis.)

7. Achievers see the development of organizational culture and capabilities as means to strategic ends. Catalysts retain this perspective, but they also see how the reverse is true: An organization's culture and capabilities provide the context within which all strategic objectives are set and implemented. See *Organizational Capability,* Ulrich and Lake.

8. The relationship between leadership agility and corporate responsibility is addressed in one of the Frequently Asked Questions in the first part of Chapter Nine.

9. These observations are based on several decades of work with leaders. For a practice-based academic study that arrives at the same conclusion, see *Theory in Practice,* Argyris and Schön. The authors examined thousands of verbatim conversations about important business and organizational issues. They found that the predominant style used to deal with differing viewpoints is unilateral assertion, but that in a significant minority of cases, the style used is one of unilateral accommodation (withholding one's views or deferring to others). Less than 10 percent used a style that was genuinely collaborative. This overall pattern has been corroborated in *Leadership and Learning,* Jentz and Woffard, and in our multi-phase research study, described in Appendix A.

10. For a clear description of mutual, post-heroic empowerment, see *The Possibilities of Organization,* Barry Oshry.

11. Even those initiatives that focus on realizing new opportunities invariably require you to solve problems and overcome obstacles.

12. Cognitive scientists have mapped a continuum that ranges from "well-structured" problems at one end to highly "ill-structured" problems at the

other ("The Structure of Ill-Structured Problems," Simon). Well-structured problems are simple and routine. They have well-established answers. Ill-structured problems are novel and complex. They have no one right answer. This spectrum directly parallels the continuum of different kinds of organizational environments described in Chapter One. In other words, the more complex your organizational environment and the more rapidly it changes, the more ill-structured the business and organizational issues you face will be.

13. On the need to use creative thinking to solve ill-structured problems, see *Breakthrough Thinking,* Nadler and Hibino; *Imaginization,* Morgan; and *Creativity in Business,* Ray and Myers. A number of experts in applying creativity to business have stressed that creative problem solving actually includes a combination of what we often think of as "creative" thinking (for example, brainstorming new ideas) and critical thinking. As Marissa Ann Mayer, Google's VP for search products and user experience, has said, "Constraints shape and focus problems and provide clear challenges to overcome. Creativity thrives best when constrained. But constraints must be balanced with a healthy disregard for the impossible," "Creativity Loves Constraints," pp. 1–2. Also see *The Creative Manager,* Evans and Russell; *A Whack on the Side of the Head,* von Oech; and *Corporate Imagination Plus,* Bandrowski.

14. Of course, to complete the process you also need to plan for and ensure implementation and to monitor and learn from the results, which brings you full cycle to the diagnostic step.

15. There are also certain personality types and thinking styles that tend to be more creative than others, but our emphasis here is on capacities that evolve further with each new stage of personal development.

16. *The Act of Creation,* Koestler. As F. Scott Fitzgerald once said, "The test of a first-rate intelligence is the ability to hold two opposed ideas in the mind at the same time and still retain the ability to function."

17. *Developing Reflective Judgment,* King and Kitchener. This research builds on the stage development research of William Perry and his associates at Harvard University (*Forms of Intellectual and Ethical Development in the College Years*). King and Kitchener have identified reflective judgment as a developmental capacity that's used to solve ill-structured problems. Their basic definition of the term is consistent with its original use by American philosopher John Dewey in *How We Think.* Their definition actually includes what we call connective awareness, but we've chosen to separate these two elements because two distinct and complementary capacities seem to be involved.

18. "Judgment" is used here not in the sense of being judgmental (highly opinionated, critical, and evaluative, a trait that's most accentuated at the heroic levels). It refers rather to a capacity for discernment, which is vital in assessing the current situation and deciding upon the best course of action to take. Taking your capacity for reflective judgment to deeper levels takes courage, because it requires you to exercise your critical thinking faculties while acknowledging that all human knowledge and judgment is ultimately subjective and uncertain. However, the more you grow in this direction, the more effective you become in collaborating with others in developing solutions that reflect an artful synthesis of creative and critical thinking.

19. *Mastering Self-Leadership,* Manz and Neck. Note that self-leadership does *not* mean being inflexible about following others when they take the lead. It simply means that you're the person who's ultimately in charge of your own development and effectiveness as a leader. The meaning we give to self-leadership agility is very similar to that used by Manz and Neck, though it's not the same in all respects. The primary differences are that we've defined five different levels of self-leadership agility, and we use our own assessment tools and coaching and training methods to facilitate this leadership agility competency.

20. Self-leadership agility is similar to certain aspects of "learning agility," as described in *The Leadership Machine,* Lombardo and Eichinger.

21. As we use the term, "developmental motivation" is what motivates you to develop *within* your current level. It does *not* refer to what motivates you to develop from one level to another. The motivation to develop into a new agility level usually includes a feeling of dissatisfaction that is related to the limitations of one's current agility level and/or a desire to experience what is possible at the next level. In this sense, the motivation for developing from one level to another is the same for every level.

22. As psychologist Carl Rogers once said, "The curious paradox is that when I accept myself just as I am, then I can change."

Putting It All Together

23. Each pair of capacities includes one that emphasizes awareness and another that emphasizes intent. All eight capacities have both mental and emotional aspects: Those that emphasize awareness have an emotional as well as mental component, and those that emphasize intent have a mental as well as emotional component. That said, the capacities that support context-setting and creative agility have a more cognitive emphasis, and those that support self-leadership and stakeholder agility have a more emotional emphasis.

Levels of Awareness and Intent

24. As we discuss further in Chapter Ten, two modes of awareness help develop the personal capacities needed for leadership agility: reflection and attention. As we use these terms, *reflection* is a mental process that occurs after an experience has occurred, allowing you to recall and think about previous thoughts, feelings, and behaviors. *Attention* refers to direct, nonconceptual awareness of physical, mental, and emotional experience in the present moment. Attention, which develops progressively as you move through the post-conventional stages, brings you into an intimate relationship with your present experience, which paradoxically gives you more perspective. In this sense, reflection and attention can both be described as a "stepping back" from your current focus.

25. Strategic thinking is a hallmark of the capacity we call "sense of purpose" at the Achiever level.

CHAPTER 4: EXPERT LEVEL

1. Tony participated in a one-semester action learning program on leadership while earning his MBA at the Carroll School of Management at Boston College. The program was taught by Bill Joiner, adjunct faculty, and William R. Torbert, a professor at the Carroll School.

Pivotal Conversations at the Expert Level

2. *Increasing Leadership Effectiveness and Reasoning, Learning and Action,* Argyris; *Theory in Practice and Organizational Learning,* Argyris and Schön; *Leadership and Learning,* Jentz and Wofford; and *The Power of Balance,* Torbert.

3. For example, other than wanting to increase his knowledge of the business, Tony minimized his need to improve. He cited only one personal trait that might be a liability (being stubborn and opinionated), which he immediately rationalized as a "healthy skepticism" that bolstered his capacity for independent, critical thinking. As discussed later in this chapter, these defensive reactions result from the Expert's relatively low level of tolerance for facing discrepancies between self-ideal and actual behavior.

4. Like Tony, Beth participated in a one-semester action learning program on leadership at the Carroll School of Management at Boston College taught by Bill Joiner and William R. Torbert. As we define it, an action learning

program incorporates training modules, coaching, learning teams, and organizational improvement projects into an integrated leadership and organizational development initiative. See *Action Learning,* Dotlich and Noel, and *Work-Based Learning,* Raelin.

5. Although Experts usually don't take the initiative to incorporate stakeholder input into their leadership initiatives, they're quite capable of doing stakeholder analyses when asked to do so.

6. The terms *advocacy* and *inquiry* were originally used in *Theory in Practice* and *Organizational Learning,* Argyris and Schön, books first published in the mid-1970s. The terms were subsequently popularized in *The Fifth Disipline* and related fieldbooks by Peter Senge and his associates.

Team Leadership at the Expert Level

7. This program was conducted under the auspices of Leadership for Change, an executive education program within the Winston Center for Leadership and Ethics at Boston College.

8. Prior to the 360-degree feedback process, the firm's CFO had talked with Carlos about these issues several times but had been frustrated with his inability to get Carlos to expand his focus.

9. You can find a description of the Agility Insight Process at www.leadership agility.com.

10. *The Wisdom of Teams,* Katzenbach and Smith.

11. In the "staff group" configuration, problem-solving discussions tend not to be group discussions but rather one-on-one interactions between the leader and an individual subordinate.

Organizational Leadership at the Expert Level

12. We do not want to give the impression that abusive behavior is a hallmark of Expert-level management. It's also not a hallmark of the assertive Expert power style. While Experts with this power style do tend to be more outwardly judgmental than leaders at subsequent agility levels, abusive behavior is the result of other factors that have shaped a manager's personality.

Expert-Level Leadership Agility Competencies

13. "Ego Development and the Problems of Power and Agreement in Organizations," Smith.

14. Compare this level of awareness and intent with the one that develops at the previous (Conformer) stage of personal development: At that stage, your level of awareness corresponds to the most basic level of abstract thought, which includes the capacity to think in hypothetical terms, the ability to see what "is" in light of what "could be." Yet abstract thinking at this stage is still superficial and stereotypical. Your level of intent is characterized by rigid mental and emotional reactions about what "should" and "should not" be. These shoulds aren't the result of personal reflection. Instead, they're unconsciously incorporated from your environment as absolute, right-and-wrong imperatives, as if there's only one right way to do things. Because this stage doesn't provide you with the emotional depth needed to tolerate the inevitable gaps that arise between these rigid ideals and life as you find it, you tend to react by being highly judgmental toward anyone, including yourself, who doesn't live up to them. For more on the Conformer stage of development, see Appendix B.

15. Many examples of this orientation are provided in Rosabeth Moss Kanter's classic, *The Change Masters*. She calls this the "segmentalist" approach to organizational change initiatives.

16. At the previous (Conformer) level, you rely on the power of personal loyalty and formal rules. We are referring here to *personal* loyalty, not, for example, to Achiever-level strategic power alliances that may have the outward appearance of personal loyalty.

17. Note that these assumptions about power and authority reinforce the tendency to keep your leadership initiatives bounded within the areas of your own authority and expertise. This is just one way in which the capacities at a particular level of agility reinforce one another.

18. The research that led to this finding was conducted by our colleague Susanne Cook-Greuter.

19. When you work with people whose agendas conflict with your own, there's a tension between getting the substantive results you want and maintaining positive working relationships. On one hand, if you continually push for your own views, others may feel disregarded. As a result, they might be less cooperative in the future or even tell others that you're hard to work with. On the other hand, if you defer to others, you won't get what you want, and others won't benefit from your point of view. At the Expert level, it's difficult to hold both sides of this tension in mind during challenging conversations, so you tend to focus on one at the expense of the other.

20. Finally, regardless of whether your predominant style is assertive or accommodative, you might simply ignore your stakeholders, partly because you

"know" you're right and partly because you don't see how it's in your interest to engage with them.

21. Tony implicitly contrasts the leaders he admires with people who *would* be afraid to stand alone on an issue. Who might these other people be? Although Tony may be thinking of specific people he works with, he's also making an unstated reference to the Conformer he used to be. In fact, one reason Experts can be rather stubborn and opinionated is that they don't want to fall back into being a person who would rather fit in than stand out.

22. Experts may oscillate between assertion and accommodation, even in the same conversation. Only at subsequent levels do managers develop the capacity to balance and even integrate these polarities.

23. The Conformer level of reflective judgment is well-suited to solving well-structured problems (problems that have one preestablished right answer).

24. *Forms of Intellectual and Ethical Development in the College Years,* Perry. This study focused on male students. *Women's Ways of Knowing,* Belenky, Clinchy, Goldberger, and Tarule, is a more recent study, which shows that women of the same age group undergo the same kind of developmental changes as they grow from the Conformer to the Expert stage. Perry's work has been confirmed and further developed in *Developing Reflective Judgment,* King and Kitchener.

25. Note how this aspect of an Expert's reflective judgment ties in with this level's assumptions about power and authority.

26. "Ego Development and the Problems of Power and Agreement in Organizations," Smith.

27. "The Experience of Support for Transformative Learning," Harris.

28. At the Expert level, in your effort to become more independent, you may even convince yourself that your self-esteem is no longer dependent on other people. However, at this level, it's not enough that *you* think you're living up to your self-ideal. If you're completely honest with yourself, you don't just want to be an expert, you also want to be admired. For example, when Tony was asked what kind of leader he wanted to be, his whole answer was couched in terms of how he wanted others to perceive him.

CHAPTER 5: ACHIEVER LEVEL
What Leadership Means to an Achiever

1. Development into the Achiever level of leadership agility requires growth into the Achiever stage of personal development. Of those managers who develop to this stage, the great majority begin to do so during their college

years. A smaller percentage develop into the Achiever stage later in life, usually between their mid-thirties and early forties. While about 90 percent of all managers reach the Expert stage, only about 35 percent of all managers grow into the Achiever stage or beyond. Currently, about 71 percent of those managers who reach this stage remain in it for the rest of their lives. The other 29 percent of Achievers (or around 10 percent of all managers) continue on to one of the more advanced stages. To see how these percentages were calculated, see the last part of Appendix A.

Pivotal Conversations at the Achiever Level

2. The steps described here refer to our Agility Insight Process. For more information on this process, visit www.leadershipagility.com.
3. This format is somewhat similar to the process we used to help Robert and his team develop new strategies for his company. For additional information about this approach, go to www.changewise.biz/os-bsp-overview.html and www.changewise.biz/os-idea_factories.html.

   Guy's coach also helped him learn the skill of *combining* advocacy and inquiry—stating your point of view and then immediately inviting others to state theirs. His coach showed him how he could use this skill at the beginning of the meeting to describe the current group dynamic, say what kind of norms he wanted instead, and ask if the group agreed. Guy used this skill again toward the end of the meeting when the group was talking about the modified procedures proposed by the subgroups: When people start in with advocacy without inquiry, one way to facilitate the discussion is to step in from time to time and essentially do the inquiry for them. For example, "What do the rest of you think about Fred's idea." Guy's coach observed that this type of leadership intervention can often slow things down in a good way and shift the tone of the conversation.

Team Leadership at the Achiever Level

4. *First Things First,* Covey, Merrill, and Merrill. Although this book doesn't use a framework of levels of leadership agility, it presents a mixture of Achiever- and Catalyst-level ideas and methods in the area of time management.
5. In a larger company, employee compensation would be housed in the Human Resource department. However, Carlos's firm had started with a recruiter and a part-time HR manager, and had only recently hired a full-time HR manager.

Leading Organizational Change at the Achiever Level

6. At that time, Mark also believed that any new health care legislation passed at the federal level would simply strengthen the market forces already at work.

7. *Good to Great,* Jim Collins, pp. 17–40.

8. A number of Achiever-level capacities are at work here, beginning with Mark's strategic foresight: He had a vivid time horizon of two to five years and a level of situational awareness that could take into account industry dynamics and a complex set of stakeholder relationships. Mark's strategic diagnosis and prescription, which was much more detailed than we've just described, reflected an ability to discern themes of continuity and change, integrate factual information and practical concepts, and envision compelling positive and negative future outcomes.

9. For research that lends credence to this probability, see "The CEO's Role in Organizational Transformation," Torbert and Rooke. In this study, the CEOs who were successful in accomplishing needed organizational transformations either operated at a post-heroic level or treated a post-heroic consultant and one or more post-heroic team members as close confidants. Like Mark after he became CEO of the merged HMO, the unsuccessful CEOs increasingly distanced themselves from post-heroic sources of influence.

Achiever-Level Leadership Agility Competencies

10. Achiever-level awareness corresponds to what most developmental psychologists consider the culmination of "formal operational thinking," a term coined by Jean Piaget. See *The Developmental Psychology of Jean Piaget,* Flavell.

11. The value-and-belief system you develop at the Achiever stage of personal development may be consistent with those that predominated in your family, school, and other institutions that shaped your upbringing, or it may differ considerably. The important thing is that, based on your own experience and reflection, you develop your own system of interrelated values and beliefs. See *Stages of Faith,* Fowler, pp. 174–183.

12. While this brief sketch of Ellen's leadership philosophy conveys some sense of what we mean by a value and belief system, what she says explicitly is only the tip of the iceberg. As would be true for anyone, writing down all the values and beliefs that compose her actual value and belief system about

leadership might require a small volume. For a more in-depth but fictional example of an Achiever-level manager's value and belief system about leadership—this one emphasizing an inclusive approach—see the chapter called "Working" in Robert Kegan's *In Over Our Heads.*

13. *Stages of Faith,* Fowler, p. 179. Let us be clear: It would be a complete misunderstanding to think that this means that Achievers reject the whole idea of external authority as illegitimate. In fact, Achievers often aspire to become authorities in their own right. It simply means that, as they think through their own view of the world, they consciously choose who and what they regard as authoritative influences in their own thinking.

14. To use the terminology of social science and management theory, Expert-level awareness tends to treat an *open system* (a system that exchanges energy and information with its environment) as if it were a *closed system* (a mechanical system whose operation does not depend on an open exchange with its environment).

15. To the best of our knowledge, the slogan "Managers do things right— Leaders do the right thing" first appeared in *Leaders,* Bennis and Nanus.

16. Whereas Achievers tend to view organizational politics as an inevitable feature of organizational life, just another reality to master, Experts often equate organizational politics with the antithesis of legitimate organizational authority.

17. The power style a leader adopts on the assertive-accommodative continuum is the result of many influences, ranging from temperament and early childhood experiences to current organizational culture. When Achievers adopt styles at the extremes of the continuum, we believe it's usually because these background factors outweigh the Achiever's normal tendency to seek some degree of balance between extremes.

18. For example, Rachel's power style, which was somewhat on the accommodative side, worked extremely well at the brokerage firm. However, when she was later recruited to work her magic at a software company, she found she wasn't assertive enough to withstand the pressure to succumb to the prevailing culture. Consequently, some of her initiatives were not as successful there.

    In complex, rapidly changing environments, Achievers are usually most effective over the long term when they assert their own views and priorities in a way that also takes others' into account. Ellen's leadership philosophy is an excellent example of the way this balance can be articulated. In practice, this is a dynamic balance, one that allows you to move back and forth between assertion and accommodation as the situation demands.

19. Here are two illustrative comments, made by two Expert-level managers at the beginning of a leadership workshop: "Can't you give us a list of the ten things that great leaders do, and then we can just go do them?" "Can't you just give us a list of all the problem personalities we have to deal with and the technique to use to handle each one?" These questions assume that a person can become a more effective leader simply by following a laundry list of external techniques and that no other change on their part is needed.

20. *Identity: Youth and Crisis,* Erikson.

21. Guilt for the consequences of your actions is more pronounced at the Achiever stage than at any other. *Ego Development,* Loevinger, pp. 13–28.

22. Research has shown that Achievers are much more likely than Experts to respond to this kind of feedback by changing their thinking and their behavior. However, Achievers tend not to be receptive to feedback that implies that their desired outcomes need to be reconsidered. Nor are they likely to act on feedback that suggests that their value-and-belief systems are biased or incomplete. See "The Experience of Support for Transformative Learning," Harris.

CHAPTER 6: CATALYST LEVEL

1. The Brundtland report, produced in 1987 by the UN's World Commission on Environment and Development, defined sustainable development as a new approach to socioeconomic development designed to "meet the needs of the present without compromising the ability of future generations to meet their own needs." It has come to refer to forms of economic development that are socially and environmentally responsible over the long term.

2. Unfortunately, these benefits were not realized. The full story is too complicated to recount here, but her boss had made a grievous business error. He wanted to cover up the error by investing such a large percentage of the corporation's capital in other activities that the investment needed to achieve the company's public commitment to emission reductions would not be possible. He ordered Brenda to collude with him in saying that while the company "aspired" to these emission reductions, it had not actually committed to doing so. Long story short, rather than compromise her integrity, Brenda left the company. Her boss wound up in jail.

What Leadership Means at the Catalyst Level

3. Research indicates that about 29 percent of those managers who reach the Achiever stage (or about 10 percent of all managers) grow into the Catalyst

stage at some point in their lifetime. (See the last part of Appendix A.) Other research on adults who have at least a college education indicates that about 12 percent of this overall population has grown beyond the Achiever stage. *In Over Our Heads*, Kegan, pp. 185–197.

Pivotal Conversations at the Catalyst Level

4. You can find information about our Pivotal Conversations programs at www.changewise.biz/pivotal_conversations.html.
5. More information about the Catalyst level of awareness and intent is provided later in this chapter and in Adam's story in Chapter Ten.

Team Leadership at the Catalyst Level

6. The other option Doug and Joan considered was to bring a sales and marketing person in to run the firm. They'd both been down that road before. They felt that type of change could be very traumatic, particularly for a firm that had just been through a difficult year.

Leading Organizational Change at the Catalyst Level

7. We were the boutique consulting firm engaged on this project. See Note 1 in Chapter One.
8. Robert settled on the seven-year time frame because he felt that, symbolically, it would help people step outside their current assumptions.
9. You can find information about our Breakthrough Strategy Process at www.changewise.biz/os-bsp-overview.html. The concept of "creative leap" as applied to strategic thinking comes from *Corporate Imagination Plus*, Bandrowski.
10. Ian was enthusiastic about switching to this approach. He felt it would be more beneficial for his client, and he felt he would learn from the experience and broaden his repertoire. His team, however, was quite skeptical. Their firm's methodology would have tested each separate idea by determining whether it could pass through a series of three criteria-laden screens. They'd seen the ideas from the Idea Factories and thought the vast majority were so "wimpy" that they'd never make it through their screens. However, when they participated in the retreat alongside the top management group, they were surprised to find that the creative connections made between initially wimpy ideas led to the development of

powerful strategic initiatives that could then be evaluated using the criteria embedded in their screens.

Catalyst-Level Leadership Agility Competencies

11. Everyone has a range of feelings that come readily to consciousness, a further range of feelings of which they are only vaguely or subliminally aware, and still other feelings that are much harder to access. The Catalyst level of awareness is helpful in gaining access to the second realm of feelings. For examples of these types of feelings, see Adam's story in Chapter Ten.

12. In the summary that follows, you'll see that each time a person moves to a new level, the eight developmental capacities increasingly overlap with one another. This is because these capacities become more fully integrated at each successive stage of personal development.

13. Business leaders at the Achiever level know that their organization and its key stakeholders operate within a context that includes the larger society and the natural environment. However, most Achievers don't find it compelling to give this broader context serious consideration, unless they're faced with serious negative consequences (fines, damaging publicity) or unless they understand that it will enhance their ability to achieve their usual business objectives. At the same time, we know from our research that some managers at the Achiever level become strongly committed to corporate social and environmental responsibility, simply because not to do so would violate their value and belief systems.

    Also note that, while two of our Catalyst exemplars are attuned to issues of corporate responsibility, the other two are not particularly concerned about these issues. In our sample, the percentage of leaders committed to social and environmental responsibility increases significantly at the Co-Creator level.

14. For more on the concept of organizational white space, see *Improving Performance: How to Manage the White Space on the Organizational Chart*, Rummler and Brache, and "Managing in the White Space," Maletz and Nohria.

15. This is not to say that Catalysts *always* take a visionary stance. It simply means that they have a depth of purpose that allows them to be visionary when the appropriate situation arises.

16. With the development of this capacity, "active listening" is no longer a technique but a genuine way of relating to another person's experience. See *Leader Effectiveness Training*, Gordon.

17. Some Catalyst leaders at the accommodative end of the power spectrum assume that being collaborative necessarily means including more people (rather than seeing collaboration as a process of mutual influence between appropriate stakeholders). Other leaders at this end of the spectrum become so wary of hierarchical decision making that they try to do away with it. This approach tends to be confusing, because the leader still retains (and, inevitably, uses) ultimate decision-making authority.

18. For example, "causal loop diagramming," a methodology used in systems dynamics, a field originally developed by Jay Forester of MIT (see www.systemsdynamics.org) and popularized in Peter Senge's *The Fifth Discipline*, is very consistent with the kind of causal thinking that develops at the Catalyst stage.

19. The accuracy with which you can put yourself into another frame of reference is an important part of Catalyst-level connective awareness (and stakeholder understanding—an example of how the eight capacities become more integrated at this level).

20. This phrase was coined by Samuel Coleridge in 1817 to refer to the willingness of readers or viewers to suspend their critical faculties to the extent of ignoring minor inconsistencies so as to enjoy a work of fiction or poetry. The meaning of phrase has since broadened to include the usage we give it here.

21. Many creative thinking techniques, such as those used in the Synectics program, are designed to tap into this capacity on a temporary basis. *Synectics: The Development of Creative Capacity*, Gordon.

22. The root meaning of paradox is "beyond opinion." For more on the value of paradoxical thinking, see *The Age of Paradox*, Handy. For a discussion of dilemma resolution, a related concept, as a central leadership task, see *Charting the Corporate Mind*, Hampden-Turner.

23. For more about the importance of problem identification and problem definition, see *Smart Thinking for Crazy Times: The Art of Solving the Right Problems*, Mitroff, and *First Things First*, Covey, Merrill, and Merrill, pp. 268–278.

24. An example from David's story would be the lack of a clear process for resolving differences between software engineers and business line managers. See the distinction between symptomatic and high-leverage solutions in *The Fifth Discipline*, Senge.

25. The idea that self-empowerment involves acknowledging and overcoming unconscious emotional dependency on the organization you work for is described in *The Empowered Manager*, Block.

26. Like all the stories and examples in this book, other than those about the five Eds, this is a true story.
27. For a helpful diagrammatic representation of the self-reinforcing dynamic of addiction in all its forms, see the "shifting the burden" system archetype described in *The Fifth Discipline*, Senge.

CHAPTER 7: CO-CREATOR LEVEL

1. Insight (or vipassana) meditation is a form of Buddhist meditation practiced primarily in southern Asia.
2. *Mindfulness* is an English translation for a term in insight meditation. Its basic meaning is direct attention to present experience.
3. Buddhist ethics include behavioral precepts, such as not killing or stealing and not engaging in slander, gossip, or abusive speech, and attitudinal precepts, such as not cultivating envy or ill-will. The underlying theme is to act in ways that benefit rather than harm others. Acting in an ethical manner is said to make it easier to practice meditation, and practicing meditation is said to make it easier to act in an ethical manner.

What Leadership Means to a Co-Creator

4. *The Five Dysfunctions of a Team*, Lencioni.
5. Research indicates that only about 5 percent of all managers develop into the Co-Creator stage. Of these, about 20 percent (or 1 percent of all managers) later develop into the Synergist stage.

Pivotal Conversations at the Co-Creator Level

6. Ken is a fully developed Co-Creator, committed to developing toward Synergist. In this situation, at least, he provides an illustration of a fully developed Co-Creator capacity for stakeholder understanding in pivotal conversations.
7. Through further discussion, Ken and his management team realized how little they'd actually shared with key employees about the company's ongoing financial condition. For example, they'd just raised prices on spa services, and people didn't understand why they weren't given pay increases as a result. They decided to make some simple charts to communicate basic financial information to employees once a quarter.

Team Leadership at the Co-Creator Level

8. Alison and Tim managed attendance at case discussions in a manner that maintained client confidentiality.

9. *TM—Transcendental Meditation,* Roth. TM is a form of meditation with roots in the Vedanta tradition of ancient India. The basic technique, which Maharishi Mahesh Yogi began to promote in the 1950s, is one of silently repeating a mantra (sound) and continually returning one's attention to it. This has the effect of quieting the mind and releasing tension within the body. Practitioners of TM are not required to adopt any religious beliefs or rituals.

Leading Organizational Change at the Co-Creator Level

10. *Civil society* refers to the totality of a society's voluntary civic and social organizations, as distinct from governmental or business organizations. Examples of civil society organizations include trade unions, professional associations, charities, religious organizations, universities, nongovernmental organizations, various advocacy groups, and so on.

    Action research, as originally formulated by social psychologist Kurt Lewin, is a type of applied social or organizational research, usually conducted by a team including both practitioners and researchers, designed to improve practice by learning from experience. The action research process follows a series of action learning cycles that include data collection, problem diagnosis, goal setting and action planning, implementation, and data collection about the effects of the action taken. See *The Practical Theorist,* Marrow, and *Action Research* (2nd edition), Stringer.

11. Graham initially practiced a form of insight meditation (see Larry's story), then switched to a more devotional style of meditation emphasizing chanting and prayer. "The underlying intent," he says, "is to promote individual joy and happiness and to help bring about a more peaceful world."

12. Although this was a local project, the problem addressed is a global one. David Korten notes that "clean water and proper sanitation are perhaps the most significant indicators of good health and long life" (*When Corporations Rule the World,* p. 41).

13. Technically, nongovernmental organizations can be for-profits, but they're typically nonprofits that get at least a portion of their funding from private sources. Their goals are typically social, cultural, legal, or environmental

rather than commercial. Some of these organizations now believe the NGO designation is too broad and prefer to be called Private Voluntary Organizations (PVOs).

14. *Critical Choices: The United Nations, Networks, and the Future of Global Governance,* Reinecke and others.

15. By 2005, more than 50 million hectares (125 million acres) of forest in more than sixty countries were being managed to FSC standards, and several thousand products were being produced using FSC-certified wood. For more information about the Forest Stewardship Council, go to www. fsc.org.

16. *EarthRight,* Hynes, and *State of the World 1986,* Brown and others.

17. "The Johannesburg Summit Test: What Will Change?" at www.johannes burgsummit.org, United Nations, Commission on Sustainable Development, and *State of the World 1999,* Brown and others. For more current information, visit the World Resources Institute portal at www.earthtrends. wri.org and see the UN's *Human Development Report 2005: International Cooperation at the Crossroads: Aid, Trade and Security in an Unequal World* at http://hdr.undp.org/reports/global/2005.

18. Graham's critique is actually more complex, but for our purposes here, we've condensed it into two key points.

19. *When Corporations Rule the World,* Korten.

20. *In Earth's Company: Business, Environment and the Challenge of Sustainability,* Frankel, and *Critical Choices: The United Nations, Networks, and the Future of Global Governance,* Reinecke and others. Of course, many people around the world are genuinely committed to ending widespread poverty and environmental degradation. The point here is that the dominant process used to address these problems isn't sufficient to change the mind-sets that drive traditional institutions.

21. From our perspective, even though some of the reports generated by the dominant global problem-solving process reflect a perspective that goes beyond the Achiever level, the process itself operates at the Achiever level of agility. GT-Nets are learning to operate at the Catalyst level. Graham offers GT-Nets a vision of their potential, which could involve growing fully into the Catalyst level and then into the Co-Creator level of organizational agility.

22. For more on the idea of creating a "container," see *Dialogue,* Isaacs.

23. *Liberating the Corporate Soul: Building a Visionary Organization,* Barrett, p. 40. For a discussion of "enlightened self-interest" within organizations, see *The Empowered Manager,* Block.

24. This collective form of reflective action has been called "societal learning and change" in a book of the same name by Steve Waddell.
25. A "community of practice" refers to the process of social learning that occurs when people with a common interest in a problem or topic collaborate over an extended period to share ideas, find solutions, and build innovations. In 1998, Etienne Wenger published *Communities of Practice,* applying it for the first time to organizational settings. Also see *Cultivating Communities of Practice,* Wenger, McDermott, and Snyder.

The Capacities of Co-Creator Leaders

26. For example, you might notice that a plan you've just advocated is based on an unexamined assumption. You might notice that you're avoiding someone because you felt unfairly blamed in your last conversation, or you might realize that you've just interrupted someone after saying you want to hear them out.
27. A former chairman of the Department of Psychology at the University of Chicago, Csikszentmihalyi is currently director of the Quality of Life Research Center at Claremont University's Graduate School of Management. He is the author of *Flow: The Psychology of Optimal Experience* and *The Evolving Self.*
28. Alison took the same attitude toward painful feelings she experienced toward the end of her tenure at the Madison Collaborative Law Group. We did not include this part of Alison's story earlier because this aspect of the Co-Creator level of awareness had already been illustrated in the stories about Larry and Ken.
29. This is just one example of the way in which different capacities, in this case situational awareness and stakeholder understanding, become more integrated at the Co-Creator level.
30. All the Co-Creators in our sample who started new organizations (other than very small coaching or consulting practices) integrated commitments to social and environmental responsibility into the way their organizations operate. All did so because of strong personal commitments. Legal compliance was not a motivation, and any public relations benefits were, at most, a secondary consideration. Achievers and Catalysts sometimes do the same thing, but Co-Creators are much more likely to make this kind of commitment.
31. Graham stressed that the work he's doing on a global scale is not more important or more advanced than that of people doing similar work on a smaller scale. "We need people working on all these levels," he said.

32. As we noted in Chapter Six, when you grow into the Catalyst level, your ability to envision future outcomes expands, allowing you to move with greater ease through short, medium, and long-term time frames. You now have the capacity to develop an innovative, personally meaningful vision that keeps you highly motivated, even if it may take ten years or longer to fully materialize. However, this doesn't mean that all post-heroic leaders are currently working toward innovative, long-term visions. Circumstances also play a role. For example, Robert didn't develop a vision of this magnitude until he became president of the oil company.

33. When you grow into the Co-Creator level, you develop a strong commitment to living your life in an authentic manner. You want to be more honest with yourself about your real feelings and motivations, and you want to live your life in a manner that truly expresses your deepest values and potentials. The more you act on this commitment, the more attuned you become to a deepening sense of life purpose. For more on the difference between quantitative and qualitative time (called *kronos* and *kairos* in ancient Greece), see *Dialogue*, Isaacs, pp. 288–290.

34. For a definition of human values that's consistent with our intended meaning here, see www.iahv.org/humanvalues.htm.

35. Co-Creators also make sure that these forums are used to revisit the organization's mission or purpose over time. For example, after two years of operation, the management team at Deep Peace reexamined and reformulated its original mission, vision, and values. Within a similar time frame, the members of Alison's law firm found that they needed to clarify its relative emphasis on mediation and litigation.

36. Graham also demonstrated this capacity when, in our interview, he was able to passionately and accurately reenact the feelings of a GT-Net leader who had very little initial interest in forming a Meta-GT-Net.

37. "Searching for Collaborative Inquiry," Joiner, pp. 6–7.

38. For a framework that shows what mutual empowerment means in a variety of different organizational role relationships, see *The Possibilities of Organization*, Oshry. For a simulation-based training program that gives participants a direct experience of the underlying stance needed for relationships based on mutual empowerment, see www.changewise.biz/os-organization-workshop.html.

39. As in Ken's encounter with Jim and in Alison's decision to leave the Madison Collaborative Law Group, win-win doesn't always mean that the parties remain in close relationship. Even though, in both cases, the parties did not come to complete agreement on the issues involved, they did come to a res-

olution about the best form for their relationship to take going forward. In retrospect, both resolutions seem to represent the best possible outcome.

40. While the meditation techniques used by the leaders cited in this chapter come primarily from different Buddhist traditions, we are not trying to promote a particular religion or form of meditation or to equate its practice with Co-Creator leadership. Alison practices Transcendental Meditation, which comes from India's Vedic tradition. In the Synergist chapter you'll meet leaders who practice forms of meditation that range from centering prayer (from the Christian tradition) to various Taoist practices. One Synergist in our sample, not featured in these chapters, practices a form of Jewish meditation. Another Synergist is a Sufi. The key factor in growing into the Co-Creator and Synergist levels is the development of a particular level of awareness and intent. Many forms of meditation can be useful in fostering this development, although application in everyday life is what makes a difference in a person's leadership. Also note that some leaders featured in these two chapters (including Srini and Marilyn) do not meditate but have developed this level of awareness and intent in other ways. Still others have combined meditation with other methods, such as personal growth workshops.

41. At more advanced levels of self-awareness, you develop an increasing ability to transform the energy locked in painful feelings by letting go of the meaning-making process and then directly and fully experiencing the emotional energy that remains.

42. For example, people like Ken and Marilyn, with a history of accommodating themselves to others' priorities, can reclaim their assertive side. Others, like Larry and Alison, whose styles are habitually more assertive than receptive, can do the reverse.

CHAPTER 8: SYNERGIST LEVEL

1. This approach is consistent with an intervention methodology called appreciative inquiry, which emerged during the early 1980s in the field of organization development. (We should note that, while this approach is sometimes used by Synergists, appreciative inquiry is also consistent with the Catalyst and Co-Creator levels of leadership agility.) See *Appreciative Inquiry,* Cooperrider, Sorensen, Whitney, and Yaeger.

2. Even though Christine uses the approach of amplifying positive energy extensively in her corporate change work, she believes that there is a time and place for tactics that draw the line on what is acceptable behavior and what

is not. For example, she felt that such tactics were especially important at the beginning of the civil rights movement.

3. See, for example, *When Corporations Rule the World*, Korten.

4. The quotes were used anonymously.

5. Christine was given a budget to hire a large consulting firm. Instead, she used the money to fund employee-initiated change projects. Although she turned no one down who requested money, she found that most people just wanted to be heard and appreciated for their efforts.

6. For information about Grameen Bank and the microlending revolution, see *Give Us Credit*, Counts.

What Leadership Means at the Synergist Level

7. Christine uses the term *story* in a way that's similar to that used in *Your Mythic Journey*, Keen and Valley-Fox, whose work in this area builds on that of mythologist Joseph Campbell.

8. The last few pages of Appendix B discuss stages beyond Synergist.

Pivotal Conversations at the Synergist Level

9. For Erikson's in-depth biographical study of the Generativity stage, see *Gandhi's Truth*.

   "A growing body of psychological research shows that being highly generative is a sign of psychological health and maturity. People who score high on measures of generativity tend to report higher levels of happiness and well being in life, compared to people who score low. High generativity is also associated with low levels of depression and anxiety." From "Generativity: The New Definition of Success," McGrath.

10. Tai chi and chi gung are forms of movement and attentional practice from the Taoist tradition of ancient China that are designed to enhance physiological, psychological, and spiritual well-being.

11. NTL refers to the National Training Laboratories.

Team Leadership at the Synergist Level

12. In most cases, new CEOs don't want to have someone around with a close, long-term relationship with the Board. Yet Stan had managed to gain the trust of each new CEO.

13. For a detailed discussion of group "containers" and "fields of conversation," see *Dialogue and the Art of Thinking Together*, Isaacs, pp. 239–290. Stan did

not follow the approach outlined by Isaacs, but his idea of setting up a container or energy field around the group was similar in spirit.

14. For an advanced version of the GE Work-Out process, see www.changewise. biz/fast_track.html.

Leading Organizational Change at the Synergist Level

15. Because Laura had a well-developed level of self-awareness, she was quite familiar with her long-standing discomfort with conflict. However, she was able to place herself in a highly conflicted situation because she had learned that she could live with this discomfort by experiencing it whenever it arose and letting it pass, just as she was doing with the grief she was still experiencing from her husband's death.

16. The health center was a large facility with seven administrators and more than a hundred employees.

17. *The Creative Manager* by Evans and Russell presents a model of the creative process that includes five phases, each of which is illustrated by Laura's story: preparation (gathering all the different viewpoints), frustration (the discomfort of holding the differing views while not yet having a solution that addressed them all), incubation (taking several weeks to mull it over), insight (her experience in the shower), and working out (testing the idea with others, then testing it in action). This model of the creative process is very similar to earlier ones, except for its insertion of the frustration phase, an addition that we've found extremely valuable.

18. We asked Laura if she does anything regularly in her life that makes it easier for her to have these kinds of intuitive insights. She said, "What I do most consistently is participate once a week in a shamanic drum circle. It's a very eclectic group of people from around the Boston area, most of whom I don't see outside that group. When we get together, we do drumming and chanting, and we do journey work together, which involves a lot of visualization. These experiences have reinforced my desire to be close to nature, and I try to give myself some quiet time to pay attention to my dream life and to sense what my heart is feeling. It's not any more complicated than that. But I would say that I do have a very rich inner life."

She also said, "I want to stress how important I think the large group meetings were, because each of the main stakeholders got to be heard by the others, and they got to understand each other's points of view. If I'd just talked with each one privately and come up with this idea totally on my own, I don't think it would have hit home. I think, in a sense, we were all 'holding the space' together, and that's what made it possible for the right solution to emerge."

19. No one other than Laura had thought of the program's alums as having a stake in the program's future. She invited some of the alums to participate in the first semester of training by talking about their medical school experiences and helping teach basic procedures, like how to take blood pressure and other vital signs. These alums were glad to participate, because they wanted to uphold the program's good reputation, wanted to stay in touch with the university, and enjoyed the opportunity to teach.

20. The new mentor program has also been beneficial for the students in a number of ways: They don't have to spend any more time with their mentor than they want to, but it gives them a special relationship, someone they can check in with throughout the program whenever they like. Because of this relationship, the students wind up learning more during the first semester, and they make fewer mistakes when they're working in the health center. Mentors also serve as an important source of feedback, and when the program is over, they can write strong letters of recommendation to go with the students' med-school applications. The health center physicians also liked the changes. With fewer volunteers in the clinic at one time and with nurse mentors to guide the remaining volunteers, patients move through the center more efficiently, and the physicians get to spend the right amount of time with their patients.

The Capacities of Synergist Leaders

21. For readers who may be familiar with meditative disciplines, the type of "awakening" described here is not an ultimate awakening but rather the beginning of a process of awakening that unfolds through many stages beyond the Synergist. See, for example, Part I of *The Meditative Mind*, Goleman.

22. While thoughts often drop away when the Synergist chooses to focus on a sensory perception, this doesn't mean that Synergists are rendered incapable of thinking! Over time, Synergists develop an ability to bring the same kind of bare attention to the flow of thoughts and emotions, and to their entire bodily presence, even though, at this stage, they still forget to do so much of the time.

23. In our Synergist sample of sixteen people, 50 percent had a regular meditation practice and about 35 percent had a "semi-regular" meditation practice. A few, like Jeff's partners, practice a more active discipline, such as hatha yoga, aikido, tai chi, or chi gung, that fosters an awareness of the

present moment. There are many types of meditation and a number of different martial arts disciplines, all of which can aid a person in transforming into and through the Synergist stage.

Each of the four leaders whose stories were featured in the Co-Creator chapter also practiced meditation. In fact, while only a few Catalysts in our sample had some kind of regular meditation practice, 40 percent in our Co-Creator sample had a regular meditation practice and another 10 percent meditated in a more sporadic way. If meditation is a primary vehicle for developing the level of awareness characteristic of the Synergist stage, why have these leaders not yet grown into the Synergist stage?

The answer goes back to the way your level of awareness and intent affects your stage of development: Research (described in the next paragraph) has shown that regular, daily meditation over the period of a year or more can, in some cases at least, assist a person in developing to the next stage. According to our research, a person evolves into the next stage (develops the capabilities of that stage) by repeatedly bringing the level of awareness and intent that lies at the heart of that stage into everyday life situations. We believe that our Co-Creators who were also meditators were able to bring enough "flow state" awareness into their everyday lives to evolve into the Co-Creator stage and that our Synergists who were also meditators were able to bring enough "present-centered" awareness into their everyday lives to evolve into the Synergist stage.

One research project studied the extent to which counseling, drug rehabilitation, Muslim or Christian groups, or regular Transcendental Meditation (TM) affected the stage development of 271 maximum-security prisoners. Controlling for overlap of membership in the various treatment programs and nineteen demographic and criminal history factors, only regular participants in the TM program experienced a significant change in developmental stage. The study examined two groups of "TM subjects"—one group that had just learned the technique and another that had been practicing regularly for the previous twenty months. On average, after 15.2 months of practice, the group of new TM subjects developed from the Conformist to the Expert stage. On average, the group of "advanced" TM subjects began the study at the Expert stage and developed to the Achiever stage ("Walpole Study of the Transcendental Meditation Program in Maximum Security Prisoners II: Longitudinal Study of Development and Psychopathology," Alexander and Orme-Johnson).

Finally, it's helpful to keep in mind that people of virtually all ages and stages have learned to meditate. Studies examining the effect of meditation on stage development have shown that people at more advanced stages tune in to the process more readily than others do and that their meditation experiences are qualitatively different (Course on Adult Development, Harry Lasker, Harvard University, Fall 1982).

24. Both Christine and Stan looked for and mobilized forces that were already moving toward desired change. This approach reflects the spirit of a post-heroic intervention methodology called appreciative inquiry. See *Appreciative Inquiry*, Cooperrider, Sorensen, Whitney and Yaeger. At the same time, it's important to note that neither Christine nor Stan focused *only* on the positive. They each did something that Christine calls "holding up the mirror"—Christine through the Readers Theater and Stan through the CEO's appearance and his own statements.

25. For more on perceiving and working with organizational energy dynamics, see "The Flow State: A New View of Organizations and Managing," Ackerman, and *In the High-Energy Zone: The 6 Characteristics of Highly Effective Groups*, Deslauriers.

26. *Answering Your Call: A Guide for Living Your Deepest Purpose*, Schuster, pp. 119–122.

27. *The Act of Creation*, Koestler, and *Fire in the Crucible: The Alchemy of Creative Genius*, Briggs.

28. For an excellent Synergist-inspired guide to working creatively with conflict, see *Unlikely Teachers* by Ringer.

29. See the distinction between "the eye of reason" and "the eye of contemplation" in *Eye to Eye*, Wilber.

30. For readers familiar with Buddhist meditation practices, in that tradition, this awareness is called *mindfulness*. See *Mindfulness in Plain English*, Gunaratana.

31. The terminology of "dropping the story line" comes from talks by Pema Chödrön. See her recent audio book, *Getting Unstuck*.

32. *Don't Push the River*, Stevens, p. 5.

33. *Don't Push the River*, Stevens, pp. 179–180.

34. *It's Me and I'm Here*, Lyon, p. xviii.

CHAPTER 9: ASSESSING LEADERSHIP AGILITY

Frequently Asked Questions

1. Kevin, the CEO of the regional hospital council, was an Expert. Mark, the health maintenance plan CEO, was an Achiever. Robert was president of the oil company and in this capacity ran his own company. Ken and Alison, who were essentially CEOs of their own organizations, were Co-Creators. Jeff, the CEO of Generativity, and Dan, the foundation CEO, were Synergists.

2. These four studies are reported in *The Power of Balance*, Torbert, pp. 43–49.

3. The rounded averages in this table differ slightly from those in the table presented in Chapter One. To understand why, see the last section of Appendix A.

4. For a book that identifies the mind-sets and skill-sets needed to be effective at specific levels of organizational responsibility, we recommend *The Leadership Pipeline*, Charan, Drotter, and Noel.

5. For example, a study of frontline manufacturing supervisors found that Achievers were more effective than Experts and that Experts were more effective than Conformers, the level prior to Expert. See "Ego Development and the Problems of Power and Agreement in Organizations," Smith.

   Another study reviewed the effectiveness of ten CEOs who attempted to revitalize their companies by leading major change initiatives. Seven CEOs, five at post-heroic levels of agility and two at heroic levels, each transformed their organization and made their company much more successful. The other three, all of whom functioned at heroic levels, led unsuccessful initiatives, and their companies suffered as a result. The two heroic CEOs who succeeded did so by stepping into post-heroic territory: In conducting their change initiatives, they treated a post-heroic consultant and one or more post-heroic team members as close confidants. By contrast, the three unsuccessful CEOs increasingly distanced themselves from post-heroic sources of influence. See "The CEO's Role in Organizational Transformation," Torbert and Rooke.

   William R. Torbert and his associates have conducted additional studies, which show that middle managers at post-heroic levels of leadership agility are more effective than those at heroic levels. These studies are cited in "Organization Transformation as a Function of the CEO's Developmental Stage," Rooke and Torbert.

6. The nature of our study is such that we feel more confident providing ballpark estimates than specific percentages. Also, remember that we are not talking about what leaders *say* about corporate responsibility. We're talking about the extent to which they actually incorporate such considerations into the initiatives they take.

7. See Brenda's summary of the chemical industry's historical stance toward environmental responsibility at the beginning of the Catalyst chapter.

Fine-Tuning Your Self-Assessment

8. For resources that can help you and your organization become more agile, see the Resources section at the back of the book.

9. When you follow through by reflecting on your experience to see what you can learn from it, then incorporate your learnings into new action

experiments (and keep going), this becomes a complete reflective action cycle.

10. This is because each level of leadership agility is rooted in a particular stage of personal development. The fact that your developmental stage tends to stabilize when you're not in transition between stages (that is, most of the time) lends a good deal of stability to your level of leadership agility. See *In Over Our Heads*, Kegan.

11. For information about an instrument you can use to assess leadership agility, visit www.leadershipagility.com.

12. Whatever level happens to be your home base, you retain the ability to downshift intentionally to earlier levels, as needed.

13. To investigate this question more rigorously, developmental psychologist Harry Lasker conducted research with graduate students at Harvard. When these students participated in highly concrete, competitive games with strict win-lose structures, they often behaved as if they were at earlier stages of development. Once the experiments were over, they returned to their previous level of functioning.

14. *Emotional Intelligence*, Goleman, p. 42.

Assessing Agility Within Your Current Level

15. For information about an instrument you can use to assess leadership agility, visit www.leadershipagility.com.

16. Sarah received this feedback in a Pivotal Conversations program she attended with a group of her colleagues.

CHAPTER 10: DEVELOPING LEADERSHIP AGILITY
Setting Leadership Development Goals

1. Sarah gained these insights by participating in one of our Pivotal Conversations programs. As we do with all participants, once she learned a more effective way to deal with a specific challenging interaction, we asked her to make a conservative estimate of what the business impact would have been if she had responded as she had now learned to respond. Sarah's estimate was one month of cycle time, which, in her case, would translate into a profit margin of $10,000 to $15,000.

2. For more on combining advocacy with inquiry, see the Pivotal Conversations sections of Chapters Four, Five, and Six. Also see our white paper, "From Disconnect to Dialogue," Joiner.

Self-Leadership in Action

3. Participants in our Pivotal Conversations programs are provided with coaching support either by us or by appropriate internal personnel. In this case, participants chose as their coach one of two senior product development managers, always someone to whom they did not report. Sarah's mentor had attended the program with her, so he was very familiar with her learning case and her leadership development goals.

4. Sarah's mentor had already been coached by one of us for several years, so he was familiar with the coaching process in general and with the reverse role-play in particular.

5. Asking Sarah how she thinks Klaus would feel would be an Achiever-level exercise. The reverse role-play, which asked her to "become" Klaus, is more consistent with the levels beyond Achiever. This example shows that people are often capable of successfully employing practices characteristic of advanced stages of development. However, they may need more guidance in using the practice, and they are not as likely as those in the relevant stage to continue it on their own.

6. Among other things, Sarah's experience shows how a successful initiative in the pivotal conversations arena can cause positive ripple effects in the team and organizational arenas.

The Power of Reflective Action

7. Our description here is a shorthand. The diagnostic step can take a number of forms, including force-field analysis (identifying the factors already facilitating a desired solution, as well as those restraining it) and appreciative inquiry, where the emphasis is on identifying and building upon positive capabilities. Problems are addressed by identifying and leveraging existing strengths.

8. If you examine the basic tasks carried out using each leadership agility competency, described briefly in Chapter Three, you'll see that each of the four competencies moves through a reflective action cycle: Context-setting agility involves scanning your environment (assessment), understanding the issues you need to address (diagnosis), and determining the outcomes you need to achieve (setting intention). Stakeholder agility includes identifying your key stakeholders (assessment), understanding what they have at stake (diagnosis), and finding ways to increase alignment (setting intention). Creative agility is a process of identifying ill-structured problems (assessment), understanding their causes (diagnosis), and generating uniquely appropriate solutions (setting intentions). Self-leadership agility

involves a clear-eyed look at your effectiveness (assessment), identifying your strengths and limitations (diagnosis), and determining leadership development objectives (setting intention). The action step in context-setting agility and stakeholder agility moves you into the other two leadership agility competencies. The action steps in creative and self-leadership agility usually merge together, as they did in Sarah's case.

9. Your internal response to your successes and failures is influenced not only by your developmental motivation but also by attitudes toward yourself that you learned in earlier periods of your life, as well as by others' current attitudes toward you.

10. The choice of a creative practice is a very individual matter. A few examples: boating, woodworking, gardening, drawing, poetry writing, needlepoint, photography, sculpting, singing, horseback riding, playing a musical instrument, and learning a new language.

11. For more details, you can access Sandy Davis's e-book *Zillience! How to Succeed in Business Without Really Frying*, at www.zillience.com.

Levels of Awareness and Intent

12. When activated, the level of awareness and intent associated with each level gradually develops your mental and emotional capacities to that level. For example, a deeper level of awareness and intent makes it easier to see the ways in which apparent opposites are connected. Therefore, the more you bring the Co-Creator level of awareness and intent to the problems you face, the more natural it becomes to see and respond to these problems with the Co-Creator level of connective awareness.

13. Whenever people develop to a new level of agility, they retain the ability to shift down to earlier levels of awareness and intent. As noted in Chapter Nine, at times this downshifting is intentional, and at other times it is unintentional.

　　The five levels of awareness correspond to stages three through seven in client-centered therapist Carl Rogers's "process conception of psychotherapy," as described in his classic *On Becoming a Person*. For a more recent and somewhat similar framework of levels of awareness, see the chapter titled "Reflection and Presence" in John Welwood's *Toward a Psychology of Awakening*.

Growing into a New Agility Level

14. In this case "thinking of the presentation as a performance" meant that Adam was preoccupied with how well he would come across to others.

However, there are also post-heroic ways to approach a presentation as a performance. See, for example, *Leadership Presence*, Halpern and Lubar.

Attentional Practice

15. *Attention* as we use the term differs from the way it is used in cognitive psychology. In that field, *attention* refers to the cognitive process of selectively concentrating on one thing while ignoring other things. In our definition, attention is a transcognitive awareness. This awareness does have a focal element. However, as it develops, it becomes increasingly spacious. See "The Vision of Action Inquiry," in *The Power of Balance*, Torbert, and *Time, Space and Knowledge*, Tulku.

16. For example, Christine has a special room set aside for prayer, meditation, drawing, and journaling, yet she doesn't have a regular, daily practice. In fact, if she's in a particularly difficult period in her life, "all these things can simply feel irritating." Yet she also knows that, in time, she'll settle down and again find these practices to be of great value.

17. Larry practices insight (or vipassana) meditation, Ken practices Zen, Jeff practices Dzogchen, and Graham practices a form of meditation rooted in Mahayana Buddhism.

18. *Relaxing into Your Being* and *The Great Stillness*, Frantzis. Depending on how they are taught, a number of martial arts disciplines can be used to cultivate present-centered awareness.

19. *Jewish Meditation*, Kaplan, and *Ecstatic Kabbalah*, Cooper.

20. *The Sufis*, Shah; *The Chasm of Fire: A Woman's Experience of Liberation Through the Teachings of a Sufi Master*, Tweedie; and *Heart, Self, and Soul: The Sufi Psychology of Growth, Balance, and Harmony*, Frager.

21. "*Centering Prayer* is a *method* of prayer, which prepares us to receive the gift of God's presence, traditionally called contemplative prayer. It consists of responding to the Spirit of Christ by consenting to God's presence and action within. It furthers the development of contemplative prayer by quieting our faculties to cooperate with the gift of God's presence. . . .

"*Christian Contemplative Prayer* is the opening of mind and heart— our whole being—to God, the Ultimate Mystery, beyond thoughts, words and emotions, whom we know by faith is within us, closer than breathing, thinking, feeling and choosing; even closer than consciousness itself. The root of all prayer is interior silence. Though we think of prayer as thoughts or feelings expressed in words, this is only one expression. Contemplative Prayer is a prayer of silence, an experience of God's presence as the ground in which our being is rooted, the Source from whom our life emerges at every moment. . . . For the Church's first sixteen centuries Contemplative Prayer was the *goal* of Christian spirituality. After the Reformation, this living tradition was virtually lost." From www.centeringprayer.com. For an introduction to centering prayer, see *Intimacy with God*, Keating.

22. See *Gratefulness: The Heart of Prayer*, Steindl-Rast.

23. The relationship between meditation and religion is a complex one. Historically, the meditation practices associated with Western religions (Christianity, Judaism, and Islam) are not well known by the general public, and the vast majority of people who belong to these religions do not have meditation practices that cultivate present-centered awareness. In the popular mind, meditation is more closely associated with Eastern religions like Buddhism, Hinduism, and Taoism. However, the great majority of Asians who identify with these religions do not have regular meditation practices either. Further, many of those who practice Eastern forms of meditation are not members of the religions in which these practices first appeared.

24. Other Synergists we interviewed practice forms of meditation rooted in teachings that acknowledge the sacred dimension of life but are not associated with a particular religion. Examples include the Gurdjieff Work (*Gurdjieff: An Introduction to His Life and Ideas*, Shirley, and *In Search of the Miraculous*, Ouspenski) and meditation methods developed by Rudolph Steiner, which Dan has practiced for decades (see Steiner's *Knowledge of the Higher Worlds and Its Attainment*).

25. *The Relaxation Response*, Benson and Klipper, and *Beyond the Relaxation Response*, Benson and Proctor.

26. *The Way of the Shaman*, Harner, and *The Corporate Shaman*, Whiteley.

27. *Feel the Fear and Do It Anyway*, Jeffers.

Attention and Leadership Agility

28. *The Physical and Psychological Effects of Meditation: A Review of Contemporary Research* (2nd ed.), Murphy and Donovan; *Zen and the Brain*, Austin.

29. Ultimately, attention will replace reflection as your home base, and you will discover that, more than anything else, you *are* your attention.

30. Bringing present-centered awareness into the nooks and crannies of your everyday life is extremely important. Some meditators keep their life "on the cushion" separate from their everyday life. In so doing, they protect some of the reactive patterns that run their lives from the transformative effect of heightened attention. For more on this topic, see *Wake Up to Your Life*, McLeod.

APPENDIX A: RESEARCH BEHIND THIS BOOK

Three Phases of Research

1. Between 1979 and 1983, Wilber published six books, all part of what he now calls "Phase 2" in the evolution of his thought. Those that most influenced our thinking at the time were *No Boundary, The Atman Project,* and *Eye to Eye.* The development of Wilber's thinking, through and beyond these writings, is a complex subject captured in *Ken Wilber: Thought as Passion,* Visser.

2. "Ego Development and Motivation: A Cross-Cultural Cognitive-Developmental Analysis of *N* Achievement," Lasker. Very shortly after he taught the course we attended, Lasker moved away from stage-development psychology and, over the course of the next twenty years, founded or co-founded a number of successful companies focusing on multimedia technology and knowledge management.

3. This "test" (an unfortunate choice of word, in our opinion) is "scored" by specially trained raters. Development of the instrument began in the 1960s. It has been extensively researched, widely used, and refined over the years. See *Measuring Ego Development,* Hy and Loevinger.

4. Many of Lasker's new insights are nicely captured in Susanne Cook-Greuter's white paper, "A Detailed Description of the Development of Nine Action-Logics in the Leadership Development Framework."

5. This approach was based on a method originally developed by William R. Torbert and Keith Merron.

6. Michael Sales (of New Context Consulting) was one of the lead consultants on the FSS project.

7. Debbie Whitestone was one of the principal investigators on this study.

8. These included studies that Torbert conducted with his colleague Dal Fisher at Boston College as well as doctoral dissertations that Torbert helped supervise. These studies are discussed further under "Research Methods" in the second part of this appendix.

9. By the year 2002, Wilber's books had been translated into twenty foreign languages, and seven had become best-sellers.

10. "The Experience of Support for Transformative Learning," Harris; "The Relationship Between Ego Development and Managerial Effectiveness Under Conditions of High Uncertainty," Merron; and "Ego Development and the Problems of Power and Agreement in Organizations," Smith. Also see "Meaning-Making and Management Action," Merron, Fisher, and Torbert.

11. *Managing for Excellence* and *Power Up,* Bradford and Cohen.

Research Methods

12. *The Power of Balance,* Torbert, pp. 43–49. Of the six studies Torbert cites, we worked with four: 37 first-line supervisors, 177 junior and middle managers, 66 senior managers, and 104 executives. We eliminated a study of 100 nurses and a study of 13 medical professionals who were each starting their own practice, because minimal management responsibilities were involved.

13. The LDP, which was created by Susanne Cook-Greuter, is essentially the same instrument as the SCT, except that a few of the thirty-six sentence-completion stems have been altered to make them more workplace-oriented (for example, "A good boss . . ."). Cook-Greuter, an expert SCT scorer originally trained by Loevinger, has scored the LDP hundreds of times and has developed validated, norm-based scoring sheets for her new sentence-completion stems.

    We initially used Cook-Greuter as our primary scorer and did our own scoring (informed by our earlier training in the SCT and by additional training from Cook-Greuter) as a double check. As time went on, we developed enough confidence both in our ability to score the LDP and in our clinical judgment to do stage assessments on our own, occasionally getting additional confirmation by engaging our "subjects" in a collaborative self-assessment process.

14. See Note 12 for Appendix A.

15. "A Detailed Description of the Development of Nine Action-Logics in the Leadership Development Framework," Cook-Greuter.

APPENDIX B: STAGES OF PERSONAL DEVELOPMENT

1. *Integral Psychology,* Wilber; *The Evolving Self* and *In Over Our Heads,* Kegan; *Ego Development,* Loevinger; *Action Inquiry,* Torbert and associates (Torbert calls his stages "action-logics"); and "A Detailed Description of the Development of Nine Action-Logics in the Leadership Development Framework," Cook-Greuter.

    While these are the only theories represented in the chart, our descriptions of pre-conventional stages (Explorer to Operator) also draw on *Childhood and Society* and *Identity: Youth And crisis,* Erikson; *The Developmental Psychology of Jean Piaget,* Flavell; Harry Lasker's course on adult development at Harvard University (Fall 1982); *The Psychological Birth of the Human Infant,* Mahler, Pine, and Bergman; *Making a Friend in Youth,* Selman and Schultz; and "The Spectrum of Development," Wilber.

Our conventional and post-conventional stages (Conformer to Synergist) incorporate the work of Erikson, Flavell, Lasker, Wilber, Kegan, Loevinger, and Cook-Greuter, as cited earlier. They also draw on "Systematic, Metasystematic, and Cross-Paradigmatic Reasoning," Richards and Commons; *Stages of Faith*, Fowler; *Developing Reflective Judgment*, King and Kitchener; and *Forms of Intellectual and Ethical Development in the College Years*, Perry.

Regarding stages beyond Synergist, see the last section of Appendix B.

There are two major stage development theories that we chose not to fully incorporate into our synthesis. One is the theory of stages of moral development developed by Lawrence Kohlberg in the 1960s and 1970s. Our stance regarding this framework is described in Note 7 for the Introduction.

We also chose not to include the Spiral Dynamics theory developed by Don Beck and Chris Cowan (building on the earlier work of Claire Graves). This is because we have questions about its empirical basis and reservations about the way its stages are described. Briefly, the Spiral Dynamics stage descriptions (which they call "v-memes") include some elements that are consistent with the findings of other stage-development theorists, but for virtually every stage, they add a significant number of additional elements that may be valid for some people at that stage but, according to other stage theories, are not generally valid for people at that stage. The result is a framework that we believe contributes unintentionally to stereotypical thinking about what people at various stages of development are like.

We invite you to make your own assessment of this framework by reading *Spiral Dynamics*, checking the empirical basis for the theory, and comparing its stages with those found in other frameworks. One way to assess the extent to which this approach engenders stereotypical thinking is to join the Spiral Dynamics e-mail discussion list. We look forward to reading *The Never Ending Quest: Clare W. Graves Explores Human Nature*, edited by Cowan and Todorovic (and others), as this book may help to resolve some of the empirical questions we have about Gravesian developmental theory.

2. In this appendix, our descriptions of stages Expert through Synergist are essentially the same as the introductory summaries found toward the beginning of each chapter in Part Two of the book.

The Three Pre-Conventional Stages

3. These and the other stages in this appendix are described in terms that apply in economically developed societies. School-related references refer to the school system found in the United States.

4. See *The Developmental Psychology of Jean Piaget,* Flavell.
5. Symbolic play often begins at around eighteen months, when children use their imagination to have concrete objects stand for other objects, as when a pillowcase becomes a superhero cape or a large cardboard box becomes a house. By age four or five, symbolic play may include building pretend structures with plastic bricks and playing games with peers like "driving the car."
6. Through the structure of language, Enthusiasts not only learn to describe basic feelings and events, they also develop the ability to follow, imagine, and verbalize increasingly elaborate stories.
7. During the ending months of the Explorer stage, object permanence gives toddlers an understanding of physical space, but no real understanding of time.

The Three Conventional Stages

8. *Stages of Faith,* Fowler.
9. This is Karen, the woman cited in the Achiever and Catalyst chapters who became a Community Development Corporation administrator.

Three Post-Conventional Stages

10. *In Over Our Heads,* Kegan, pp. 185–197. Most people who grow into the Catalyst stage do so in their mid-twenties or beyond.

FAQs About Developmental Stages

11. See *The Essential Piaget,* Piaget; *Essays on Moral Development,* Vol. 1: *The Philosophy of Moral Development,* Kohlberg; *Ego Development,* Loevinger; and *The Evolving Self,* Kegan.
12. *Making a Friend in Youth,* Selman and Schultz.
13. We encountered this insight in Harry Lasker's course on adult development, Harvard University (Fall 1982). Also see our discussion of emotional hijacking in Chapter Nine.
14. Also from Harry Lasker's course.
15. Also from Harry Lasker's course.
16. We are indebted to Tara Brach for this formulation. See her book *Radical Acceptance.*

Stages Beyond Synergist

17. One exception was Erik Erikson, whose Generativity and Integrity stages implied growth beyond the Achiever stage. See *Erik Erikson: The Growth of His Work*, Coles.
18. *The Atman Project*, Wilber.
19. This is the term Wilber uses in his framework as it appears in the charts presented toward the end of *Integral Psychology*.
20. On page 206 of *Integral Psychology*, Wilber attempts to compare his framework with Torbert's. Wilber's comparison is accurate through Torbert's Achiever stage but is not accurate after that.

    To clarify the relationship between Cook-Greuter's most advanced stages and those articulated by Torbert: Using data from advanced-stage individuals who responded to the Leadership Development Profile and drawing on the literature on transpersonal development, Cook-Greuter posits two stages beyond what we call the Co-Creator stage. The first she calls *Construct-Aware*. The second she calls *Unitive*. (See "From Post-Conventional Development to Transcendence," Miller and Cook-Greuter, especially the figure on p. xxvi.) According to our understanding of Torbert's most advanced stages, Cook-Greuter's Construct-Aware and Unitive stages both fall within what we might call Torbert's Alchemist "zone" of development ("zone" implying multiple stages). More specifically, we believe that her Construct-Aware stage corresponds to our Synergist stage, while her Unitive stage corresponds to the stage beyond Synergist, though, as she herself acknowledges, some aspects of her Unitive stage "may confound several distinct higher levels of consciousness." "A Detailed Description of the Development of Nine Action-Logics in the Leadership Development Framework," Cook-Greuter.

∿ References

Ackerman, L. "The Flow State: A New View of Organizations and Managing," in J. D. Adams (ed.), *Transforming Work*. (2nd ed.) Alexandria, Va.: Miles River Press, 1998.

Alexander C. N., and Orme-Johnson, D. W. "Walpole Study of the Transcendental Meditation Program in Maximum Security Prisoners II: Longitudinal Study of Development and Psychopathology," in C. N. Alexander and others (eds.), *Transcendental Meditation in Criminal Rehabilitation and Crime Prevention*. New York: Haworth Press, 2003.

Argyris, C. *Increasing Leadership Effectiveness*. Malabar, Fla.: Krieger, 1976.

Argyris, C. *Reasoning, Learning, and Action: Individual and Organizational*. San Francisco: Jossey-Bass, 1982.

Argyris, C., and Schön, D. A. *Organizational Learning*. Reading, Mass.: Addison-Wesley, 1978.

Argyris, C., and Schön, D. A. *Theory in Practice: Increasing Professional Effectiveness*. San Francisco: Jossey-Bass, 1974.

Association of Career Firms International. Untitled article on Lee Hecht Harrison Fortune 500 leadership survey, June 10, 2004. Available online: www.aocfi.org/news/06-10-2004_2.html. Access date: March 26, 2006.

Austin, J. H. *Zen and the Brain: Toward an Understanding of Meditation and Consciousness*. Cambridge, Mass.: MIT Press, 1998.

Baker, C., Durante, C., and Sanín-Gómez, E. "Agile Government: It's Not an Oxymoron." *Executive Agenda: Ideas and Insights for Business Leaders*, 2004, *7*(1), 57–65.

Bandrowski, J. F. *Corporate Imagination Plus: Five Steps to Translating Innovative Strategies into Action*. New York: Free Press, 1990.

Barrett, R. *Liberating the Corporate Soul: Building a Visionary Organization*. Boston: Butterworth-Heinemann, 1998.

Beck, D. E., and Cowan, C. C. *Spiral Dynamics*. Malden, Mass.: Blackwell, 1996.

Belenky, M. F., Clinchy, B. M., Goldberger, N. R., and Tarule, J. M. *Women's Ways of Knowing: The Development of Self, Voice, and Mind.* (10th anniversary ed.) New York: Basic Books, 1997.

Bennis, W. G. *The Unconscious Conspiracy: Why Leaders Can't Lead.* New York: AMACOM, 1976.

Bennis, W. G., and Nanus, B. *Leaders: Strategies for Taking Charge.* (2nd ed.) New York: HarperBusiness, 1997.

Benson, H., and Klipper, M. Z. *The Relaxation Response.* (Updated and expanded ed.) New York: Quill, 2001.

Benson, H., and Proctor, W. *Beyond the Relaxation Response: How to Harness the Healing Power of Your Personal Beliefs.* New York: Times Books, 1984.

Berens, L., and Nardi, D. *The 16 Personality Types: Descriptions for Self-Discovery.* Huntington Beach, Calif.: Telos, 1999.

Block, P. *The Empowered Manager: Positive Political Skills at Work.* San Francisco: Jossey-Bass, 1987.

Boyatzis, R. E., and McKee, A. *Resonant Leadership: Renewing Yourself and Connecting with Others Through Mindfulness, Hope, and Compassion.* Boston: Harvard Business School Press, 2005.

Brach, T. *Radical Acceptance: Embracing Your Life with the Heart of a Buddha.* New York: Bantam, 2003.

Bradford, D. L., and Cohen, A. R. *Managing for Excellence: The Leadership Guide to Developing High Performance in Contemporary Organizations.* Hoboken, N.J.: Wiley, 1997.

Bradford, D. L., and Cohen, A. R. *Power Up: Transforming Organizations Through Shared Leadership.* Hoboken, N.J.: Wiley, 1998.

Briggs, J. *Fire in the Crucible: The Alchemy of Creative Genius.* New York: St. Martin's Press, 1988.

Brown, L. R., and others. *State of the World, 1986: A Worldwatch Institute Report on Progress Toward a Sustainable Society.* New York: Norton, 1986.

Brown, L. R., and others. *State of the World, 1999: A Worldwatch Institute Report on Progress Toward a Sustainable Society.* New York: Norton, 2001.

Charan, R., Drotter, S., and Noel, J. *The Leadership Pipeline: How to Build the Leadership-Powered Company.* San Francisco: Jossey-Bass, 2001.

Chödrön, P. *Getting Unstuck: Breaking Your Habitual Patterns and Encountering Naked Reality.* (Recording). Boulder, Colo.: Sounds True, 2004.

Coles, R. *Erik Erikson: The Growth of his Work.* New York: Plenum, 1970.

Collins, J. C. *Good to Great: Why Some Companies Make the Leap—and Others Don't.* New York: HarperBusiness, 2001.

Cook-Greuter, S. R. "A Detailed Description of the Development of Nine Action-Logics in the Leadership Development Framework," 2005. Paper available for download at www.harthillusa.com; click "On the Development of Action Logics (3/01/05) (pdf)" under "White Papers." Access date: June 1, 2006.

Cook-Greuter, S. R. Leadership Development Profile (LDP). n.d. Harthill USA. Available online: www.harthillusa.com. Access date: March 26, 2006.

Cooper, D. *Ecstatic Kabbalah.* Boulder, Colo.: Sounds True, 2005.

Cooperrider, D. L, Sorensen P. F., Whitney, D., and Yaeger, T. F. *Appreciative Inquiry: Rethinking Human Organization Toward a Positive Theory of Change.* Champaign, Ill.: Stipes, 2000.

Counts, A. *Give Us Credit.* New York: Crown, 1996.

Covey, S. R., Merrill, R., and Merrill, R. R. *First Things First Every Day: Because Where You're Headed Is More Important Than How Fast You're Going.* New York: Simon & Schuster, 1997.

Cowan, C., and Todorovic, N. (eds.). *The Never Ending Quest: Clare W. Graves Explores Human Nature.* Santa Barbara, Calif.: ECLET, 2005.

Csikszentmihalyi, M. *Flow: The Psychology of Optimal Experience.* New York: HarperCollins, 1990.

Csikszentmihalyi, M. *The Evolving Self: A Psychology for the Third Millennium.* New York: HarperCollins, 1993.

Davis, I. "How to Escape the Short-Term Trap." *Financial Times,* Apr. 11, 2005. Available online: www.mckinsey.com/aboutus/mckinseynews/pressarchive/pdf/FT_Op-ed_April_11,2005.pdf. Access date: March 26, 2006.

Davis, S. *Zillience! How to Succeed in Business Without Really Frying: Practical Ways to Methodically Increase Your Resilience and Enhance Your Capacity to Thrive* (e-book and pamphlet versions), Hudson, Mass.: ChangeWise, 2006. Available online: www.changewise.biz/rw/. Access date: March 26, 2006.

Deslauriers, P. *In the High-Energy Zone: The 6 Characteristics of Highly Effective Groups.* Makawao, Hawaii: Inner Ocean, 2002.

Dewey, J. *How We Think.* Mineola, N.Y.: Dover, 1997. (Originally published 1910.)

Dotlich, D. L., and Noel, J. L. *Action Learning: How the World's Top Companies Are Re-creating Their Leaders and Themselves.* San Francisco: Jossey-Bass, 1998.

Dove, R. *Response Ability: The Language, Structure, and Culture of the Agile Enterprise.* Hoboken, N.J.: Wiley, 2001.

Erikson, E. H. *Identity: Youth and Crisis.* New York: Norton, 1968.

Erikson, E. H. *Childhood and Society.* New York: Norton, 1993.

Erikson, E. H. *Gandhi's Truth: On the Origins of Militant Nonviolence.* New York: Norton, 1993.

Evans, R., and Russell, P. *The Creative Manager: Finding Inner Vision and Wisdom in Uncertain Times.* San Francisco: Jossey-Bass, 1992.

Flavell, J. H. *The Developmental Psychology of Jean Piaget.* Princeton, N.J.: Van Nostrand, 1963.

Fowler, J. W. *Stages of Faith: The Psychology of Human Development and the Quest for Meaning.* San Francisco: Harper San Francisco, 1981.

Frager, R. *Heart, Self, and Soul: The Sufi Psychology of Growth, Balance, and Harmony.* Wheaton, Ill.: Quest Books, 1999.

Frankel, C. *In Earth's Company: Business, Environment and the Challenge of Sustainability.* Gabriola Island, B.C., Canada: New Society, 1998.

Frantzis, B. K. *Relaxing into Your Being.* Fairfax, Calif.: Energy Arts, 2001.

Frantzis, B. K. *The Great Stillness: Body Awareness, Moving Meditation and Sexual Chi Gung.* Fairfax, Calif.: Energy Arts, 2001.

Gilligan, C. "In a Different Voice: Women's Conceptions of Self and of Morality." *Harvard Education Review,* 1977, *47,* 481–517.

Goldman, S. L., and Graham, C. B. (eds.). *Agility in Health Care: Strategies for Mastering Turbulent Markets.* San Francisco: Jossey-Bass, 1999.

Goldstein, J. *The Experience of Insight.* Boston: Shambhala, 1987.

Goleman, D. *The Meditative Mind: The Varieties of Meditative Experience.* Los Angeles: Tarcher, 1988.

Goleman, D. *Emotional Intelligence: Why It Can Matter More Than IQ.* New York: Bantam Books, 1995.

Goleman, D. *Working with Emotional Intelligence.* New York: Bantam Books, 1998.

Goleman, D., Boyatzis, R., and McKee, A. *Primal Leadership: Realizing the Power of Emotional Intelligence.* Boston: Harvard Business School Press, 2002.

Gordon, T. *Leader Effectiveness Training, L.E.T: Proven Skills for Leading Today's Business into Tomorrow.* (1st Perigee ed.) New York: Berkley, 2001.

Gordon, W.J.J. *Synectics: The Development of Creative Capacity.* New York: HarperCollins, 1961.

Greenleaf, R. *Servant Leadership.* Mahwah, N.J.: Paulist Press, 1977.

Gunaratana, B. H. *Mindfulness in Plain English.* Boston: Wisdom, 2002.

Gunneson, A. *Transitioning to Agility: Creating the 21st Century Enterprise.* Reading, Mass.: Addison-Wesley, 1997.

Halpern, B. L., and Lubar, K. *Leadership Presence: Dramatic Techniques to Reach Out, Motivate, and Inspire.* New York: Gotham Books, 2003.

Hamel, G., and Valikangas, L. "The Quest for Resilience." *Harvard Business Review,* Sept. 2003, *81*(1), 52–63.

Hampden-Turner, C. *Charting the Corporate Mind: From Dilemma to Strategy.* Cambridge, Mass.: Blackwell, 1994.

Handy, C. B. *The Age of Paradox.* Boston: Harvard Business School Press, 1994.

Harner, M. *The Way of the Shaman.* (10th anniversary ed.) San Francisco: Harper San Francisco, 1990.

Harris, C. "The Experience of Support for Transformative Learning." Unpublished doctoral dissertation, Harvard Graduate School of Education, Harvard University, 2002.

Hy, L. X., and Loevinger, J. *Measuring Ego Development.* Mahwah, N.J.: Erlbaum, 1996.

Hynes, H. P. *EarthRight.* Rocklin, Calif.: Prima,1990.

Isaacs, W. *Dialogue and the Art of Thinking Together: A Pioneering Approach to Communicating in Business and in Life.* New York: Doubleday/Currency, 1999.

Jeffers, S. *Feel the Fear and Do It Anyway.* (1st ed.) San Diego: Harcourt Brace Jovanovich, 1987.

Jentz, B. C., and Woffard, J. W. *Leadership and Learning: Personal Change in a Professional Setting.* New York: McGraw-Hill, 1979.

Joiner, B. "From Disconnect to Dialogue: Transforming Business Results Through Pivotal Conversations," 2002. Available online: www.changewise.biz/tips_and_tomes.html. Access date: March 26, 2006.

Joiner, B. "Searching for Collaborative Inquiry." Unpublished doctoral dissertation, Harvard Graduate School of Education, Harvard University, 1982.

Kanter, R. M. *The Change Masters: Innovations for Productivity in the American Corporation.* New York: Simon & Schuster, 1983.

Kaplan, A. *Jewish Meditation: A Practical Guide.* New York: Schocken Books, 1985.

Katzenbach, J. R., and Smith D. K. *The Wisdom of Teams: Creating the High-Performance Organization.* New York: HarperBusiness, 2003.

Keating, T. *Intimacy with God.* New York: Crossroad, 1994.

Keen, S., and Valley-Fox, A. *Your Mythic Journey.* Los Angeles: Tarcher, 1989.

Kegan, R. *In Over Our Heads: The Mental Demands of Modern Life.* Cambridge, Mass.: Harvard University Press, 1994.

Kegan, R. *The Evolving Self: Problem and Process in Human Development.* Cambridge, Mass.: Harvard University Press, 1982.

Keirsey, D. *Please Understand Me II: Temperament, Character, Intelligence.* Del Mar, Calif.: Prometheus Nemesis, 1998.

Kidd, P. T. *Agile Manufacturing: Forging New Frontiers.* Reading, Mass.: Addison-Wesley, 1994.

King, P. M., and Kitchener, K. S. *Developing Reflective Judgment: Understanding and Promoting Intellectual Growth and Critical Thinking in Adolescents and Adults.* San Francisco: Jossey-Bass, 1994.

Koestler, A. *The Act of Creation.* New York: Macmillan, 1969.

Kohlberg, L. *Essays on Moral Development,* Vol. 1: *The Philosophy of Moral Development.* San Francisco: Harper San Francisco, 1981.

Korten, D. *When Corporations Rule the World.* (2nd ed.) San Francisco: Berrett-Koehler, 2001.

Kotter, J. P. *A Force for Change: How Leadership Differs from Management.* New York: Free Press, 1990.

Kroeger, O., and Thusen, J. M. *Type Talk, or How to Determine Your Personality Type and Change Your Life.* New York: Delacorte Press, 1988.

Lasker, H. "Ego Development and Motivation: A Cross-Cultural Cognitive-Developmental Analysis of *N* Achievement." Unpublished doctoral dissertation, Department of Sociology, University of Chicago, 1978.

Lawler, E. E., III, and Worley, C. G. *Built to Change: How to Achieve Sustained Organizational Effectiveness.* Hoboken, N.J.: Wiley, 2006.

Leaf, C. "Temptation Is All Around Us: Daniel Vasella of Novartis Talks About Making the Numbers, Self-Deception, and the Danger of Craving Success." *Fortune,* Nov. 4, 2002.

Lencioni, P. *The Five Dysfunctions of a Team: A Leadership Fable.* San Francisco: Jossey-Bass, 2002.

Levinson, D. J., and others. *The Seasons of a Man's Life.* New York: Knopf, 1978.

Loevinger, J. *Ego Development: Conceptions and Theories.* San Francisco: Jossey-Bass, 1976.

Lombardo, M. M., and Eichinger, R. W. *The Leadership Machine: Architecture to Develop Leaders for any Future.* Minneapolis: Lominger, 2001.

Lyon, H. C., Jr. *It's Me and I'm Here! From West Point to Esalen: The Struggles of an Overachiever to Revitalize His Life Through the Human Potential Movement.* New York: Delacorte Press, 1974.

Mahler, M. S., Pine, F., and Bergman, A. *The Psychological Birth of the Human Infant: Symbiosis and Individuation.* New York: Basic Books, 1975.

Maletz, M. C., and Nohria, N. "Managing in the White Space." *Harvard Business Review,* Feb. 2001, pp. 102–111.

Manz, C. C., and Neck, C. P. *Mastering Self-Leadership: Empowering Yourself for Personal Excellence.* (3rd ed.) Upper Saddle River, N.J.: Prentice Hall, 2003.

Marrow, A. J. *The Practical Theorist: The Life and Work of Kurt Lewin.* New York: Teachers College Press, 1977.

Mayer, M. A. "Creativity Loves Constraints." *Business Week,* Feb. 13, 2006, pp. 1–2.

McCann, J. E. "Building Agility and Resiliency During Turbulent Change." Teleconference sponsored by Human Resource Planning Society, Dec. 14, 2004.

McCann, J. E. "Organizational Effectiveness: Changing Concepts for Changing Environments." *Human Resource Planning,* March 2004.

McGrath, D. "Generativity: The New Definition of Success." *Spirituality and Health,* Fall 2001. Available online with registration: www.spiritualityhealth.com.

McLeod, K. *Wake Up to Your Life: Discovering the Buddhist Path of Attention.* San Francisco: Harper San Francisco, 2001.

Merron, K. "The Relationship Between Ego Development and Managerial Effectiveness Under Conditions of High Uncertainty." Unpublished doctoral dissertation, Harvard Graduate School of Education, Harvard University, 1985.

Merron, K., Fisher, D., and Torbert, W. R. "Meaning-Making and Management Action," *Group and Organization Studies,* 1987, *12,* 257–286.

Miller, M. E., and Cook-Greuter, S. "From Post-Conventional Development to Transcendence," in M. E. Miller and S. Cook-Greuter, *Transcendence and Mature Thought in Adulthood: The Further Reaches of Adult Development.* Lanham, Md.: Rowman and Littlefield, 1994.

Mitroff, I. I. *Smart Thinking for Crazy Times: The Art of Solving the Right Problems.* San Francisco: Berrett-Koehler, 1998.

Morgan, G. *Imaginization: New Mindsets for Seeing, Organizing and Managing.* Thousand Oaks, Calif.: Sage, 1997.

Murphy, J., and Gilligan, C. "Moral Development in Late Adolescence and Adulthood: A Critique and Reconstruction of Kohlberg's Theory." *Human Development,* 1980, *23,* 77–104.

Murphy, M., and Donovan, S. *The Physical and Psychological Effects of Meditation: A Review of Contemporary Research with a Comprehensive*

Bibliography. (2nd ed.) Sausalito, Calif.: Institute of Noetic Sciences, 1997.

Nadler, G., and Hibino, S. *Breakthrough Thinking.* (2nd ed.) Rocklin, Calif.: Prima, 1994.

Oleson, J. *Pathways to Agility: Mass Customization in Action.* Hoboken, N.J.: Wiley, 1998.

Oshry, B. *The Possibilities of Organization.* Boston: Power and Systems, 1986.

Ouspenski, P. D. *In Search of the Miraculous: Fragments of an Unknown Teaching.* (new ed.) San Diego: Harcourt, 2001.

Perry, W. G., Jr. *Forms of Intellectual and Ethical Development in the College Years: A Scheme.* San Francisco: Jossey-Bass, 1999.

Piaget, J., Gruber, H. E., and Voneche, J. J. (eds.) *The Essential Piaget.* Northvale, N.J.: Aronson, 1995.

Preiss, K., Goldman, S. L., and Nagel, R. N. *Cooperate to Compete: Building Agile Business Relationships.* New York: Van Nostrand Reinhold, 1996.

Raelin, J. A. *Work-Based Learning: The New Frontier of Management Development.* Reading, Mass.: Addison-Wesley, 1999.

Ray, M., and Myers, R. *Creativity in Business.* New York: Doubleday, 1986.

Reid, H. G., and Yanarella, E. J. "Critical Political Theory and Moral Development: On Kohlberg, Hampden-Turner, and Habermas." *Theory Society,* 1977, *4,* 479–500.

Reinecke, W. H., and others. *Critical Choices: The United Nations, Networks, and the Future of Global Governance.* Ottawa: International Development Research Centre, 2000.

Richards, F. A., and Commons, M. L. "Systematic, Metasystematic, and Cross-Paradigmatic Reasoning," in M. L. Commons, F. A. Richards, and C. Armon, C. (eds.). *Beyond Formal Operations.* New York: Praeger, 1984.

Ringer, J. *Unlikely Teachers: Finding the Hidden Gifts in Daily Conflict.* Portsmouth, N.H.: One Point Press, 2006.

Rogers, C. R. *On Becoming a Person: A Distinguished Psychologist's Guide to Personal Growth and Creativity.* Boston: Houghton Mifflin, 1961.

Rooke, D., and Torbert, W. R. "Organization Transformation as a Function of the CEO's Developmental Stage." *Organization Development Journal,* 1998, *16*(1), 11–28.

Rooke, D., and Torbert, W. R. "Seven Transformations of Leadership," *Harvard Business Review,* April 2005, pp. 66-76.

Roth, R. *TM—Transcendental Meditation.* (rev. and updated ed.) New York: Fine, 1994.

Rowan, R. *The Intuitive Manager.* Boston: Little, Brown, 1986.

Rummler, G. A., and Brache, A. P. *Improving Performance: How to Manage the White Space on the Organizational Chart.* (2nd ed.) San Francisco: Jossey-Bass, 1995.

Schein, E. H. *Career Dynamics: Matching Individual and Organizational Needs.* Reading, Mass.: Addison-Wesley, 1978.

Schuster, J. P. *Answering Your Call: A Guide for Living Your Deepest Purpose.* San Francisco: Berrett-Koehler, 2003.

Selman, R. L., and Schultz, L. H. *Making a Friend in Youth: Developmental Theory and Pair Therapy.* Hawthorne, N.Y.: Aldine de Gruyter, 1998.

Senge, P. "Creating Desired Futures in a Global Economy." *Reflections,* 2004, 5(1), 1–12.

Senge, P. M. *The Fifth Discipline: The Art and Practice of the Learning Organization.* New York: Doubleday/Currency, 1990.

Shah, I. *The Sufis.* New York: Anchor Books, 1990. (Originally published 1964.)

Sheehy, G. *Passages: Predictable Crises of Adult Life.* New York: Dutton, 1976.

Shirley, J. *Gurdjieff: An Introduction to His Life and Ideas.* Los Angeles: Tarcher, 2004.

Simon, H. "The Structure of Ill-Structured Problems." *Artificial Intelligence,* 1973, 4, 181–201.

Smith, S. "Ego Development and the Problems of Power and Agreement in Organizations." Unpublished doctoral dissertation, School of Government and Business Administration, George Washington University, 1980.

Steindl-Rast, D. *Gratefulness: The Heart of Prayer: An Approach to Life in Fullness.* New York: Paulist Press, 1984.

Steiner, R. *Knowledge of the Higher Worlds and Its Attainment.* (3rd ed.; G. Metaxa, trans. H. B. Monges and L. D. Monges, rev.) New York: Anthroposophic Press, 1970. (Originally published 1904.)

Stevens, B. *Don't Push the River (It Flows by Itself).* Lafayette, Calif.: Real People Press, 1970.

Stringer, E. T. *Action Research.* (2nd ed.) Thousand Oaks, Calif.: Sage, 1999.

Taylor, S. "The Present State of Leadership and Strategies for Preparing Future Leaders." Webinar presentation sponsored by Center for Creative Leadership, March 2005.

Torbert, W. R. "The Vision of Action Inquiry," in W. R. Torbert, *The Power of Balance: Transforming Self, Society, and Scientific Inquiry.* Thousand Oaks, Calif.: Sage, 1991.

Torbert, W. R. *The Power of Balance: Transforming Self, Society, and Scientific Inquiry.* Thousand Oaks, Calif.: Sage, 1991.

Torbert, W. R., Cook-Greuter, S., and others. *Action Inquiry: The Secret of Timely and Transforming Leadership.* San Francisco, Calif.: Berrett-Koehler, 2004.

Torbert, W. R., and Rooke, D. "The CEO's Role in Organizational Transformation." *Systems Thinker,* September 1999, *10*(7), 1–5.

Tulku, T. *Time, Space and Knowledge: A New Vision of Reality.* Emeryville, Calif.: Dharma, 1977.

Tweedie, I. *The Chasm of Fire: A Woman's Experience of Liberation Through the Teaching of a Sufi Master.* Tisbury, Wiltshire, U.K.: Element Books, 1979.

Ulrich, D., and Lake, D. *Organizational Capability: Competing from the Inside Out.* Hoboken, N.J.: Wiley, 1990.

United Nations Development Programme (UNDP). *Human Development Report 2005: International Cooperation at a Crossroads: Aid, Trade and Security in an Unequal World,* 2005. Available online: http://hdr.undp.org/reports/global/2005. Access date: March 27, 2006.

United Nations World Commission on Environment and Development. *The Brundtland Report: Our Common Future.* Oxford, England: Oxford University Press, 1987.

United Nations, Commission on Sustainable Development. "The Johannesburg Summit Test: What Will Change?" Sept. 25, 2002. Available online: www.johannesburgsummit.org/html/whats_new/feature_story41.html. Access date: March 26, 2006.

Visser, F. *Ken Wilber: Thought as Passion.* Albany: State University of New York Press, 2003.

von Oech, R. *A Whack on the Side of the Head: How You Can Be More Creative.* (3rd ed.) New York: Warner Books, 1998.

Waddell, S. *Societal Learning and Change: How Governments, Business and Civil Society Are Creating Solutions to Complex Multi-Stakeholder Problems.* Sheffield, U.K.: Greenleaf, 2005.

Welwood, J. *Toward a Psychology of Awakening.* Boston: Shambhala, 2000.

Wenger, E. *Communities of Practice: Learning, Meaning, and Identity.* Cambridge, U.K.: Cambridge University Press, 1998.

Wenger, E., McDermott, R., and Snyder, W. *Cultivating Communities of Practice: A Guide to Managing Knowledge.* Boston: Harvard Business School Press, 2002.

Whiteley, R. *The Corporate Shaman: A Business Fable.* New York: HarperBusiness, 2002.

Wilber, K. *The Atman Project: A Transpersonal View of Human Development.* Wheaton, Ill.: Quest Books, 1980.

Wilber, K. "The Spectrum of Development," in K. Wilber, J. Engler, and D. B. Brown, *Transformations of Consciousness.* Boston: New Science Library, 1986.

Wilber, K. *A Brief History of Everything.* (2nd ed.) Boston: Shambhala, 2000.

Wilber, K. *Integral Psychology: Consciousness, Spirit, Psychology, Therapy.* Boston: Shambhala, 2000.

Wilber, K. *Theory of Everything: An Integral Vision for Business, Politics, Science, and Spirituality.* Boston: Shambhala, 2000.

Wilber, K. *Eye to Eye: The Quest for the New Paradigm.* (3rd ed., rev.) Boston: Shambhala, 2001.

Wilber, K. *No Boundary: Eastern and Western Approaches to Personal Growth.* Boston: Shambhala, 2001.

Wilber, K., Engler, J., and Brown, D. B. *Transformations of Consciousness: Conventional and Contemplative Perspectives on Development.* Boston: New Science Library, 1986.

Zaleznik, A. "Managers and Leaders: Are They Different" *Harvard Business Review,* 1977, 55(5), 67–78.

~~~ Resources

A special Web site has been established to keep you up to date on the latest leadership agility resources: www.leadershipagility.com.

This Web site is designed to meet the needs of two groups of people: managers and leadership development professionals. Its purpose is to give you up-to-date access to the latest leadership agility resources:

Assessment tools

Talks, seminars, and tele-seminars

Articles and white papers

Consulting on leadership development strategy

Action learning programs

Leadership agility workshops in each of the three action arenas:

- Pivotal conversations
- Team leadership
- Leadership of organizational change

Leadership agility coaching

Training and certification programs for coaches and workshop leaders

Manuals and support services for increasing personal resilience

If you're interested in developing more agile teams and organizations, you can find information about relevant consulting, training, and coaching services at www.changewise.biz.

～ Acknowledgments

This book was more than four years in the making, the result not only of our own efforts but also those of many others who provided much appreciated guidance and encouragement along the way.

We first want to acknowledge and thank Bill Torbert, who introduced us to one another. Bill also introduced each of us to stage-development psychology, and he either conducted or supervised much of the early research that established the relationship between developmental stages and effective leadership. Bill, you have been a timely mentor and a friend in the true sense of the word.

We also want to acknowledge our clients, interviewees, and students: the leaders who made this book possible. We thank you for what you've shared with us and for your courage in experimenting toward more agile and effective forms of leadership. It is a privilege to observe your remarkable achievements.

We thank our agent, Sabine Hrechdakian, for having the perspicacity to comprehend what this book could be, even when it was little more than a gleam in our eyes. Sabine, we appreciate the intelligence and business savvy with which you guided us at many pivotal moments during this process.

We thank Susan Williams of Jossey-Bass for her enthusiasm and willingness to take a chance on first-time authors with an ambitious book idea. We were also very fortunate to have Byron Schneider as our developmental editor. Byron, your thoughtful advice and collaborative spirit made you an absolute pleasure to work with. We also thank our official reviewers, who fearlessly dug into the material in its more inchoate form and emerged with excellent suggestions that had a decisive effect on the final product.

We also thank Susanne Cook-Greuter for her flawless scoring and interpretation of the Leadership Development Profile. Your expertise and support was a welcome contribution to this project. And we thank

Dane Hewlett for his generosity in sharing his own research findings on the more advanced stages of development, for expanding our sample of leaders at these stages, and for initiating at Villanova University the first study group on the book. Susanne and Dane, we look forward to your continued contributions to the field.

We extend a special acknowledgment to Sandy Davis, a pioneer in the field of resilience and long-time partner in ChangeWise, for his steadfast support and encouragement and for his unfailing commitment to practice.

We greatly appreciate Alice Josephs for her well-developed sensibilities and sheer tenacity in editing the entire manuscript. We thank Sahib-Amar Khalsa for her cheerful, fast, and dependable production of high-quality interview transcripts. And we are grateful to others who provided helpful feedback on earlier drafts of the book: Debbie Whitestone, Jeff Drust, Mark Horowitz, Paul Joiner, Michael Luftman, Roberta Prada, Jean Tennyson, and Mark Weissman.

Stuart Horwitz provided invaluable guidance and encouragement during the proposal phase. We appreciate your insight, your humor, and your friendship. Tara Brach, Chris Cavanaugh, Kristin Cobble, Jill Docking, Deborah Dumaine, Sara Ellis, Vivian Everett, Marion Freiberg, Trevor Goldfisher, George Goldsmith, Nina Krushwitz, Marc Lesser, Bill Novak, Bill Ryan, Steven Schatz, Abby Seixas, Ann Tannenbaum, and Tom Wilson also provided helpful advice and encouragement.

Finally, we want to thank our teachers, from whom we've learned many valuable practices and perspectives.

Bill Joiner
Stephen Josephs

⟶ The Authors

Bill Joiner is a seasoned leadership and organization development consultant with thirty years of experience completing successful projects with companies based in the United States, Canada, and Europe. Known for his ability to custom-tailor his work to meet specific client objectives, he speaks about leadership agility and helps companies design leadership development strategies and action learning programs that foster this vital competency. He has facilitated scores of leadership development programs, creative strategy sessions, and organizational change projects, and he serves as a coach to senior leaders undertaking team and organizational change initiatives. He also teaches at the Center for Leadership and Ethics at Boston College. He has a doctorate in organization development from Harvard University and an MBA. He can be reached at bj@changewise.biz.

Stephen Josephs's twenty-five-year executive coaching practice has grown through decades of training and research. In the 1970s he began "modeling" exemplary leaders, identifying the unconscious thought processes that allowed them to outperform others by significant margins. Currently, with his knowledge of business performance, psychology, and mind-body disciplines, he helps leaders attain new levels of agility. In working with clients, Stephen guides them in achieving two results: their leadership makes a difference, and they enjoy who they become in the process. A skilled performer himself (classical guitar and improvisational theater), he uses the arts to raise the fun quotient in business. He has a doctorate from the University of Massachusetts and master's degrees from Harvard and Antioch Universities. He can be reached at sj@changewise.biz.

Josephs and Joiner are founders of ChangeWise, a leadership and organization development firm with offices in Boston and San Francisco: www.changewise.biz.

Index